The Changing Chinese Legal System, 1978–Present

The Changing Chinese Legal System, 1978–Present

Centralization of Power and
Rationalization of the Legal System

Bin Liang

Routledge
Taylor & Francis Group
New York   London

First published 2008
by Routledge
270 Madison Ave, New York, NY 10016

Simultaneously published in the UK
by Routledge
2 Park Square, Milton Park, Abingdon, Oxon OX14 4RN

Routledge is an imprint of the Taylor & Francis Group, an informa business

© 2008 Taylor and Francis

Typeset in Sabon by IBT Global

1006074155

Library of Congress Cataloging in Publication Data
Liang, Bin.
The changing Chinese legal system, 1978–present : centralization of power and rational-
ization of the legal system / Bin Liang.
p. cm. — (East Asia, history, politics, sociology, culture)
Includes bibliographical references and index.
ISBN 978-0-415-95859-2 (hardback : alk. paper)
1. Law reform—China—History. 2. China—Economic policy. 3. China—Politics and
government. 4. China—Social policy. I. Title.
KNQ470.L53 2008

340'.30951—dc22   2007024393

ISBN10: 0-415-95859-8 (hbk)
ISBN10: 0-203-92854-7 (ebk)

ISBN13: 978-0-415-95859-2 (hbk)
ISBN13: 978-0-203-92854-7 (ebk)

Praise for *The Changing Chinese Legal System, 1978–Present*

Bin Liang has extended some of the classical legal research on power and prediction in this book. It reaches systematically far beyond the Chinese legal system, and may prove to be a classic itself. It is timely and important, especially in light of the pace and space of globalization.

Pat Lauderdale, School of Justice, Arizona State University

Chapter 3

Contents

List of Tables and Figures

Tables

Figures

Acknowledgments

Though I intend to keep it short, I do owe my appreciation and gratefulness to many people who directed, contributed, and helped in this research. First, because this research expanded on my doctoral dissertation finished at Arizona State University 5 years ago, I am indebted to all my committee members, including Dr. Pat Lauderdale, Dr. Gray Cavender, and Dr. John Johnson. Dr. Lauderdale deserves special thanks as he provided further encouragement and inspiration on my works in my postgraduation years, including this book. In addition, my doctoral dissertation research was partially supported by a research grant from the Associated Students of Arizona State University (ASASU). The grant released part of my financial burden during my field research in China. I would like to take this opportunity to express, once again, my gratefulness for the research support.

Second, many people and friends, both in the United States and in China, kindly provided their assistance to my research while I was collecting data. I would like to express my special thanks to Tang Qianhong, Xu Min, Liu Zheng, Zu Like, and judges working in the research group at the Qing Yang Court in Chengdu city. Third, I would like to thank my former colleague Dr. Cynthia Dobson, who read through my manuscript and provided many suggestions to my final writing. Fourth, Kim Reyes, from the Writing Center of the Oklahoma State University-Tulsa, kindly provided her professional editorial assistance in my preparation of this book. Finally, with appropriate permissions, significant parts of two previously published journal articles were used as the bases for my discussions in both Chapter 4 and Chapter 5. In Chapter 4, a significant portion was adapted from Bin Liang, "Severe strike campaign in transitional China," *Journal of Criminal Justice*, 2005, 33(4), pp. 387–399, with permission from Elsevier; in Chapter 5, a significant portion was adopted from Bin Liang and Pat Lauderdale, "China and globalization: Developments in economic and legal change," *Journal of Developing Societies*, 2006, 22(2), pp. 197–220, by Sage Publications.

About the Author

Bin Liang is an assistant professor in the Department of Sociology at Oklahoma State University-Tulsa. He received his Ph.D. and J.D. from Arizona State University. He has published articles on studies related to crime and the legal system in China. His current research interests include globalization and its impact on the Chinese legal system, crime and deviance in China, · and the drug court in Tulsa County, Oklahoma.

Abbreviations

ACR	Antidumping and Countervailing Regulation of the PRC
ADR	Alternative Dispute Resolution
ALL	Administrative Litigation Law
ARA	Administrative Review and Approval
ASEAN	Association of South East Asian Nations
CCCPLC	Chinese Communist Central Political and Legal Committee
CCP	Chinese Communist Party
CCPCC	Chinese Communist Party Central Committee
CIETAC	China International Economic and Trade Arbitration Commission
CPL	Civil Procedural Law
EU	European Union
FDI	Foreign Direct Investment
FIE	Foreign Invested Enterprise
FTA	Free Trade Area
GATT	General Agreement of Tariffs and Trade
GDP	Gross Domestic Product
GNP	Gross National Product
MOJ	Ministry of Justice
MPS	Ministry of Public Security
NPC	National People's Congress
NBSC	National Bureau of Statistics of China
PRC	People's Republic of China

SEZ	Special Economic Zone
SOE	State-owned Enterprise
SPC	Supreme People's Court
SPP	Supreme People's Procuratorate
UNCTAD	United Nations Conference on Trade and Development
WIPO	World Intellectual Property Organization
WTO	World Trade Organization

1 Introduction

This book examines the changing Chinese legal system within the scope of China's political economy during the second half of the 20th century and the early years of the 21st century. In approximately 60 years, China experienced two dramatic changes: In 1949, the Chinese Communist Party (CCP) successfully unified mainland China and founded a new China as a socialist nation. In the next three decades, the new communist government tried to safeguard and build the country at the same time and to follow Marxist–Leninist–Maoist instructions both economically and politically. During this period, the function of law and the legal system was reduced to serve the communist government as an instrument. As a result, China suffered significantly from the chaos caused by endless class struggle. This period of time was usually labeled as the "rule of man."

Since 1978, China has entered a new phase. The Chinese government first kicked off economic reform and the "open door" policy and then initiated its legal reform. Dramatic changes in the reform era significantly transformed the nation in the next 30 years. Economically, China quickly caught up to other technically advanced nations in the world and began to actively participate in the global economic system. Legally, realizing the disaster of the lawlessness caused by the rule of man, the Chinese government was determined to build an effective legal system with distinct Chinese characteristics. Although not without limitations, China's growing legal system quickly became a new means, relied on both by the CCP for its governance and by Chinese citizens as a safeguard for their increasing individual rights. It is those dramatic changes in the legal system of China, especially after 1978, that are central to this research.

In this opening chapter, I present my research questions and theoretical framework. Then I review previous relevant studies and discuss how my work may further contribute to this field. Next I introduce my research sources and discuss important methodological issues that I encountered in my research. Finally I lay out the structure of this book.

RESEARCH OBJECTIVES AND
THEORETICAL FRAMEWORK

This research examines the changing Chinese legal system over approximately the past six decades. I am interested in both substantive changes in China's legal system, and, more important, in a theoretical understanding of those dramatic changes (e.g., what caused those changes, how those changes are connected, and what will happen next). Both substantive changes and theoretical understandings are indeed related: The former are sources for my analyses, and the latter are the conceptual maps. The ultimate goal of this research is to gain a better understanding of economic, political, and essentially legal changes in China within the global context.

Specific research questions are addressed in different chapters. In Chapter 2, I look at economic changes both before and after the reform. Key questions here include these: What are major economic changes? What are the characteristics of those changes, especially after 1978? How did the Chinese government make those changes possible? What is the impact of those changes on China's practice of Marxism? Next, in Chapter 3, I examine China's political and legal reforms after 1978 and ask the following questions: What are the characteristics of China's legalization process? What is the function of this process? What are the limitations of this process? What is the relation between legal reform and political reform? In Chapter 4, I focus on crime and punishment issues in the new era and explore key questions such as these: What means are taken by the government to combat rising crime rates in the new era? What is the effect of such crime control and punishment? How do societal changes after the reform impact crime and crime control? In Chapter 5, I expand my discussion into the global context and ask the following questions: What is the understanding of globalization by the Chinese government? How does the Chinese government respond to the global system? What is the impact of China's globalization on its domestic legal system? Finally, in Chapter 6, I examine the current judicial system based on my empirical court observations. Questions addressed in this chapter include these: How does the court handle its daily work, both substantially and procedurally? Who are the regular players in the court system? What potential problems exist within the current system? What are the factors that influence the operation of court reform? Through key questions in these chapters, I move from economic changes in China to political and legal changes, then to social and cultural changes, and finally to the context of the global system.

In his study of crime control and punishment in the current U.S. and U.K. societies, Garland (2001) paid attention first to political, economic, and cultural changes of the new era. He argued that these new changes transformed the social conditions that supported the old criminal justice system, gave rise to new perceptions of crime control, and shaped new crime control and criminal justice practices of the present period. Drawing on the same analytical approach, I review and analyze dramatic changes of the Chinese legal system since 1978 within the changing economic, political, and cultural environment of the new era.

Theoretically, I rely on Marx and Weber's classical theories in my analyses of the economic and political changes and explore relations between the economic base and the political as well as the legal systems. Then I bring in Durkheim's theory in my discussion of new crime control and punishment in China and show how we can gain a better understanding of China's current crime and punishment beyond the legal scope. Finally, I turn in particular to the world-economy theory in my analysis of China's globalization. The world-economy theory helps us understand the progress of world globalization, the nature of such a process, and its impact on China (and especially its legal system).

PREVIOUS STUDIES[1]

Study of the Chinese legal system has its own history along with the development and growth of China. Before 1980, there were very few studies on the Chinese legal system. Works done by scholars such as Cohen (1968, 1970) and V. H. Li (1978) gave a good description of the communist legal system under the leadership of the CCP. These comparative works emphasized the differences between communist practices and Western legal practices.

Entering the 1980s, scholars expanded their research on the Chinese legal system. Several trends were observable in this period. First, as a continuation of the efforts in the 1970s, scholars noticed the initial development of the legal system after the reform (see, e.g., Mayer, 1989). Studies on the criminal justice system in general (see, e.g., Leng, 1985; Rojek, 1985), on crime punishment (Scobell, 1988; Tifft, 1985), and on police administrative power and control (Bracey, 1989; Ward, 1985) in particular all showed new signs of legal changes besides heavy reliance on analyses of the communist practices. Second, a group of scholars started examining China's low crime rate and recidivism rate. Their comparative works such as studies on the correctional system (Bracey, 1988; Hobler, 1989) were written as introductions to the U.S. audience of how the Chinese legal system was able to maintain such effective crime control. Some other scholars turned their focus to Chinese culture and legal traditions for potential answers (see, e.g., Bracey, 1985; Cohen, Edwards, & Chen, 1980; Kim, 1981). Third, in an effort to explain the Chinese legal system to audiences from other legal and cultural backgrounds, some scholars applied concepts used in the study of the Western legal and social systems, such as social control, in their studies of the Chinese legal system (see, e.g., Rojek, 1989; Troyer, Clark, & Rojek, 1989). To some extent, there is an opposing focus between the last two groups: On the one hand, an emphasis on the uniqueness of the Chinese culture and its legal traditions may lead to the argument of culture determinism; on the other hand, the application of Western-generated value-laden concepts, such as social control, in Chinese society tends to ignore social and cultural differences, and leads to problems associated with culture imperialism (S. Zhu, 1992).

The study of the Chinese legal system blossomed after 1990. Studies have been expanded in several directions since then. First, many studies focused on new laws in China on foreign trade, investment, and other business-related activities (see, e.g., Alford, 1995a; Corne, 1997; Feinerman, 1994; Y. Feng, 1992; Potter, 1992, 1995; X. Yan, 1992). These studies served a clear purpose for foreign businessmen and investors in China. Second, studies of crime, crime control, and punishment in China have been deepened and expanded into many subfields, such as juvenile delinquency (see, e.g., important works by Bakken, 1993, 1995; Bao, Hass, & Pi, 2007; Fu, 1992; Xiang, 1999; L. Zhang, 2003; L. Zhang & Messner, 1995), the death penalty (see Boxer, 1999; Liang, Lu, Miethe, & Zhang, 2006; H. Lu & Zhang, 2005; Monthy, 1998; Scobell, 1990), gang and organized crime (see A. Chen, 2005; Gao & Song, 2001; L. Zhang, Messner, Lu, & Deng, 1997), workplace theft and official offense (see L. Zhang & Messner, 1999; L. Zhang et al., 2000), sexual offenses (see Anderson & Gil, 1998; Gil & Anderson, 1999; H. M. Tanner, 1994a), official corruption (see Gaylord & Levine, 1997; Levy, 1995; Sun, 2001), money laundering (see Ping, 2006; S. Yang, 2002), the prison system and prisoners (see Seymour & Anderson, 1998; L. Zhang, Messner, & Lu, 1999; Zhou, 1991), criminal defendants' confession and legal representation (see H. Lu & Miethe, 2002, 2003), anticrime campaigns (see Gil & Anderson, 1998; H. M. Tanner, 1994b, 1999; M. S. Tanner, 2000), new public order crimes (Keith & Lin, 2006), and recidivism and crime prevention (see Deng, Zhang, & Cordilia, 1998; Friday, 1998; J. Liu, 2005; Zhong & Broadhurst, 2007). Third, studies on policing and police power in China clearly traced new changes after the reform and showed the different roles played by the police, people's new conceptions about the police work, and adjusted relationships between the police and the community (see Biddulph, 1993; Cao & Hou, 2001; Dutton, 1992; Dutton & Lee, 1993; Fu, 1990, 1993; H. Lu, 1998, 1999; Wong, 1994, 2002). Fourth, given changes in the legal system in China, more scholars started working on analyses of the legal reforms and transitions (see Diamant, Lubman, & O'Brien, 2005; Dicks, 1995; Epstein, 1991; Gallagher, 2006; J. Li, 1996; Lo, 1995; Lubman, 1996; Peerenboom, 2002a; Potter, 1994b, 1998, 1999, 2004; Zheng, 1998; S. Zhu, 1989; Zou, 2006). This was the time that the term *legal reform* first appeared in scholars' works. Uncertain about the nature of the new reform, some scholars questioned the effect of China's legalization and pointed out limitations of the Chinese legal reform compared with the Western model of the rule of law (see Dellapenna & Morton, 2000; Keith, 1991, 1994; Turner, Feinerman, & Guy, 2000; Vermeer & d'Hoohe, 2002; S. Zhao, 2006a). Fifth, legal scholars with Chinese backgrounds have started publishing works from their perspectives, with a mixed expectation of both introducing the emerging legal system to the Western audience (a going-out approach) and analyzing issues in the Chinese legal system based on Western models and lessons (a bringing-in approach; see Bao et al., 2007; Cao, 2007; J. Chen, 1995, 1999; X. Chen, 2002; J. Liu et al., 1998; H. Lu & Miethe, 2007; C. Wang & Zhang, 1997; G. Wang & Mo, 1999; J. Wang, 1997; Wong, 2000, 2001a, 2001b). Sixth, the study of the Chinese legal tradition has been expanded in two directions. On the one hand, studies traced backward to ancient Chinese legal traditions and tried to show the continuity of those traditions (see, e.g., Dikotter, 2002; MacCormack, 1996; Peerenboom, 1993). For this group, the emphasis was on the legal traditions in the past. On the other hand, some scholars focused on the most recent development of the Chinese legal system and tried to show the impact of legal traditions on the current legal reforms (see, e.g., Michelson, 1998a, 1998b; Ren, 1997). For this group, the focus was on the present. In any event, studies in both directions made significant contributions to a deeper understanding of what Chinese legal traditions are and how they impact current legal reform. Finally, some scholars began to pay special attention to the growing court system in China (see R. C. Brown, 1997; Lubman, 1999; Woo, 1999). This is consistent with the changes of the legal system in the new era when the court is gaining more and more power.

Even though the study of the Chinese legal system has been tremendously expanded in the last two decades, there is still a need for further studies for a number of reasons. First, the changing nature of the current legal system made many previous studies obsolete, and keeping up with recent developments is critical to an understanding of the current Chinese legal system. Second, the Chinese legal system shows a character of complexity in the current transitional period. New elements are introduced into the system even while the old practices are still lingering. This situation is further complicated by different levels of development in different regions (e.g., the east coast vs. the west inner land; the urban vs. the rural). Third, to date, only a small number of studies are based on firsthand data collected from field research.[2] There are definite practical reasons (e.g., lack of access) for such a scarcity. This research fills this gap using my empirical observations of the current judicial system (see Chapter 6). Finally, with a few exceptions (e.g., Feinerman, 1995; Keith & Lin, 2006; Liang & Lauderdale, 2006; Potter, 2001a, 2001b; Zou, 2006), previous studies failed to examine China's legalization process in a global context. In recent years, China definitely increased its pace of integration into the global system, and in 2001 China became a member of the World Trade Organization (WTO). In this research, I pay special attention to China's globalization and address its impact on China's domestic legalization (see Chapter 5), in the hope that this effort will draw more attention to this critical issue.

RESEARCH SOURCES AND METHODOLOGY

Due to the nature of my research, I draw mainly on three different sources of data: published resources, court observations, and interviews. In Chapters 2 through 5, I focus on China's economic and political-legal changes, crime and punishment in the new era, and the integration of China's political economy into the global system. Conducted at the macro level, my analyses rely heavily on published materials (e.g., research articles, reference sources, and online information). Next, in Chapter 6, I focus on the operation and function of the current judicial system at the micro level, using my empirical observations and interviews conducted in China in 2002.

Published Resources

Besides reviewing previous studies, I spent a significant amount of time doing library research and collecting data from reference sources to analyze economic, political-legal, and social changes over the years. For example, I paid numerous visits to the National Library of China (http://www.nlc.gov. cn/), the largest library in China, and reviewed various statistical journals and periodicals (see a list of these collections in the references). As a result, I was able to produce many meaningful tables based on longitudinal data retrieved from these collections. On the one hand, I was amazed by the completeness of some data, especially in the early years before 1978; on the other hand, very few data are available on some sensitive issues. For example, I failed to find consistent and systematic data on the severe strike campaign (*yanda* in Chinese), an issue that I address in Chapter 4.

Due to the nature of these data (i.e., all are collected and reported by governmental agencies), there is always a question as to their validity. One main critique is that the Chinese governmental agencies manipulated the numbers on purpose, for example, overestimating data on economic growth[3] and underrecording crimes (discussed and tested in Yu, 1998; Yu & Zhang, 1999). Facing the critique, the National Bureau of Statistics of China (NBSC) on the one hand tried to counter such accusations (e.g., pointing out incentives for *underreporting* of local economic growth),[4] and on the other hand made efforts to improve its data collection and adopted international standards to increase the openness of its data.[5] Recently, in August 2006, the NBSC established a special committee that deals with reports and whistle-blowing on statistical manipulations and showed its determination for further improvement.[6]

Even though such data are not unproblematic, scholars heavily rely on them in their research because they are the best available, and there are signs that China's statistical data reporting is improving with the development of the country's economy and its integration into the global system. In addition, the validity of data I collected should not be questioned indiscriminately. For example, concern about the governmental manipulation depends on the nature of the data. For many politically insensitive data (e.g., population growth, growth of the court system and lawyers), there is less or little incentive for manipulations. For other sensitive data (e.g., the unemployment rate[7]), however, governmental embellishments are more likely.

With those concerns in mind, I do utilize those longitudinal data in my research, and my focus is on changes over the years. In such a way, even if the data are skewed due to systematic errors (e.g., the governmental manipulations), this skew does not affect the general pattern of the changes.

Online Information

With the increasing development of new technologies, the Internet has become a necessary tool and to some extent an important part of people's lives in the new era.[8] How to use the Internet as a means to collect data and conduct research is a new issue facing scholars (see Greenberg & Lakeland, 1998; Jones, 1999).

I have been collecting online information since 1996. My collection process definitely grows with the increased Internet use by the Chinese government and other agencies and institutions. Unlike conducting surveys and interviews on the Internet, my collection of Internet information stays at the basic level. Once I find a piece of useful news, I print a hard copy and sort the news into different categories. The true methodological issue here is to explain where I get the information and how to verify the correctness and accuracy of the information.

There are three main online sources I use. First is news information from the Internet version of the *People's Daily* (*renmin ribao*) (http://www.snweb. com.cn). The *People's Daily* is the official newspaper of the Chinese Communist Party Central Committee (CCPCC). Often called the "Party's paper" (*dangbao*), it is the leading national newspaper (Yuan, 1995). Due to its nature, there is clearly the same concern as outlined earlier; that is, the news here is carefully embellished by the central government. On the other hand, this careful review and approval provides an extra guarantee for the existence of the subject matter once the matter is published, although there is a question about the magnitude of the matter. Besides, utilizing governmental data exactly serves one purpose of my research; that is, to explore the policy changes or potential moves by the Party and the central government.

The second major online source of information is from the most popular search engine in China, *xinlang wang* (http://www.sina.com.cn/). The news section of this search engine provides much more information from various avenues other than the *People's Daily*. Although it is still subject to general censorship by the Chinese government, it does provide information from a relatively more independent and objective perspective. The relative freedom enjoyed by it, however, can cause trouble for researchers. For example, there is sometimes a question about the accuracy of the information reported by some local newspapers. A careful judgment has to be made by the researcher based on the source of the news, the nature of the subject matter, and other considerations.

The last major online source is directly related to my study of the legal system. In recent years, many official legal Web sites have been opened, such as the Web site for the People's Courts (http://www.chinacourt.com.cn), the China legal publicity Web site (run by the Ministry of Justice at http://www. legalinfo.gov.cn/), the *Legal Daily* Web site (http://www.legaldaily.com.cn/), and the Web site for the All China Lawyers Association (http://www.acla. org.cn). The advantage of these Web sites is obvious. News and articles from them discuss exact topics relevant to my research. Because of the expertise, information obtained here tends to be more systematic and accurate compared with information from the second source already mentioned. The major concern is, once again, the governmental control over the agencies and institutions that operate these Web sites. For example, a significant number of news items under the People's Courts Web site are almost identical with news items in other official newspapers (e.g., the *People's Daily*), a clear sign that the Web site is serving political functions for the central government.

Online information serves three purposes for my research. First, I use it to double-check the longitudinal data I collect from published sources. Numerical data online tend to be sporadic but sometimes increase my confidence in the published data after a comparison of information from the two sources. Second, online information provides meaningful qualitative data both theoretically and substantively. Third, online information is the best available source for the most recent changes in China.

One final word about the online information is the problem of dead links. Due to the constantly changing nature of the Internet, some of the links I provide in this study might no longer be valid. For this reason, I have kept the original hard copies for researchers who would like to verify the data.

Court Observations

In 2002, I conducted my court observations in two large cities in China, Beijing[9] and Chengdu.[10] In the next sessions, I lay out the settings of my observation and discuss case selections and potential problems with my presence in the courtroom.

Court Settings and Access

In 2001, I got to know Judge T,[11] a visiting judge from Chengdu, while we were in Phoenix. After Judge T went back to China, we kept in contact, and finally I decided to pay him a visit in Chengdu as part of my field research. By then Judge T was working at the People's Court in Qing Yang District (the Qing Yang Court) in Chengdu, Sichuan province. He used to work at the Chengdu Intermediate People's Court (the Chengdu Court) before he joined the Qing Yang Court. His position at the district court and connection with the intermediate court turned out to be very helpful to my study.

On my second day in Chengdu, Judge T introduced me to several young judges in a research group at the Qing Yang Court. The research group is an official division of the Court, and people in the research group usually do annual court reports, study difficult legal issues, discuss ongoing cases with presiding judges, and make suggestions if necessary. I quickly became a friend of the group even though they respectfully called me "teacher Liang."[12] This affiliation helped me with my courtroom access at the Qing Yang Court. In addition, I could talk to them after my observation and clarify questions I had with regard to both procedural and substantive issues.

In fact, I had little problem in gaining courtroom access at the Qing Yang Court. All courtrooms were located within one huge building. For example, criminal courtrooms were on the first and second floors, administrative courtrooms were on the third floor, and civil cases were tried in courtrooms on the fourth and fifth floors. I went to different courtrooms for the cases I wanted to hear. Sometimes, I checked with chief judges (*tingzhang*) first so that I could arrange my observations according to their schedules.

The Chengdu Court is not very far from the Qing Yang Court (about 2 miles away), and it is located in a much nicer building: bigger, newer, and with better facilities (see Figure 1.1 for a courtroom outlook inside the court building). Judge T intended to introduce me to his friends who were judges there to help me with my research. I was concerned, however, about the

Figure 1.1 Courtroom outlook inside the court building.

Illustration: The four letters above the courtroom door, "Take law seriously."

impact that his introduction might have and decided to go to the Court as a normal visitor.

It was not difficult to get into the huge court building, even though the guards at the front door made it look quite intimidating (just keep in mind that this is the *People's* Court). The real hurdle was with the case schedule. Unlike people who went to the Court for litigation purposes and knew where they should go, I had no clue which courtrooms were going to have trials. Eventually, the courtroom cleaners turned out to be helpful. I simply checked with them because they knew exactly what was going on in each courtroom, and it was their duty to open the courtrooms where there would be trials on that day.

After my trip to Chengdu, I decided to observe cases at comparable levels in Beijing, and I chose the Beijing First Intermediate Peoples' Court (the Beijing First Court)[13] and the People's Court in Hai Dian District (the Hai Dian Court). The Beijing First Court is located in Shi Jing Shan District. Like the Chengdu Court, the court building looks very nice and is well equipped. Unlike the Chengdu Court, however, anyone who wants to sit in the courtroom has to get an observer or witness card at the front door. The number of cards is limited, and they appear to be issued on a first come, first served basis. To get an observer card, you have to show your personal ID and explain exactly which case you are going to watch.

There is a large electronic screen outside the reception room that is supposed to show daily case schedules. I usually got a card for the earliest case possible, either in the morning or in the afternoon after the official break (from noon to 1 p.m.). After I finished watching one case, I immediately checked with the cleaners (again!), and moved to the next possible case. When the courtroom was in use, the door was closed and an indicator light was on. This made any intrusion very unlikely. In other words, when I finished watching one case, I could not watch any ongoing case, but had to wait for the next one to begin.

The Hai Dian Court turned out to be the most difficult one for courtroom access. Like the Beijing First Court, an observer card was required for all visitors, including the parties' relatives. The courtroom facility, however, in no way matched the intermediate court. More often, the courtroom was so small that only a few (e.g., three) observers could be accommodated in each case (see Clark & Feinerman, 1996). There was also a large electronic screen outside the court building, but it was not working on my first visit. Because I was unable to tell which case I was about to observe, the security guard refused to issue me an observer card. When I told him that the electronic screen was not working, he answered, "If it's not working, it means that there is no case scheduled." It was plainly not true, and I saw many people go into and out of the court building that day. Even when the electronic screen was working, it showed only criminal cases for some reason. This made my civil case observations almost impossible.[14] As a result, I managed to watch only two civil cases at the Hai Dian Court.

In sum, compared with courts in Chengdu, my court access was much more restricted in Beijing. Various difficulties, such as geographical distance (e.g., the sheer distance between the Beijing First Court and the Hai Dian Court made any travel between them impossible on the same day), restricted control of the courtroom (e.g., the witness card), and unexpected access difficulties (e.g., problems with the electronic screen) all made my research more difficult.

Cases Observed

I observed a total of 54 cases: 34 in Chengdu and 20 in Beijing. Among them, 26 were civil cases, 22 were criminal cases, 5 were administrative litigation cases, and another's nature was unclear. I list all cases in tables (see case summary tables Appendix B), including information such as date, time, trial place, composition of the judge panel, secretary, nature of the case, trial procedure, both parties, and their representations. In 12 cases I was able to watch only part of the trial because of my late entry.

In terms of the nature of these cases, two instances are worth mentioning. First, three cases (20, 22, and 24) at the Chengdu Court turned out to be special because a trial exam for the leading judge was arranged. All parties in these cases were equipped with microphones for recording purposes, and the leading judges certainly tried their best in those cases. It did not appear that parties in those cases were informed about the exam beforehand. All parties, however, were cooperative (e.g., moving toward the microphone and raising their voices when so requested). Second, I found many people were swarming into a huge courtroom one day at the Beijing First Court; this aroused my curiosity, and I followed them into that courtroom. Rather than a normal case, it was the first creditors' meeting in a bankruptcy case (41). Hundreds of creditors showed up, and it was a quite interesting and unique experience.

There was not a particular order for my case selection. Due to the nature of my research, more systemic sampling such as random sampling was not possible. What I did was to try to balance different types of cases if possible. Therefore, my case sample was not an accurate representation of all cases. Based on my experience at four different courts, however, I found that many issues were common indeed, and this increased my confidence for discussions. Finally my analyses should not be expanded to courts at other levels (e.g., the high people's courts, or the people's tribunals). Given the fact that there are more than 10,000 people's tribunals in the country handling more than 1.5 million cases a year,[15] we would expect less formal problem-solving approaches at the ground level. I am confident, though, that my analyses should be valid for district courts and intermediate-level courts in, at least, big cities, and the court structure in both cities theoretically should be the model for courts in less developed areas in the future.

My Status as an Observer

Because trials are open to the public according to law,[16] my observer status was not a problem most of the time. However, it was not foolproof. For example, I was waiting for a case at the Chengdu Court one day, and as usual I was the only observer. Right before the trial, the judges noticed me, and one judge asked about my presence. I told them that I was about to observe the case. "Okay, it's alright," he answered. During the trial, two other female judges noticed my note-taking, and they approached me and checked my status again after the trial. They told me that I should not have taken notes in the courtroom without their permission.[17]

There were several other instances, in both Chengdu and Beijing, in which the presiding judges checked my status before the trial. My general impression is that judges did not want their cases examined by observers, and they allowed observations reluctantly.[18] As time went on, I definitely improved my skills. The more I got to know the court system, the more I learned how to avoid those embarrassing moments. The tip is indeed simple: Enter the courtroom as late as possible so that the presiding judges do not have much time to question you, because everyone including the judges wants to get the trial done as soon as possible!

It is difficult to estimate the impact of my presence in the courtroom. Most of the time (especially when there were other observers), my presence did not appear to have an effect on the trial. In some cases, however, it could have had an impact. For example, one presiding judge at the Qing Yang Court, not knowing me then, was very relaxed in the first case I observed. He was standing beside the secretary, rather than sitting behind his judge table, and putting his hands in his pockets. In the next case after I was introduced to him, he went back to his judge table and never left the table throughout the trial. In the third case (a divorce case), both parties (the husband and wife) noticed my presence and requested a private trial. The judge had to take a recess and explain to me (saying "sorry") why I could not observe the case based on law. It seemed that he started treating my presence seriously and differently after we got to know each other. Near the end of my Chengdu trip, Judge T invited me to give two lectures at both the Qing Yang Court and the Chengdu Court. At this time I was formally introduced to judges at both Courts. On the next day, judges in the courtroom clearly treated me as a guest and respectfully called me "teacher Liang." In short, once the judges knew who I was, they tended to treat me differently (e.g., with respect), and therefore they might be more careful with the way they tried cases.

Interviews

In addition to court observations, I conducted interviews. My interview selection was based on a theoretical or judgmental sampling, a form of nonprobability sampling that depends on the researcher's ability to make decisions about what to observe based on constraints such as opportunity, personal interests, resources, and, most important, the problem to be investigated. Detailed knowledge is expected from the informed interviewees with a purpose to substantiate or guide my analyses.[19]

My interviewees consisted mainly of judges, lawyers, and legal scholars and students, and sometimes I was able to talk to parties in the cases and other laymen. Although I managed to talk to several people in a more formal manner (e.g., I explained to them my research purpose, asked their permission, and then started conversations), I gained more information through informal, natural conversations with people who happened to run into my research and were willing to share with me their experiences and knowledge. For people I interviewed formally, I let the interviewees choose the interview location so that they would feel more comfortable. Most of these interviews were conducted at their homes or offices, and a few were conducted at my home or in a restaurant. The interview usually lasted about an hour.

In my experiences with less formal interviews, it was difficult to draw a line between a planned interview conducted at a specific place and a more casual, but conscious conversation that could happen anywhere incidentally. For instance, I tried to talk to some legal scholars (such as Professor Zhu Suli from Beijing University and Professor He Bingson from China University of Political Science and Law) in a formal, planned interview, but my time was limited each time and the result was very minimal. On the other hand, an encounter by chance could become a valuable source. For instance, I was sitting in a case at the Chengdu Court one day. During an official break, the appellee (i.e., the defendant in the appeal) of the case, a lawyer in Chengdu, approached me, and we started chatting (at this moment, about the case at hand, of course). After the trial, he invited me to his law office and ended up treating me to lunch. We had a very meaningful talk during the lunch.

My status as a foreign researcher turned out to be suspicious to some people (especially to officials). Before I went on my trip, a friend recommended her aunt and uncle, both judges working at the Beijing First Court, as potential interviewees. When I contacted them over the phone, my friend's aunt kept asking me about my research purpose, and I sensed her hesitation and unwillingness to talk to me. Eventually I canceled the interview plan.

In all cases, I did not use a tape recorder. Sometimes I took notes while the other party was talking, and sometimes I waited until the other party left. It is difficult to tell which method worked better. I found note-taking during a conversation very helpful in two aspects. First, it definitely helped with information tracking and data collection: I rarely missed important things in the conversation. Second, the process of taking notes helped my own thinking, probing, and further questioning, as I often picked up another question to clarify the unclear. If not for my note-taking, I probably would have missed some useful questions. The main concerns for such note-taking were the reaction of the interviewee and the interference with the natural flow of the conversation. I was afraid that the interviewee would take it as impolite or become more nervous or cautious in responding to my questions. Both would affect the outcome of our conversation. However, it did not seem to bother my interviewees based on my observation once they started talking to me. Another point about my interview was that my structured questions did not go as well as expected. Sometimes my interviewees were baffled by those questions and tried to guess my question (perhaps to cater to my research). Instead, the most fruitful data came from the interviewees' own stories. When judges and attorneys started telling me about an interesting case they had been personally involved in, I always found more follow-up questions. The storytelling style closed our distance, made the respondents more relaxed, and indeed produced more meaningful results.

In sum, my interview experience tells me that as a researcher, learning to engage oneself in natural and unexpected conversations with people who have experience and knowledge on the research subject is very important and sometimes produces very meaningful data, especially when one's access to formal interviews is limited.

ORGANIZATION OF THE BOOK

This book contains seven chapters. In Chapter 1, I present my research questions and analytical frameworks, review previous relevant studies, and discuss my research sources and methodology. In Chapter 2, I describe the dramatic changes that happened in the economic structure in China after 1978. In the prereform era, following orthodox Marxism, the CCP tried to transform various nonpublic economic activities into public ownerships under a planned economy. The function of the legal system was reduced to a tool for class struggle. After the economic reform in 1978, the CCP seemed to have made a 180-degree turn; nonpublic economic activities reemerged and indeed thrived in the next three decades. At the same time, various means of capital accumulation, operation, and management were borrowed from developed nations to facilitate China's economic development. The market economy eventually replaced the planned economy as the main economic mode in 1993. Amazingly, these tremendous changes were made possible through a series of reinterpretations of Marxism, and China still claims itself as a socialist nation.

In Chapter 3, I focus on the rebuilding of the political and legal system in the reform era. Responding to economic reforms, substantive changes were made to the structure of the legal system through a process of systemization and bureaucratization. Serving the needs of economic development, China's legal system shows a character of lagging behind at present. China's legal reform should be studied as part of the ongoing political reform. Consistent with Weber's analysis, I argue that the legalization process has been pushed forward through a process of centralization of both political and social control power, contrary to the decentralization of economic power. The Chinese government adopted legal reform as a new means of governing national affairs and therefore relegitimating its political power and control in such a transitional era.

In Chapter 4, I study one main function of the legal system, crime and punishment, and discuss the dramatic social changes in the reform era. Even though the legal system was rebuilt and strengthened after 1978, China suffered from rising crime rates. New crimes and criminal groups emerged and made up a significant part of the crime picture. Facing the problem, the Chinese government adopted a severe strike campaign approach to stop crime. Longitudinal statistical data, however, do not support the government's claimed success of the campaign. In contrast, the campaign approach did serve other functions, such as raising people's awareness of crime, seeking public support for crackdowns, and strengthening the fading moral boundary (in a Durkheimian sense). I argue that the roots of the crime problem lie in the deepened stratification of the society and the fading of communist ideological control in a process of social transition.

In Chapter 5, I put China's economic, political, and legal reforms into the global context and analyze both the impact of globalization on China and China's influence on the world economy. China's understandings of the world-economy and globalization are seemingly confusing. They are a mixture of the modernization theory, the world-economy paradigm, and critiques of unequal treatment in world economic activities and ideologies imposed by leading Western nations. The Chinese government is using globalization to facilitate China's economic development, to utilize both economic and legal changes to strengthen its political and social control, and to save its one-party political system at home.

In Chapter 6, I focus on one key branch of the legal system, the judicial system in China. Based on my court observations in both Beijing and Chengdu, I show that all of the major changes (economic, political, and cultural) described previously at the macro level are reflected in the current judicial system. The current court system has been in a process of systemization and seeking more power and relative independence both internally and externally. As part of the political reform, however, its progress has been limited by the political structure and the Party's ideological control. In addition, traditional influences, such as preferences for mediation (over litigation) and substantive justice (over procedural justice), lack of respect (from the masses), and lack of guaranteed power (from the political structure) still have major influences on the building and operation of the judicial system.

Finally, in the concluding chapter, I summarize all of the substantive chapters (Chapters 2–6) and put them into a systematic framework. Then, I draw some conclusions from my study and highlight potential contributions for future studies. The study of China's political economy is indeed related to other nations' developments within the global context. The nature and progress of China's socialist market economy provides a meaningful example of how a third-world, peripheral, socialist nation increases its integration and moves toward the core of the world system, and, in particular, an analysis of China's legalization process contributes to a general understanding of how a nation can utilize its political and legal reforms to make progress within the global system.

2 Economic Reform and Reinterpreted Marxism

In this chapter, I examine the economic bases for China's legal system in two different historical periods. One is the prereform era, covering the historical period from 1949 to 1978,[1] and the other is the reform era after 1978. In the prereform era, doctrinal Marxism was adopted and practiced by the government. Economically, socialist transformations were taken to eradicate various nonpublic ownerships. Ideologically, "Maoist Thought" was praised as the true Marxism appropriate to China's specific case. As a result, the legal system was used as a tool to serve the interests of the proletarian dictatorship.

After 1978, China initiated economic reform and practiced the "open door" policy. Economically, nonpublic ownerships reemerged and contributed significantly to China's economy in the next three decades. On the other hand, the state-owned enterprises (SOEs), as the main representative of the public ownerships, experienced tremendous difficulties in the reform era, although the government tried various means to revitalize them. To boost the economy, the Chinese government also borrowed from Western nations many means for capital accumulation, production, and management. With the transition of the economic structure, the market economy eventually replaced the planned economy as the main economic mode in China. Despite all those changes, the CCP kept claiming China as a socialist nation through a series of reinterpretations of Marxism. These reinterpretations both incorporated the dramatic changes and allowed the government to keep its ideological name in the new era.

PREREFORM ERA UNDER DOCTRINAL MARXISM: 1949–1978

1949 marked a turning point in Chinese history. It not only indicated the founding of a new China, but also represented a dramatic social change in which China turned into a socialist country based on Marxism. Chinese people had to adjust to the new society and accept the new ideology quickly.

Socialist Economic, Political, and Social Structure

In the early 1950s, China had a variety of different economic ownerships, besides the SOEs, such as individual economies made up of peasants and handicraft-men, economic cooperatives in rural areas, and individual and national (private) capitalist economic forms.[2] These nonpublic economic organizations were recognized and protected under the *Common Program* (the temporary national Constitution) adopted by the Chinese People's Political Consultative Conference in 1949 (cited in Gong, Xia, & Liu, 1999, p. 94). The fate of these economic forms and organizations, however, seemed doomed in the new socialist nation because of their nonpublic nature. Modeled on the structure of the formal Soviet Union, the first Constitution of China, passed in 1954, clearly provided that nonpublic economic forms should be restricted and transformed gradually into either state-owned or collective-owned economic entities subject to the socialist planned economy (Gong et al., 1999; see also Xin, 1999). By 1956, socialist transformations were accomplished in urban areas, and people's communes were formed throughout the country in rural areas to help the transition of collective ownerships to ownerships by the whole people (see Chin, 1983).

Corresponding to the planned economy, the CCP wanted a static society governed by state plans politically and socially. Administrative organizations were set up nationwide, from ministries at the central government to neighborhood committees in local communities, to help the governance of the central government. Ideologically, Chairman Mao Zedong classified all contradictions (*maodun* in Chinese) during this period into two kinds and made clear distinctions between the antagonistic (people vs. enemy) and the nonantagonistic (people vs. people) contradictions. High-pressure dictatorship (e.g., through criminal punishment) should be adopted only against the enemies (see Clark & Feinerman, 1996; Fu, 1993; V. Yang, 1996). As a consequence, one's political classification (*chengfen*) became a means for political control, critical to one's life and career.

On January 9, 1958, the Standing Committee of the first National People's Congress passed the Regulations of the People's Republic of China on Residence Registration. It required each family in urban areas to register at local public security departments and to hold a valid registration booklet. In the booklet, name, birth date, occupation, family members, residence, family status (agricultural or nonagricultural), gender, place of birth, and more details were recorded (see Mathaus, 1989; T. Zhang, 2001). The household registration (*hukou*) system drew a distinction between the rural and the urban, bound people (especially peasants) to their native places (e.g., lands), and made migration and social transition very difficult, if not completely impossible. It was a means of political administration, and it also became an effective means of social (status) control.[3]

In urban cities, the workplace (*danwei*) exercised tight control over its workers. Its functions went beyond pure supervision over one's work performance and extended to governance over one's political performance (usually connected with one's work performance), one's after-work life (e.g., mass entertainment organized by *danwei*), and one's private life as well (e.g., marriage matches). To a large extent, it became another means of social control by the central government (see Walder, 1986; Yuan, 1995). Combined with other control mechanisms such as one's personal files (*dang'an*) and class labels (*chengfen*), the household registration and *danwei* all had a great impact on people's lives in this historical period. Within such a system, the function of law and the legal system was reduced to be a governmental tool.

Law as a Tool for Class Struggle

Based on orthodox Marxism, the Chinese communist government strongly repudiated Western democracy and its justifications of an autonomous legal system (e.g., ideas of separation of power and checks and balances). Rather, it declared that law is associated with the nature of the state and therefore by no means impartial. It is a tool for the maintenance of state domination (P. M. Chen, 1973). Consistent with this understanding, class struggle had been viewed as an effective means to push forward development of society since the founding of the new China. From the "Anti-Rightists" campaign and the "Great Leap Forward" movement in the 1950s to the Cultural Revolution in the 1960s and 1970s, law and the legal system were used as tools for class struggle, and their existence and functions were subject to politicians' discretions. In 1959, for instance, the Ministry of Justice (MOJ) and the Bureau of Legislative Affairs (under the State Council) were both closed, followed by abolishment of justice bureaus in provinces, autonomous regions, and municipalities (Xin, 1999).

In addition, a mass-line policy was adopted in the whole country, and people were motivated to participate in the building of the socialist country and in class struggle (V. H. Li, 1978). The mass-line policy called for popular justice at the community level and encouraged greater involvement and mobilization of the masses to manage their own affairs, to resolve their own conflicts, and to achieve self-policing and discipline as well as mutual policing.[4] All these movements further weakened the function of China's nascent and brittle legal system. In the heyday of class struggle during the Cultural Revolution period (1966–1976), state legal systems were severely paralyzed. For example, in this 10-year period, the Third Session of the National People's Congress (NPC), as the national legislative organization, could not hold its regular meetings, even though the national Constitution required its annual meetings. Only one law, the Platform for the Development of the National Agriculture from 1958 to 1967, was made during this period. The revised Constitution in 1975 contained merely 30 articles, a sharp reduction from a total of 106 articles in the 1954 Constitution. The People's Procuratorates were completely abolished and regrouped into public security organizations.[5]

The remaining organizations of the legal system also could not function normally in this period. It was not unusual that the *Gong, Jian, Fa* (police, procuracy, and court) were smashed by extremely feverous youths, the Red Guards, in social movements (see Bracey, 1988; Gold, 1991). This period of time was later described by scholars as lawless or a period of the "rule of man."

As summarized by J. Chen (1999), the characteristics of the justice and legal system during this period were evident in three aspects. First, the Marxist concept of law was used as a tool to remold society, to suppress class enemies, and to enforce party policies rather than to protect individual rights. Second, justice was both politicized and popularized. Social and legal distinctions were made based on one's (political) class membership and the implementation of the mass line led to mass trials for ideological indoctrination. Third and finally, extrajudicial organizations, procedures, and measures were often utilized to impose sanctions and settle disputes. These three features exactly represented *natures, forms*, and *operations* of the legal system during this historical period.

Marxism and Chinese Traditions

It should be noted that Chinese communist law was not a product of Marxism alone. It was also a product of Chinese traditions.[6] The combination of Marxism and Chinese traditions, however, is not a simple addition. Rather, it is a complex process.

On the one hand, the new communist system was built on the destruction of the old traditional system. For example, the feudalistic self-sufficient economic system was replaced with the socialist mode of production; the local traditional power of *Zu* (the kinship) as a form of social control was detached and weakened (see S. Zhu, 1992; see also Chao, 1982, and H. C. Hu, 1948, for more detailed studies of traditional *Zu* in China); the new Marriage Law enacted by the government in 1950 dramatically challenged and changed traditional family roles ensuring equal rights for both sexes in the family and weakening the traditional authority of the elderly and men (see Troyer et al., 1989; L. Zhang & Messner, 1995); and in the educational system, Marxism publicly replaced traditional Confucianism as the dominant theory and ideology being taught in schools.

On the other hand, Chinese traditions also seemed to facilitate the dramatic shift and the adoption of Marxism in the new society. Scholars have already pointed out some commonalities between Marxian practices and Chinese traditions. First, both emphasized moral and ideological education and internalization, and law and the legal system were only secondary as means to reach the ends (see V. H. Li, 1978; Ren, 1997; S. Zhu, 1992). Second, based on Marxism, the CCP maintained that national and Party's interests are by definition synonymous with those of the masses. Individuals' rights were granted from above and only so long as they may serve the overall societal good (see Polumbaum, 1994). This practice was consistent with traditional Confucian views of individualism, in which one's value was realized through the fulfillment of one's duties and responsibilities in certain social groups (Ren, 1997). Third, class distinctions in the new China were not unfamiliar to Chinese people because under Confucianism, traditional Chinese society was hierarchical and class-based (P. M. Chen, 1973). All those seemingly common features to a large extent helped China's transition into a communist nation.

In their domestic research, many Chinese scholars drew a line between the prereform era and the reform era after 1978 and viewed them as a contrast between the traditional legal system and the modern legal system. They held that the traditional legal system was closely connected with and indeed originated from the Chinese economic base (dominantly a self-sufficient and agricultural economy), political base (centralized, planned administrative policies based on the rule of man), and culture base (group-centered rights over individual rights). In comparison, the modern legal system was connected with advanced market economy and democratic political organizations (see, e.g., Gong et al., 1999; Zuo & Zhuo, 2000). They further suggested that the transition from the traditional model to the modern model is inevitable and necessary for China's further development.

REFORM ERA UNDER REINTERPRETED MARXISM AFTER 1978

1978 marked a watershed in Chinese history. After the 3rd plenary session of the 11th Central Committee, the CCP officially acknowledged that "the principle contradiction in China today is no longer class struggle but between the growing material and cultural needs of the people and the backwardness of social production" (cited in Leng, 1985, p. 36). This call was to end the class struggle that had persisted in China for more than 20 years and to shift the government's priority back to economic development. In the next three decades, China's economy quickly took off and began to catch up with advanced developed nations. For example, in 1978, both the gross national product (GNP) and the gross domestic product (GDP) were a little more than 364 billion yuan, and the per capita GDP was just 381 yuan. Then the GDP grew at an average of 9.6% (adjusted) per year from 1979 to 2005.[7] By 2005, both GNP and GDP reached more than 18.3 trillion yuan (more than a 1,198% index increase with 1978 = 100), and the per capita GDP jumped to 14,040 yuan (more than a 878% index increase with 1978 = 100; see Table 2.1). The most recent data reported China's GDP as 20.94 trillion yuan in 2006, a 10.7% increase from 2005.[8] Next, I take a closer look at the transition and focus on how the changes were made possible.

Table 2.1 Gross National Product (GNP), Gross Domestic Product (GDP) and Per Capita GDP

Year	GNP (100 Million Yuan)	GDP (100 Million Yuan)	Index of GDP (1978 = 100)	Per Capita GDP (Yuan)	Index of Per Capita GDP (1978 = 100)
1978	3,645.2	3,645.2	100.0	381	100.0
1979	4,062.6	4,062.6	107.6	419	106.1
1980	4,545.6	4,545.6	116.0	463	113.0
1981	4,889.5	4,891.6	122.1	492	117.5
1982	5,330.5	5,323.4	133.1	528	126.2
1983	5,985.6	5,962.7	147.6	583	137.9
1984	7,243.8	7,208.1	170.0	695	156.8
1985	9,040.7	9,016.0	192.9	858	175.5
1986	10,274.4	10,275.2	210.0	963	188.2
1987	12,050.6	12,058.6	234.3	1,112	206.6
1988	15,036.8	15,042.8	260.7	1,366	226.3
1989	17,000.9	16,992.3	271.3	1,519	231.9
1990	18,718.3	18,667.8	281.7	1,644	237.3
1991	21,826.2	21,781.5	307.6	1,893	255.6
1992	26,937.3	26,923.5	351.4	2,311	288.4
1993	35,260.0	35,333.9	400.4	2,998	324.9
1994	48,108.5	48,197.9	452.8	4,044	363.3
1995	59,810.5	60,793.7	502.3	5,046	398.6
1996	70,142.5	71,176.6	552.6	5,846	433.9
1997	77,653.1	78,973.0	603.9	6,420	469.4
1998	83,024.3	84,402.3	651.2	6,796	501.4
1999	88,189.0	89,677.1	700.9	7,159	534.9
2000	98,000.5	99,214.6	759.9	7,858	575.5
2001	108,068.2	109,655.2	823.0	8,622	618.7
2002	119,095.7	120,332.7	897.8	9,398	670.4
2003	135,174.0	135,822.8	987.8	10,542	733.1
2004	159,586.7	159,878.3	1,087.4	12,336	802.2
2005	183,956.1	183,084.8	1,198.7	14,040	878.9

Note. Data from *China Statistical Yearbook* (2001, 2005, 2006); *China Statistical Abstract* (2002). Data collected in the *China Statistical Yearbook* over time sometimes do not match (due to revisions). The most recent data are used.

Reemergence of Nonpublic Modes of Production

Major changes in socialist economic structure have been made possible with changes to the modes of productivity in both rural and urban areas. In rural areas, the contract responsibility system replaced collective commune production and greatly promoted farmers' incentives and enhanced agricultural production. In a little more than 25 years, the gross output value of farming increased more than 16-fold, from 111.76 billion yuan in 1978 to 1.96 trillion yuan in 2005. Along with the increase, production in forestry, animal husbandry, and fishery all developed quickly in rural areas (see Figure 2.1).

The successful experience in rural areas prompted the expansion of the reform into industrial sectors. Non-state-owned models of organizations, such as township and village enterprises, (foreign) joint ventures, wholly foreign enterprises, and private enterprises were gradually reintroduced into industrial sectors after almost 30 years of suppression. Those nonpublic productive activities were deemed the "tail of capitalism," and there were calls for them to be collectivized and eliminated under the 1975 and 1978 versions of Constitution. After 1978, however, it was those nonpublic modes of production that greatly contributed to China's economic development. Table 2.2 shows how quickly the individual-owned industry and other types of industries have grown over the years in terms of their total size (number of industrial enterprises) and overall output value, as compared to both state-owned and collective-owned industries. In the 1950s,

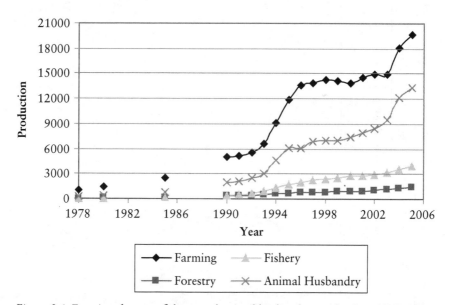

Figure 2.1 Farming, forestry, fishery, and animal husbandry production, 1978–2005.

Source: (1) *China Statistical Yearbook* (2005, 2006); (2) *China Statistical Abstract* (2002).

Table 2.2 Number of Industrial Enterprises and Gross Industrial Output Value by Ownerships

	Number of Industrial Enterprises (Unit: 10,000)					Gross Output Value (Unit: 100 Million Yuan)				
Year	Total*	State-Owned Industry	Collective-Owned Industry	Individual-Owned Industry	Other Industries	Total	State-Owned Industry	Collective-Owned Industry	Individual-Owned Industry	Other Industries
1952						349	144.97	11.38	71.79	120.86
1957	16.95	4.96	11.90			704	378.54	133.97	5.84	185.65
1962	19.74	5.30	14.44			920	808	112		
1965	15.77	4.59	11.18			1,402	1262.78	139.22		
1970	19.51	5.74	13.77			2,117	1854.70	262.30		
1975	26.29	7.50	18.79			3,207	2600.56	606.44		
1978	34.84	8.37	26.47			4,237	3289.18	947.82		
1979	35.50	8.38	27.12			4,681	3673.60	1007.70		
1980	37.73	8.34	29.35		0.04	5,154	3915.60	1231.36	0.81	24.49
1981	38.15	8.42	29.68		0.05	5,400	4037.10	1329.38	1.90	31.40
1982	38.86	8.60	30.19		0.07	5,811	4326.00	1442.42	3.40	39.40
1983	39.25	8.71	30.46		0.08	6,461	4739.4	1663.14	7.50	50.40
1984	43.72	8.41	35.21		0.10	7,617	5262.70	2263.09	14.80	76.70
1985	46.32	9.37	36.78	334.78	0.17	9,716	6302.12	3117.19	179.75	117.41

1986	49.93	9.68	40.04	478.45	0.21	11,194	6971.12	3751.54	308.54	163.06
1987	49.36	9.76	39.21	555.33	0.39	13,813	8250.09	4781.74	502.39	278.77
1988	50.00	9.91	39.54	614.81	0.55	18,224	10351.28	6587.49	790.49	495.32
1989	50.54	10.23	39.59	612.42	0.72	22,017	12342.91	7858.05	1057.66	758.44
1990	50.44	10.44	39.11	617.60	0.88	23,924	13063.75	8522.73	1290.30	1047.56
1991	50.48	10.48	38.92	638.67	1.08	26,625	14954.58	8783.00	1287.00	1599.58
1992	50.21	10.33	38.45	685.40	1.42	34,599	17824.15	12135.00	2006.00	2633.57
1993	52.01	10.47	38.33	797.12	3.21	48,402	22724.67	16464.00	3861.00	5352.06
1994	53.18	10.22	38.51	800.74	4.45	70,176	26200.84	26473.00	7082.00	10421.35
1995	59.21	11.80	41.36	568.82	6.03	91,894	31219.66	33622.64	11820.57	15230.87
1996	57.88	11.38	39.48	621.07	7.02	99,595	36173.00	39232.18	15429.82	16582.25
1997	53.44	9.86	35.79	597.47	7.79	113,733	35968.00	43347.17	20376.13	20982.01
1998	16.51	6.47	4.77	603.38	5.27	119,048	33621.00	45730.00	20372.00	27270.00
1999	16.20	5.07	4.26		7.87	126,110	35571.00	44607.00	22928.00	32962.00
2000	16.29	5.35	3.78		7.16		40554.37	11907.92		53609.45
2001	16.88	4.76	3.52				42502.6	11811.5		

Note. Data from *China Statistical Yearbook* (1980–2001) and *China Statistical Abstract* (2002). Data collected in the *China Statistical Yearbook* over time sometimes do not match (due to revisions). The most recent data are used.
*The total reported here includes only the number of all state-owned and non-state-owned above designated size industrial enterprises.

nonstate- and collective-owned industries still made contributions to the national gross output, and did so significantly in the early 1950s. They were, however, totally gone in the 1960s and 1970s. Only after the 1980s did they reemerge on the national stage. By the mid-1980s, the number of nonstate- and collective-owned industries already far exceeded the total number of state- and collective-owned industries. Around the turn of the new millennium, the gross output value of nonstate and noncollective industries had already caught up to that of state and collective industries and showed an explosive increase in 20 years.

The new energy brought by non-public-owned sectors was also evident in their competitive average wages for workers, as compared with state-owned and collective-owned sectors (see Table 2.3). After their reemergence, the average wage of non-public-owned sectors kept up with that of state-owned sectors and clearly outperformed the collective-owned units. It is also worth mentioning that the state-owned units were able to keep increasing their wage levels in the 1990s and in the new millennium only after serious internal struggles and after going through major overhauls[9] (see later discussion on the SOEs). Because of their accelerating development, non-public-owned sectors started absorbing more and more labor (see Table 2.4). In 1994, the number of workers employed by nonpublic sectors already surpassed that of urban collective-owned units, and in 2002, it also passed the shrinking SOEs. Percentagewise, in 1978, the number of employees of SOEs represented 18.5% of the total number of employees; the shares for urban collective-owned units and private and self-employed individuals were 5% and 0.037%, respectively. By the end of 2005, the share for the SOEs dropped to 8.6% and the share for the urban collective-owned units dropped to 1.1%, but the share for private and self-employed individuals increased to 14.1%.

The development of non-public-owned economies was accompanied by new understandings of their roles in the whole structure of the socialist economy. In 1981, the 6th Plenum of the 11th Central Committee acknowledged that a certain scope of economic activity by individual laborers was a *necessary supplement* to public ownership (cited in Lardy, 2002). This acknowledgment was reaffirmed in the 1982 Constitution, which recognized that nonpublic ownership activities were working as a *necessary and beneficial complement* to the socialist economy (cited in S. Zhu, 1989). By 1997, nonstate sectors were viewed as an *integral* part of China's socialist market economy (Lardy, 2002), and it was further emphasized that both public and nonpublic ownership activities should expand and develop hand in hand.[10] By 2000, private firms were granted an equal footing with state-owned firms in the socialist market economy. On February 24, 2005, the State Council published its *Opinions on Development of Non-Public-Owned Economies* to further facilitate the growth of various non-public-owned economies and encourage them to enter works previously closed to them. Official data in 2005 and 2006 showed that non-public-owned economies already

Table 2.3 Average Wage of Staff and Workers and Related Indexes

	Average Money Wage (Yuan)				Indexes (Preceding Year = 100), Average Real Wage			
Year	Total	State-Owned Units	Urban Collective-Owned Units	Units of Other Types of Ownership	Total	State-Owned Units	Urban Collective-Owned Units	Units of Other Types of Ownership
1978	615	644	506		106.0	106.2	105.1	
1979	668	705	542		106.6	107.5	105.1	
1980	762	803	623		106.1	106.0	106.9	
1981	772	812	642		98.8	98.6	100.5	
1982	798	836	671		101.3	101.0	102.5	
1983	826	865	698		101.5	101.5	102.0	
1984	974	1,034	811	1,048	114.8	116.4	113.1	
1985	1,148	1,213	967	1,436	105.3	104.8	106.6	122.5
1986	1,329	1,414	1,092	1,629	108.2	108.9	105.5	106.0
1987	1,459	1,546	1,207	1,879	100.9	100.5	101.6	106.0
1988	1,747	1,853	1,426	2,382	99.2	99.3	97.9	105.0
1989	1,935	2,055	1,557	2,707	95.2	95.4	93.9	97.7
1990	2,140	2,284	1,681	2,987	109.2	109.7	106.6	108.9
1991	2,340	2,477	1,866	3,468	104.0	103.2	105.6	110.5
1992	2,711	2,878	2,109	3,966	106.7	107.0	104.1	105.3
1993	3,371	3,532	2,592	4,966	107.1	105.7	105.9	107.9
1994	4,538	4,797	3,245	6,303	107.7	108.7	100.2	101.5
1995	5,500	5,625	3,931	7,463	103.8	100.4	103.7	101.4
1996	6,210	6,280	4,302	8,261	103.8	102.6	100.6	101.7
1997	6,470	6,747	4,512	8,789	101.1	104.2	101.7	103.2
1998	7,479	7,668	5,331	8,972	107.2	106.7	103.1	98.3
1999	8,346	8,543	5,774	9,829	113.1	112.9	109.7	111.0
2000	9,371	9,552	6,262	10,984	111.4	110.9	107.6	110.9
2001	10,870	11,178	6,867	12,140	115.2	116.2	108.9	109.7
2002	12,422	12,869	7,667	13,212	115.5	116.2	108.9	109.7
2003	14,040	14,577	8,678	14,574	112.0	112.3	112.2	109.3
2004	16,024	16,729	9,814	16,259	110.5	111.1	109.5	108.0
2005	18,364	19,313	11,283	18,244	112.8	113.6	113.2	110.4

Note. Data from *China Statistical Yearbook* (2001, 2005, 2006) and *China Statistical Abstract* (2002).

Table 2.4 Number of Employed Persons by Ownership (Unit: 10,000 People)

Year	Total	State-Owned Units	Urban Collective-Owned Units	Private Enterprises and Self-Employed Individuals (Both Urban and Rural Areas)
1978	40,152	7,451	2,048	15
1979	41,024	7,693	2,274	32
1980	42,361	8,019	2,425	81
1981	43,725	8,372	2,568	113
1982	45,295	8,630	2,651	147
1983	46,436	8,771	2,744	231
1984	48,197	8,637	3,216	339
1985	49,873	8,990	3,324	450
1986	51,282	9,333	3,421	483
1987	52,783	9,654	3,488	569
1988	54,334	9,984	3,527	648
1989	55,329	10,108	3,502	2,142
1990	65,749	10,346	3,549	2,274.3
1991	65,491	10,664	3,628	2,491.5
1992	66,152	10,889	3,621	2,699.5
1993	66,808	10,920	3,393	3,312.0
1994	67,455	11,214	3,285	4,424.2
1995	68,065	11,261	3,147	5,569.5
1996	68,950	11,244	3,016	6,188.2
1997	69,820	11,044	2,883	6,791.1
1998	70,637	9,058	1,963	7,823.5
1999	71,394	8,572	1,712	8,262.5
2000	72,085	8,102	1,499	7,476.5
2001	73,025	7,640	1,291	7,474
2002	73,740	7,163	1,122	8,153
2003	74,432	6,876	1,000	8,936
2004	75,200	6,710	897	9,605
2005	75,825	6,488	810	10,725

Note. Data from *China Statistical Yearbook* (2001, 2005, 2006) and *China Statistical Abstract* (2002).

contributed more than 50% of China's total GDP annually,[11] and there is little doubt that they will keep growing.

Stagnating State-Owned Enterprises and Their Reforms

As the backbone of the socialist economy, the SOEs have been facing the challenge of non-public-owned sectors since the commencement of China's economic reform. Under the increasing competition, all the problems associated with the SOEs, such as excessive debts, skyrocketing inflation, redundant workers, heavy social burdens, and lack of efficiency, hindered economic performance and development of SOEs (X. Wang, 1998). Having been shifted from the sole legitimate enterprise type to the dominant one with other important supplements, SOEs had to find ways to keep their dominant status. As early as in the late 1980s and early 1990s, some scholars in China outlined reform plans and argued that the leading role of the state-owned economy should be transformed from a quantitative mode to a guidance mode (see Special Topic Team, 1989–1990). In 1997, Xiao Zhuoji published an article, "The Major Breakthrough of Ownership Theory," in the *People's Daily* and argued that "the dominance of public ownership should be measured by both 'quantity' and 'quality,' but the latter is more important. It is not accurate to use quantity as the criterion of the judgment (of dominance) as people usually do." Indeed, transitions have been moving toward this direction in practice. In 2001, for instance, non-public-ownership laborers outnumbered workers in the public sector in Beijing for the first time, with a total of 3.37 million employed people (53.5% of all employed workers). One major reason cited for such a transition was the restructuring of SOEs into various nonpublic sectors.[12]

Realizing the problems of SOEs, the Chinese government tried various means to revitalize the energy of SOEs and increase their competitiveness. Plans were proposed to separate the "ownership right" from the "right of operation," with an aim to realize the autonomy of the enterprises and to grant SOEs more economic self-determination rights.[13] The ideal separation of the daily operation right from the ownership right, however, turned out to be difficult. In principle, the State-Owned Enterprise Law (1988) provided that property in SOEs shall be owned by the whole people and the state shall exercise the property rights on behalf of the whole people. At the same time, the state functioned as the regulator of the business environment in which SOEs operated. However, SOEs also had certain legal obligations and rights over the assets entrusted to them, and bore responsibilities for managing daily operations as well as assuming liabilities. As SOEs transacted their business, they created legal relationships with other economic actors in the market. Due to these complex relationships, the task of separation inevitably experienced practical difficulties (see J. Chen, 1995; World Bank, 1997b).

In practice, various steps were taken to reach the goals of the SOEs reform. First, the financial power of enterprises was expanded from 1978 to

1984, and enterprises were given the right to retain and utilize part of their profits. Second, from 1984 to 1992, more management power in addition to financial power was granted to enterprises, and the old administrative relations between the state and enterprises were adjusted or replaced, giving enterprises more independent status in the market. As a result, state subsidies to SOEs were gradually reduced. In 1985, the total subsidies to SOEs represented 9.9% of China's GDP, but they were sharply reduced to 3.9% by 1994 (see Table 2.5).

After 1992, another reform move was adopted to transform and diversify public ownerships into different forms (X. Wang, 1998). The trial at this last phase clearly went beyond the boundary of the original plans. Two new approaches were proposed in principle and put into practice. First, small and less important SOEs were encouraged to diversify into other economic forms (what has been practiced exactly since 1992), and, second, recapitalization (e.g., securitization) was encouraged for big and key SOEs as an alternative to total privatization. The goal was to allow workers in these enterprises to become legal ownership shareholders.[14] In the new millennium, it was further proposed that foreign investment should be utilized as a means to regroup and recapitalize SOEs.[15] In November 2003, for example, Li Rongrong, Chairman of the State-Owned Assets Supervision and Administration Commission of the State Council, reported to the media that from 1998 to 2002 a total of 442 state-owned industrial enterprises (including corporate state-owned enterprises) were restructured and recapitalized through public offerings, and that a total of 743.6 billion yuan was raised (including overseas investment of 35.2 billion yuan) as a result.[16] It is obvious that the SOE reforms indicated a much deeper level of economic structural transformation than mere efforts to improve some outmoded enterprises.

Capitalization

Since the adoption of the "open door" policy, the Chinese government has been learning lessons from more advanced capitalist nations. Replacing the old models under the planned economy, the Chinese government borrowed more effective means to improve capital accumulation, production, and operation. I focus on three examples here: issuance of domestic and foreign debts, land transactions, and formation of a stock market.

Issuance of Debts

Soon after the reform, the Chinese government started issuing bonds as domestic debts to accumulate necessary capital for economic development. Table 2.6, based on data from the World Bank, shows how quickly the total amount of domestic debt increased from about 4 billion yuan in the early 1980s to around 200 billion yuan in the late 1990s. It also shows the changing sources of domestic debts. Bonds issued to individual households skyrocketed

Table 2.5 Subsidies to State Enterprises, 1985–1994 (Percentage of GDP)

	1985	1986	1987	1988	1989	1990	1991	1992	1993	1994
Total	9.9	9.9	10.2	7.0	6.9	6.2	5.8	7.5	6.3	3.9
Through the budget	7.5	7.5	7.2	6.4	6.9	6.4	5.2	3.9	3.1	2.2
Through the financial sector	2.4	2.4	3.0	0.6	−0.1	−0.2	0.6	3.6	3.2	1.7

Note. From World Bank (1996, p. 18).

Table 2.6 China's Domestic Debt (in Billions of Yuan)

Year	Issued to Enterprises	To Households	To Financial Institutions	Total
1982	2.4	2.0		4.4
1983	2.1	2.1		4.2
1984	2.0	2.2		4.2
1985	2.2	3.8		6.0
1986	2.3	4.0		6.3
1987	7.2	4.5		11.7
1988	3.5	8.8	6.6	18.9
1989	4.3	18.1		22.4
1990	12.6	9.3	7.1	29.0
1991	2.0	19.94	7.0	28.94
1992		38.9		38.9
1993		31.48	7.0	38.48
1994	2.00	111.77		113.77
1995		142.89	39.19	182.08
1996		212.62		212.62
1997		241.2		241.2
1998		195.35		195.35
Total	42.6	1,048.95	66.89	1,158.44

Note. From *World Bank* (1994, 1999).

in the 1990s and became the main source of debt in the late 1990s, in contrast to debts issued to enterprises. Official data by the NBSC for subsequent years reported even higher numbers as compared with those of the World Bank. From 1998 to 2004, the domestic debts issued increased from 322.8 billon yuan to 672.6 billon yuan (*China Statistical Yearbook*, 2005). The numbers in 2005 and 2006 further reached 704 billion and 888 billon yuan, respectively (National Debt Association of China, http://www.ndac.org.cn/index.jsp). From 1998 to October 2002, the Chinese government issued long-term debts worth 510 billion yuan and invested heavily in infrastructure construction. These investments reportedly contributed to China's GDP increase by 1.5% in 1998, 2% in 1999, 1.7% in 2000, and 1.8% in 2001.[17]

At the same time domestic debts were growing, China gained access to increasing quantities of foreign exchange through the sale of bonds on international markets. In 1982, China issued its first international bond worth 10 billion yuan in Tokyo. The second private placement of another 5 billion-yuan issue also was transacted in Tokyo a year later. In 1984 the Bank of China issued 20 billion yuan in bonds through a public offering, again in Japan, and by the end of 1988 a total of 39 bond issues, valued at $4.25 billion U.S., had been sold in various international markets such as Tokyo, Singapore, Luxembourg, London, Frankfurt, and Hong Kong (Lardy, 1994). The issuance was accelerated in the early 1990s. By 1992 and 1993, figures and projections from the World Bank already ranked China the seventh and eighth largest among all developing-country issuers of international bonds (Lardy, 1994). The NBSC data showed that China's foreign borrowing increased from less than 3 billion yuan in 1985 to a record high of 35.8 billion yuan by 1993 and then fell back to 14.5 billion yuan by 2004 (*China Statistical Yearbook*, 2005).

Land Transactions

Because of the nature of socialism, all land automatically belongs to the whole population. After the reform, people started realizing the lucrative nature of land. Similar to changes that happened to the SOE properties, the land-use right, a new legal concept, was introduced and institutionalized in 1986 when the Land Management Law was promulgated. In 1988, the commercial use of land was sanctioned by an amendment to the Constitution (J. Chen, 1999). Once the land use right was separated from the ownership right, it became commercially transactionable. In September 1988, a 50-year lease of a 5,321-square-meter residential site was awarded following a bid at a price of 200 yuan per square meter in Shenzhen, Guangdong province. In November of the same year, another 50-year lease for a 46,355-square-meter residential site was made at a price of 368 yuan per square meter. A month later, a new round of bidding for another piece of land resulted in an even higher price of 611 yuan per square meter (Oechsli, 1988). Those transactions opened the door for a new means of capitalization and operation.

Once the door was opened, land transactions expanded quickly to include not only individual residential areas but also huge chunks of open, state-owned land. In July 2002, a public auction was held at Hai Dian District in Beijing for the use right to a piece of state-owned land, the first state-owned land transaction. This 96 million-square-meter site was eventually sold at 53 million yuan.[18] In August of the same year in Xi'an, Shanxi province, a similar public-owned land transaction went through at a price of 41.5 million yuan.[19]

Stock Market

The formation and development of China's stock market is another example of how Western capitalist means were borrowed and practiced under the socialist market economy. Before the reform, stock issuance was viewed as a capitalistic means of exploitation. The new stock market established in the 1990s, however, has become one of the most important ways of capital accumulation and operation in China. In December 1990 and July 1991, stock exchanges were opened in Shanghai and Shenzhen, respectively. In the first year, only 15 companies dared to try the once forbidden apple with a total market capitalization of 10.9 billion yuan.[20] It took little time, however, before people accepted the new test, and China's stock market started expanding with incredible speed. By 2004, more than 1,300 companies had gone through public offerings, and the total market capitalization jumped to 4.8 trillion yuan in 2000 before it cooled off to 3.7 trillion yuan by 2004 (see Table 2.7).[21] The most recent data reported that a total of 1,434 companies had gone through public offerings by the end of 2006, and the total market capitalization reached an all-time high of 8.9 trillion yuan.[22] In addition, the stock market was increasingly diversified in types of shares with less restriction (see Table 2.8). In 2001, for example, the B-share was allowed to open to mainland citizens, and this greatly encouraged the development of the B-share market.[23] In the same year, China's B-share market experienced the highest increase in the world.[24] By October 2002, China's stock market became the third largest in Asia, behind only Japan and Hong Kong.[25] In December 2002, foreign investors also received permission to invest in domestic stocks.[26]

After the opening of the stock market, the Chinese government tried to adjust the stamp tax over the years as another means to control the young stock market. In 1990, the stamp tax was set at 0.6%. It was lowed to 0.3% in 1991 to stimulate the market. In 1997, it was increased to 0.5% but quickly fell back to 0.4% in 1998. In 1999, the stamp tax rate for the B-share was lowered to 0.3%. In 2001, the rate was lowered again to 0.2% for all shares.[27] From 1991 to 2000, the total stamp tax collected by the government reached more than 146 billion yuan.[28] China's stock market has gradually become a major contributor to the market capital accumulation. From 1991 to 2001, the total market capitalization accumulated reached 772.7 billion yuan.[29] In 1992, the total market capitalization of the stock market was a little more than 104 billion yuan, 3.89% of China's GDP, but it jumped to 4.8 trillion yuan by 2000, representing 48.47% of China's total GDP. Only after the new millennium did China's stock market cool down and start decreasing (see Table 2.9), before it again surged in 2006, when market capitalization represented 44% of China's GDP.[30]

Socialist Market Economy

After those dramatic changes happened, the Chinese government realized that the old planned economy could not be kept any longer, and both practical and theoretical adjustments had to be implemented. Soon after the reforms in the early 1980s, plans were proposed to supplement the planned

Table 2.7 Stock Transactions in Shanghai and Shenzhen Stock Exchanges

Year	Number of Companies		Number of Stocks		Value of Shares Traded (Unit: 100 Million Yuan)		Market Capitalization (Unit: 100 Million Yuan)		Transaction Volume (Unit: 1 Million Shares)		Transaction Value (Unit: 100 Million Yuan)	
	Shanghai	Shenzhen	Shanghai	Shenzhen	Shanghai	Shenzhen	Shanghai	Shenzhen	Shanghai	Shenzhen	Shanghai	Shenzhen
1991	8	7			2.72	38	29.42	80				
1992	29	29			46.94	171	558.4	490				
1993	106	77	123	95	423.94	437.68	2195.69	1335.32	14741.81	7914.66	2340.54	1286.66
1994	171	120	203	142	586.96	381.93	2600.13	1090.48	65676.03	35657.88	5735.07	2392.55
1995	188	135	220	161	587.00	351.22	2525.66	948.62	51382.72	19148.06	3042.63	932.99
1996	293	237	329	270	1408.74	1458.29	5477.81	4364.57	110188.37	143126.06	9114.82	12217.35
1997	383	362	422	399	2513.47	2690.95	9218.07	8311.17	121568.19	134433.70	13763.17	16958.66
1998	438	413	477	454	2947.45	2798.14	10625.91	8879.73	112795.49	102615.07	12386.11	11158.14
1999	484	463	525	504	4294.69	3964.27	14580.47	11890.70	156038.27	137200.61	16965.79	14353.81
2000	572	514	614	560	8481.33	7606.19	26930.86	21160.08	243765.39	232072.82	31373.86	29452.79
2001	646	514	690	550	8382.11	6081.06	27590.6	15931.6	181995.4	133233.3	22709.4	15595.8
2002	715	509	759	551	7467.3	5017.26	25363.7	12965.4	178109.6	123509.9	16959.1	11031.4
2003	780	507	824	548	8201.14	4977.38	29804.9	12652.8	269272.9	147035.5	20824.1	11291.1
2004	837	540	881	582	7350.88	4337.76	26014.3	11041.2	360774.2	221999.1	26470.6	15863.4
2005	834	547										

Note. From *Almanac of China's Finance and Banking* (2001, 2005); *World Bank* (1995); the *People's Daily*, February 24, 2002; and *China Statistical Yearbook* (2006).

Table 2.8 Stock Issuance Over Time

	Stock (Share) Issuance (100 Million)				Capital Raised (100 Million Yuan)				
Year	Total	Share A	H&N	B	Total	Share A	H&N	B	Rights Issued
1991	5.00	5.00			5.00	5.00			
1992	20.75	10.00		10.75	94.09	50.00		44.09	
1993	95.79	42.59	40.41	12.79	375.47	276.41	60.93	38.13	81.58
1994	91.26	10.97	69.89	10.40	326.78	99.78	188.73	38.27	50.16
1995	31.60	5.32	15.38	10.90	150.32	85.51	31.46	33.35	62.83
1996	86.11	38.29	31.77	16.05	425.08	294.34	83.56	47.18	69.89
1997	267.63	105.65	136.88	25.10	1,293.82	825.92	360.00	80.76	170.86
1998	105.56	86.30	12.86	9.90	841.52	778.02	37.95	25.55	334.97
1999	122.93	98.11	23.05	1.77	944.56	893.60	47.17	3.79	320.97
2000	512.03	145.68	359.26	7.10	2,103.08	1,527.03	562.21	13.99	519.46
2001	141.48	93.00	48.48		1,252.34	1,182.13	70.21		430.64
2002	291.74	134.20	157.54		961.75	779.75	181.99		56.61
2003	281.43	83.64	196.79	1.00	1,357.75	819.56	534.65	3.54	74.79
2004	227.92	54.88	171.51	1.53	1,510.94	835.71	648.08	27.16	104.54
2005	576.05	13.80	553.25		1,882.51	338.13	1,544.38		2.62

Note. From *China Statistical Yearbook* (2005, 2006).

Table 2.9 Proportion of Market Capitalization to GDP (100 Million Yuan)

Year	GDP[a]	Market Capitalization	% of GDP	Value of Shares Traded	% of GDP
1992	26,923.5	1,048.13	3.89	217.94	0.81
1993	35,333.9	3,531.01	9.99	861.62	2.44
1994	48,197.9	3,690.62	7.66	964.82	2.00
1995	60,793.7	3,474.00	5.71	937.94	1.54
1996	71,176.6	9,842.37	13.89	2,867.03	4.03
1997	78,973.0	17,529.23	22.20	5,204.43	6.59
1998	84,402.3	19,505.64	23.11	5,745.59	6.81
1999	89,677.1	26,471.17	29.52	8,213.97	9.16
2000	99,214.6	48,090.94	48.47	16,087.52	16.21
2001	109,655.2	43,522.19	39.69	14,463.16	13.19
2002	120,332.7	38,329.12	31.85	12,484.55	10.38
2003	135,822.8	42,457.72	31.26	13,178.52	10.10
2004	159,878.3	37,055.57	23.18	11,688.64	7.31
2005	183,956.1	32,430.28	17.63	10,630.51	5.78

Note. From *Almanac of China's Finance and Banking* (2001, 2005), and *China Statistical Yearbook* (2006).
[a]The most recently revised GDP data reported in the *Chinese Statistical Yearbook* (2006) are used.

economy with market regulations, and this was the first step in making adjustments (World Bank, 1997a). Next, the term *commodity economy* was proposed to meet the needs of the new market under the planned economy (see J. Chen, 1995; World Bank, 1997a). Although the difference between a commodity economy and a market economy was vague, the government showed a strong reluctance to use the term *market economy* at that time because of its association with capitalism. In 1987, the CCP acknowledged that China's socialism was still at a preliminary stage. Rather than "carried out on the basis of a highly-developed capitalism as orthodox Marxism suggested, China's socialism was constructed in backward industrial conditions, with backward productive forces and an underdeveloped commodity economy" (Lo, 1995, p. 29). This acknowledgment paved the way for further structural changes.[31] For example, income derived from bonds and shares was viewed as unearned under orthodox Marxism. At the preliminary stage of socialism, however, it became acceptable to receive some income that did not come from one's own labor (Epstein, 1991).

In 1988, Zhao Ziyang, General Secretary of the CCP, rejected the orthodox Marxist dichotomy that characterized socialism and capitalism in terms of a planned and a market economy, and this rejection gave rise to the development of the Chinese market economy (Lo, 1995). Under the new interpretation, a market economy no longer belonged to capitalism and could be used as a means by socialist countries to regulate the economy as a supplement to the planned economy. From 1989 to the early 1990s, the official position was that China's economy was an economy with "organic integration with both planned and market regulations" (World Bank, 1997a). The triumph of the market economy over the planned economy, however, looked unstoppable. In 1993, the market economy officially replaced the planned economy in the revised Constitution as the main economic mode at the socialist preliminary stage. Since then, the official term has been the "socialist market economy with Chinese characteristics."

Two things are worth mentioning during this series of name changes (from the planned economy to the commodity economy and then to the market economy). First, as some scholars pointed out, these name changes did not bring something new to Chinese reform as far as specific measures were concerned. Rather, the significance lay in the justification for introducing those new names or notions. It was a strong indicator that the Chinese government had gradually discarded old ideological boundaries based on orthodox Marxian doctrines. The adoption of "socialist market economy with Chinese characteristics" was more like a license to allow capitalist practices in the economic domain (see J. Chen, 1999; Solinger, 1993). Second, the Chinese government did not give up Marxism as its official theoretical guidance, at least literally, even though so many changes were made that clearly departed from orthodox Marxian doctrines. Instead, all these changes were made possible through a series of reinterpretations of Marxian theories in China.

Reinterpreted Marxism After 1978

In a sense, Marxism in China was always a revised Marxism, different from other socialist nations' practices in reality (see discussions by Frank, 1980; Hopkins et al., 1996; Lowe, 1996; Lukes, 1985; Wallerstein, 1984). What has been reinterpreted since 1978, however, marks a significant digression from the Marxism upheld before 1978.

From the beginning of its revolution, the CCP adopted Marxism-Leninism as its theoretical guidance. Later, with the establishment of Mao Zedong's power in the Party, the "Mao Zedong Thought" became the dominant thought, and it was officially accepted by the CCP in its 7th Party Congress in 1945 (Yuan, 1995). After the birth of the new China, Marxism-Leninism-Maoism was further indoctrinated as the absolute truth by the Party. On the one hand, the term is a historical product embedded in three giants in different countries and in different periods. On the other hand, it shows the flexibility (or perhaps confusion) of the underlying theory. Different from the Stalinist command economy model based on official bureaucratization, Mao adopted a social-mobilization model based on the mass-line policy as a way to avoid mistakes committed by the Soviet Communist Party (Van Ness, 1984). Although substantially different, both China and the former Soviet Union claimed their systems as true socialism under Marxism.

After 1978, the CCP under Deng Xiaoping's leadership ended class struggle and shifted the Party's priority back to economic development. This was viewed as correcting Mao's mistakes made in the Cultural Revolution and revalidating the fundamental Marxian theory that the economic base determines the superstructure. Further, Deng broke the conventional boundaries of socialism and capitalism by claiming that "social practice (praxis) is the only criterion of seeking truth."[32] Under such a standard, all effective means, no matter whether named capitalism or socialism, could be used to enhance economic production at the socialist preliminary stage.

One result of these new economic and social changes was a strong challenge to people's old ideology. In his dissertation, Tanner (1994) described an example of how some older generations reacted to the fact that workers in SOEs had been fired and become unemployed: "Unemployed! Our baby's rice-bowl is broken! Heaven! Isn't this going back to the old days? How could a socialist country's workers also become unemployed?" Quite a few angered workers pressed their fingers to the manager's nose: "Are you the communist party's factory manager, or are you a capitalist?" (p. 180). This example showed how difficult it was for some people to face the dramatic changes after the reform. Nevertheless, people had to accept the rising unemployment rate and enterprise bankruptcies after the bankruptcy law was introduced in 1986 (for works about the bankruptcy law, see Cao, 1998a, 1998b). In the educational system, Marxism and Leninism started receding too, similar to what had happened to China's traditional moral teachings (e.g., Confucianism) decades before. In 1993, for example, the People's University in Beijing abolished 17 courses on Marxism and Leninism and introduced new courses such as marketing, international trade, and real estate management (Nai-kwai Lo, 1993). Many scholars believed that Deng's pragmatism demolished the ideological basis of Maoism, but it also failed to find a new way to unify people's thoughts and therefore created an ideology void (see W. Chen, 1998; Wai, 1994).

Nevertheless, Dengism (Deng Xiaoping's theory) was gradually established by the Party as another living Marxism in China after Maoism.[33] The official interpretation was that Maoism changed China from a semifeudal and semicolonial society to a new socialist society, and Dengism changed China into a country under the socialist market economy with Chinese characteristics.[34] Under Deng's theory, the market economy does not belong to capitalism any more, and it is consistent with the necessity of socialist economic division and productions.[35] As expected, Dengism was finally put into the CCP Charter in the 15th Party's Congress and listed as one of the main guidelines along with Marxism, Leninism, and Maoism in the revised 1999 Constitution.[36] Now the term became Marxism-Leninism-Maoism-Dengism.

After Deng's death, his successor Jiang Zemin put forward his theory, and not surprisingly this was viewed as the latest development of Marxism in China.[37] On July 1, 2001, Jiang outlined his "Three Represents" theory in a speech given for the celebration of the 80-year anniversary of the founding of the CCP. The gist of the new theory argued that in the new century the CCP must represent "the development trend of China's advanced production forces, the orientation of China's advanced culture, and the fundamental interests of the Chinese people."[38] After this July 1 speech, the media was filled with laudatory commentaries and tried to establish this "Three Represents" theory as the most recent development of living Marxism in China.[39] It was proposed that Jiang's theory should be added into the CCP Charter in the 16th Party's Congress, and the true standard and judgment should be "Marxism, Leninism, Mao's Thought, Deng's Theory and Jiang's 'Three Represents' principles"[40]. In 2002, Jiang's theory was indeed added into the amended Party Charter.[41] It is ironic that the list is getting longer as each generation of the CCP leaders tries to establish his name as part of it, and it is also remarkable to see how Marxism incorporated so many divergent theories and practices through reinterpretations in China.

Because of these reinterpretations, the Chinese government was able to hold onto its socialist nature ideologically. In these reinterpretations, media propaganda played a huge role in two discernible ways. First, socialism was reemphasized each time as the only viable system for China. It was argued that capitalism, although it has gone through many improvements, has never changed its fundamentals with its exploitive and colonial expansionary nature. It is inevitable that socialism eventually will take the place of capitalism.[42] Second, theories have been proposed to explain differences between a socialist market economy and a capitalist market economy. Justifications were made to show new market economic relations (e.g., the remunerative principle "from each according to its ability, to each according to its contribution") could exist at an early stage of socialism according to traditional Marxian economic theory, and how these relations are fundamentally different, because of their socialist nature, from the exploitative relations in capitalist nations.[43] As confusing as they were, the bottom line seemed to be that if China holds to socialism as the basic system, any capitalist means could be borrowed and utilized for the building of Chinese socialism. An answer, however, has not been provided as to how China can hold to a socialist system after its economic and political structures are changed. In 2002, an interesting economic incident was noticed in China, when overproduced milk was dumped in several big cities such as Nanjing and Chengdu. The milk-dumping incident used to be taught as a standard example of capitalist economic crises in Marxian textbooks. In a little more than 20 years after the reform, China experienced the same incident. A commentator sighed over the fact that no one dared to admit it as a sign of economic crisis.[44] This incident showed precisely the painful struggle; that is, how to reconcile common characteristics and functions of economic structures with different theories because of (the presumed) divergent natures in systems.

In summary, dramatic changes have happened in the economic structure in China during the reform era. It is not accurate to say that those capitalist functions and experiences were completely new to Chinese society because many of them did exist before the CCP came to power. What happened in the reform era was, in a sense, a return to what had been repressed and eradicated in the prereform era. The CCP, however, still managed to hold to Marxism as its dominant theoretical guidance, as it tried to revise and reinterpret Marxism to incorporate new changes, both theoretically and practically.

CONCLUSION

In this chapter, I tried to pinpoint the dramatic changes that happened to the economic base in China after 1978 as a comparison to the prereform era. In the prereform era, doctrinal Marxism had been adopted and practiced economically, politically, and legally. Consistent with the planned economy, the function of law and the legal system was reduced to facilitating administrative policies and mainly used as a tool in class struggle. In the reform era, the economic structure was dramatically changed. Various nonpublic economic activities were revived and thrived. Capitalist means of production and management were introduced into the economic system, and a market economy was eventually adopted and established.

Substantively, many changes in the new era represented a resurgence of what had been labeled as "functions with capitalist nature" in the prereform era. In 20 years, however, Chinese society had to adjust to new modes of production, forms of capitalization, and economic and social organizations. In a way, the major challenge came more from ideological struggles and transitions. Amazingly, all these dramatic changes were claimed as credits in a series of reinterpretations of living Marxism in China. This showed to some extent the struggle by the leaders of the CCP. On the one hand, they had to answer new calls to cater to both economic and social changes, and, on the other hand, they tried to save the Party's ideological consistency and control under Marxism. In such a transition, political and legal reforms began to serve an important function, a topic that I address in the next chapter.

3 Legalization and Centralization of Power

In the last chapter, I outlined the dramatic changes that occurred in the economic structure of China after 1978. In this chapter, I move on to examine changes at the political and legal level in the new era. Along with economic changes, the Chinese legal system also changed its role. Serving immediate economic needs, the rebuilding of the legal system has been emphasized and accelerated in recent years. As a result, we witnessed the systemization and bureaucratization of the legal system (in a Weberian sense), even though the process was definitely colored by Chinese characteristics. In this legalization process, various legal branches such as the court, the procuratorate, and the lawyers were (re)established and strengthened; legal study and education were restored and encouraged; and new notions such as legal professionalism and rule of law were proposed and put into practice.

Following the trajectory of China's economic development, scholars proposed a decentralization theory. Although this approach has its merits on the economic domain, I argue that caution be used when scholars apply and expand this term into other domains. Instead, China's legal reform should be studied in a broader scope; that is, as part of the ongoing political reforms in China. Consistent with Weber's analysis, the systemization and bureaucratization of the legal system has been carried out through a process of centralization of both political and social control power, contrary to the decentralization of economic power. The Chinese government adopted legal reform as a new means of governing national affairs and tried to legitimate and maintain its own political power and control in the new era.

CHANGING LEGAL SYSTEM: ITS LEGALIZATION, SYSTEMIZATION, AND BUREAUCRATIZATION

Reinterpreting the Function of Law and the Legal System

After 1978, realizing that the rule of man was a mistake and had had disastrous consequences, the Chinese government started its legal reform. The first step was to reinterpret the function of law and the legal system. Before the reform, law was viewed ideologically as a tool for the proletarian dictatorship and used to differentiate the people from the enemy and punish the latter. This understanding was consistent with the practice of the traditional Chinese legal system in which criminal law clearly dominated. After the reform, the process of legalization had to move beyond the scope of criminal law to answer the need for economic development. As a result, the function of law as a tool for class struggle was deemphasized as only one of many characteristics of law (although it cannot be totally discarded under Marxian theory). Instead, the material character of law (i.e., law is determined by its economic base) was emphasized, and it demanded law be used to support and facilitate the economic base (see Y. Wang & Zhang, 1992). In addition, it was pointed out that legal means should be used to solve not only contradictions between the people and the enemy, but also contradictions among people. The authority of law and the legal system and the presumed equality and fairness all make legal means a powerful weapon to handle economic and administrative problems in the new era.[1] Once the importance of legalization was recognized theoretically, legal practice quickly expanded. In 1999, for the first time, the Constitution was revised to guarantee that "the People's Republic China practices ruling the country in accordance with the law and building a socialist country of law."[2]

Increasing Lawmaking and Legislative Functioning

After the new China was founded in 1949, the NPC and its Standing Committee promulgated a number of laws and regulations to establish a legal system for the new government. This effort, however, was completely disrupted by class struggle, especially in the Cultural Revolution period. By 1979, most of the laws and regulations enacted in the earlier years had already become invalid (Xin, 1999). The first task of China's legalization in the reform era, therefore, was to create new laws and regulations.

Table 3.1 shows the number of laws and regulations passed by the NPC, its Standing Committee, the State Council, and local people's congresses over the years. It clearly shows a growing lawmaking process. During this process, new laws were enacted, and many important ones (e.g., the Constitution, the Criminal Law, the Criminal Procedure Law) were amended several times, catering to the needs of the new era. In addition, the lawmaking process became more systematic, and there were signs that the NPC and its Standing Committee gained more power and became less subject to the Party's control (see Keith, 1997; Shih, 1999; M. S. Tanner, 1999). In July 2000, the Standing Committee of the NPC passed the Legislative Law of the People's Republic of China (*lifa fa*) and formalized the lawmaking procedure.[3] From 1978 to August 2002, the NPC and its Standing Committee passed 301 laws, seven law interpretations, and 122 decisions regarding laws. It was officially announced that China had accomplished its task of building a preliminary legal system.[4]

Table 3.1 Laws and Regulations Passed by the NPC, Its Standing Committee, the State Council, and Local People's Congresses

Year	Laws Made by NPC and Its Standing Committee	Decisions Regarding Laws Made by NPC and Its Standing Committee	Administrative Regulations Enacted by State Council	Local Regulations Made by Local People's Congresses
1953–1957	479			
1979–1986	56	51		
1986	11	4	80	186
1987	6	5	76	219
1988	9	12	45	242
1989	8	3	43	307
1990	13	7	45	326
1991	12	4	32	277
1992	12	5	27	258
1993	13	7	49	281
1994	11	7	40	722
1995	22	2	30	820
1996	19	3	25	577
1997	12	12	47	1,362
1998	11	9	24	700
1999	16	8	29	699
2000	13	2	27	648
2001	19	4	46	
2002	16	8	24	
2003	10	5	28	
2004	18	5	32	

Note. From *Law Yearbook of China* (1986–2005), J. Wang (1988, p. 45), The *People's Daily*, February 27, 2002; February 19, 2003.

Systemization and Bureaucratization of the Legal System

Along with the accelerated lawmaking process, China's legalization put a strong emphasis on rebuilding its legal system.

Development of the Court System

The Chinese government rejuvenated the judicial system, which was almost completely paralyzed in the Cultural Revolution. Under the old ideology, the judicial system had a minimum role to play, and it ranked last in the list of all three legal branches (i.e., *Gong, Jian,* and *Fa,* or police, procuracy, and court). After the reform, however, power and roles of the judicial system grew as its function was greatly expanded into the economic, political, and social domains.

Figure 3.1 shows the ascending trend of various types of cases accepted by the courts of the first instance over the years when the judicial system was becoming one of the most popular organizations in China. Several features are obvious. First, it shows an amazing increase in cases. In 1978, the total number of cases accepted by the courts was 447,755. The number skyrocketed to more than 5 million after 1996, reached a record high of 5,692,434 in 1999, and then slowly decreased to 5,161,170 by 2005. In 27 years, the total number of cases increased more than tenfold. When broken down, data showed remarkable increases in all types of cases. From 1978 to

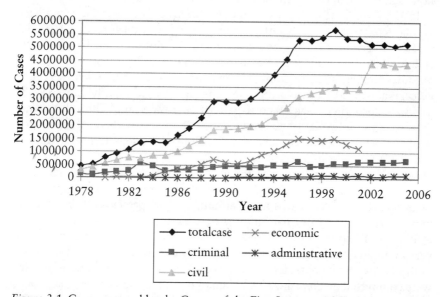

Figure 3.1 Cases accepted by the Courts of the First Instance, 1978–2005.

Source: (1) *Law Yearbook of China* (1987-2001); (2) *China Statistical Yearbook* (2001, 2005, 2006).

2005, the numbers increased more than 13-fold for general civil cases and almost fourfold for criminal cases; economic dispute cases increased more than 295-fold from 1980 to 2001; and administrative cases increased more than 181-fold from 1983 to 2005.

Second, the distribution of court cases changed dramatically. In 1978, criminal cases represented more than 30% of all cases. However, its share steadily decreased, except in 1983 due to an official crackdown initiated by the government (see Chapter 4). By the end of the 20th century, criminal cases represented only about 10% of total cases (13% in 2005). As expected, civil litigations clearly outgrew criminal cases after the reform. Civil litigations represented about 60% of the total cases over the years after economic dispute litigations were separately reported from the general civil cases category. Along with the rapid development of the economy, the share of economic dispute cases increased quickly to more than 20% in the mid-1980s and stabilized at around 25% by the end of the 20th century.

In 1982, the Civil Procedural Law (CPL) took effect, and for the first time Chinese citizens could sue the government or its officials for administrative misconduct. In 1990, the new Administrative Litigation Law (ALL) further guaranteed citizens' administrative litigation rights (see Potter, 1994a). However, the growth of administrative litigations struggled, and by 2005 it represented only a minimal 1.8% of total cases. Table 3.2 shows that a significant number, an average of 40%, of all accepted cases were withdrawn, and citizens managed to win (i.e., to get unfavorable administrative decisions against them reversed) only in about 15% of those cases.

In 1994, the State Compensation Law became effective, and it gave a legal avenue to citizens who sought monetary compensation for official administrative misconduct. The good plan again did not seem to be effectively and consistently implemented as expected. Table 3.3 presents information on state compensation in administrative litigation cases handled by courts. Percentage-wise, cases favoring compensation varied greatly from 18.7% to 53.2%, and there was no clear pattern over the years.[5] Table 3.4 shows compensation information in criminal cases handled by the procuratorates. A lower percentage of compensation is expected compared with that of compensation in administrative litigation cases, given the close relationship between the procuratorates and the public security organizations. Again, it was difficult to predict the outcome when the percentage of compensated cases varied from 18.7% to 40.3%, although higher percentages appeared in more recent years.[6] Information on the compensation amount is extremely lacking, and, based on media reports, the actual amount (per capita) was very minimal on average and it varied greatly case by case.[7] Take Liu Rongbin's case as an example here. On May 25, 2000 a burglary and a murder were committed in Chanzhou city, Hainan province. On February 12, 2001, Liu Rongbin was charged with these crimes by the local procuratorate. On May 14, the Hainan Intermediate Court convicted Liu and sentenced him to death. On appeal, the Hainan High Court reversed the conviction and

Table 3.2 Information on Administrative Litigation Cases

Year	Cases Accepted	Cases Terminated	Affirmed Cases	Reversed Cases	Rulings Modified	Cases Withdrawn	Others
1987	5,240	4,677					
1988	8,573	8,029	3,929	916	422	2,171	
1989	9,934	9,742	4,135	1,364	587	2,966	690
1990	13,006	12,040	4,337	2,012	398	4,346	947
1991	25,667	25,202	7,969	4,762	592	9,317	2,562
1992	27,125	27,116	7,628	5,780	480	10,261	851
1993	27,911	27,958	6,587	5,270	430	11,550	4,121
1994	35,083	34,567	7,128	6,547	369	15,317	5,206
1995	52,596	51,370	8,903	7,733	395	25,990	8,349
1996	79,966	79,537	11,549	11,831	1,214	42,915	12,028
1997	90,557	88,542	11,230	12,279	717		1,863
1998	98,350	98,390	13,036	15,214		47,817	9,376
1999	97,569	98,759	14,672	15,251		44,395	9,491
2000	85,760	86,614	13,431	13,635		31,822	14,078
2001	100,921	95,984	15,941	12,943		31,083	
2002	80,728	84,943	15,520	11,042		26,052	
2003	87,919	88,050	16,356	10,377		27,811	
2004	92,613	92,192	16,393	11,636		28,246	
2005	96,178	95,707	15,769	16,895		28,539	
2006		95,052	37,360	14,250		32,146	

Note. From *Law Yearbook of China* (1987–2005); 2005–2006 data from the SPC 2006 and 2007 annual work reports to the NPC, in the *People's Daily*, March 20, 2006; March 22, 2007; 2005 data from the *China Statistical Yearbook* (2006).

sent it back to the Intermediate Court for retrial. On February 19, 2002, the local procuratorate finally dismissed the case against Liu. In June, Liu requested state compensation for the 549 days he was imprisoned from the arrest to the final release. By December 2002, the Intermediate Court and the local procuratorate decided to award Liu a total of 23,771 yuan based on a national average wage standard of 43.3 yuan per day.[8]

Third, the internal structure of the court system has become more specialized to achieve a more efficient system. After the founding of the new China,

Table 3.3 Information on State Compensation Cases, Administrative Litigations

Year	Cases Accepted	Cases Terminated	Cases in Favor of Compensation (% of Terminated Cases)
1995	197	154	64 (41.6%)
1996	398	291	74 (25.4%)
1997	531	425	226 (53.2%)
1998	1,632	1,431	482 (33.7%)
1999	4,396	4,675	
2000	3,797	3,914	733 (18.7%)
2001	N/A	N/A	N/A
2002	2,818	2,642	879 (33.2%)
2003	3,016	3,124	1,065 (34.1%)
2004	3,298	3,134	932 (29.7%)
2005		2,991	
2006		2,323	

Note. From *Law Yearbook of China* (1996–2005); 2005–2006 data from the SPC 2006 and 2007 annual work reports to the NPC, in the *People's Daily*, March 20, 2006; March 22, 2007.

about 2,000 courts were established nationwide. To meet the increasing need after the reform, the number of courts was increased to more than 3,000 and stabilized at 3,500 in the 1990s (see Table 3.5). With the expansion of the court system, the number of people working in courts at all levels grew as well (see Table 3.6). Specialized divisions or chambers (*ting* in Chinese) were established to cope with different types of cases within the court system. For example, since the early 1980s, courts at all levels managed to establish separate chambers to govern economic disputes. Later, special administrative litigation chambers were established to handle administrative litigations. By 1988, administrative litigation chambers were established at 26 high courts, 242 intermediate courts (63.5% of all intermediate courts), and 1,154 district courts (39% of all district courts). In the same year, the Supreme People's Court (SPC) also established its administrative litigation chamber (Tan, 2000).

The Procuratorate System and Legal Aid Organizations

After the legal reform, the abolished People's Procuratorates were reestablished and expanded quickly along with the development of the court system

Table 3.4 State Compensation in Criminal Cases Handled by the Procuratorates

Year	Cases Accepted	Cases Investigated	Cases in Favor of Compensation (% of Investigated Cases)	Total Value of Compensation (in Yuan)
1995	199	71	20 (28.2%)	
1996	379	235	44 (18.7%)	290,330
1997	669	464	96 (20.7%)	
1998	1,936	798	252 (31.6%)	13,695,000
1999	1,994	1,329	327 (24.6%)	11,800,000
2000	2,447	2,430	925 (38.1%)	42,930,000
2001			384	
2002			777	
2003	4,934		1,438	
2004	1,878	1,835	740 (40.3%)	

Note. From *Law Yearbook of China* (1996–2005); 2004 data were posted at Chinacourt.org, April 19, 2005.

(see Table 3.5). In 1986, the total number of the people's procuratorates at all levels reached 3,491, the number fluctuated in the late 1990s due to organizational restructures, and then it stabilized around 3,600 in the new millennium. The number of people working in the system increased steadily with the growth of the organization. In 1986, 140,246 people worked in the system, and the number reached 228,374 in 2000 (see Table 3.7 for more detailed personnel information).

In 1994, the MOJ in China proposed to establish a legal aid (*falü yuan-zhu*) system nationwide with a goal of providing high-quality free legal assistance for all who need it.[9] By the end of 1996, there were only three legal aid organizations at the provincial level (in Sichuan, Guangdong, and Beijing), but the program has expanded very quickly since then. On August 22, 2001, Tibet established its legal aid center, and as a result China's legal aid system covered all provinces. In July 2003, the Regulations on Legal Aid was passed by the State Council, and it became effective in September.[10] By the end of 2006, there were 3,150 legal aid organizations nationwide with more than 11,700 official workers.[11] In 1999 the legal aid system provided assistance in 91,726 cases, and the number jumped to 310,000 in 2006; similarly the financial support for the legal aid system was increased from 27.8 million yuan in 1999 to 370 million yuan in 2006 (see Table 3.8 for information over the years). Despite such quick development, numerous

Table 3.5 Growth of the Court System and the Procuratorates System

Year	Court System		Procuratorate System	
	Number of All Courts	*Number of All People*	*Number of All Procurators*	*Number of All People*
1949–1951	2,000			
1986	3,404	188,825	3,491	140,246
1987	3,435	194,388	3,487	153,072
1988	3,435	214,930	3,495	165,399
1989	3,014		3,582	171,815
1990	3,422	194,836	3,599	176,028
1991	3,424	200,134	3,533	179,870
1992	3,493		3,563	183,726
1993			3,655	187,778
1994			3,662	194,456
1995			3,616	208,320
1996			4,052	215,521
1997	3,556		3,846	221,912
1998			3,712	223,999
1999			4,142	226,157
2000			3,910	228,374
2001			3,692	226,839
2002			3,624	208,207
2003			3,649	209,622
2004			3,630	211,230

Note. From *Law Yearbook of China* (1987–2005).

problems such as lack of funding and staffing and uneven regional development were quickly identified and reported.[12]

Lawyers and Lawyering

Before the legal reform, lawyers had never played a significant role in the legal system. In 1979, a little more than 2,000 lawyers worked in less than

Table 3.6 Personnel Composition of the People's Courts

Year	Total	Presidents of Courts	Chief Judges	Presiding Judges	Assistant Presiding Judges	Secretary	Security Staff	Others
1981	117,585	9,083	19,222	15,466	16,203	23,393	11,650	22,268
1982	143,941	10,203	24,637	19,365	21,881	29,168	12,436	26,251
1983	149,372	9,851	25,476	20,675	26,847	28,693	13,480	24,404
1984	157,974	9,670	29,731	22,585	25,182	28,039	13,200	29,567
1985	179,558	9,905	32,283	25,769	26,272	35,686	13,516	36,123
1986	188,825	10,217	34,310	26,355	27,636	37,246	14,244	38,817
1987	194,388	10,681	36,679	35,765	34,070	40,977	12,842	23,374
1988	214,930	10,534	39,095	33,307	36,085	46,479	12,652	36,778
1990	194,836	10,816	42,685	35,613	42,346	50,965	12,411	
1991	200,134	11,096	45,311	36,345	45,707	49,714	11,961	

Note. From *Law Yearbook of China* (1987–2000).

700 law firms in the whole nation. With the quick development of the legal system, law became a popular profession. The number of law firms as well as the number of lawyers quickly increased. By the year 2005, China had 12,988 law firms with a total of 153,846 lawyers (both full-time and part-time; see detailed information in Table 3.9).[13] Moreover, the organization of law firms has been changing. In the 1980s, all law firms were state-owned firms, consistent with the nature of China's economic structure. By the end of the 1980s, cooperative law firms, another form of organization, were allowed to exist, and developed quickly over the years. Since the mid-1990s, the number of partner-type law firms grew as most cooperative law firms changed their organizations into partnerships. By early 2005, 70% of all law firms existed in various forms of partnerships in China.[14]

Even as domestic law firms were growing, foreign law firms also opened offices in China. In 1992, five firms became the first group of foreign law firms to open offices in Beijing and Shanghai, and another seven law firms from Hong Kong kicked off operations in mainland China. The momentum kept going, and by April 13, 2004, a total of 129 foreign law firms and 42 Hong Kong law firms had opened branches in a number of major cities in China[15] (see Table 3.10 for breakdown information).

Once the number of lawyers grew, organizations and regulations were set to control this new social group. In 1986, the All China Lawyers Association was founded and became a powerful organization for regulating

Table 3.7 Personnel Composition of the People's Procuratorates

Year	Total	Chief Procurators	Procurators	Assistant Procurators	Secretary	Security Staff	Others
1986	140,246	9,932	55,138	32,260	24,069	9,118	9,729
1987	153,072	10,122	59,330	33,996	25,786	8,954	14,884
1988	165,399	10,444	64,543	37,392	26,577	8,527	17,916
1989	171,815	10,704	67,378	41,891	25,843	8,689	17,310
1990	176,028	11,088	70,717	44,529	22,943	7,394	19,357
1991	179,870	11,456	73,613	45,816	21,624	6,818	20,543
1992	183,726	11,723	77,052	46,979	20,186	7,018	20,768
1993	187,778	11,924	82,125	47,448	18,545	9,279	18,457
1994	194,456	12,290	87,221	47,591	17,962	10,451	18,941
1995	208,320	12,655	95,544	48,270	20,763	10,307	20,781
1996	215,521	13,217	98,816	44,958	25,439	10,484	22,697
1997	221,912	13,328	102,258	44,338	26,386	10,697	24,905
1998	223,999	13,387	105,904	37,633	30,279	10,697	26,099
1999	226,157	13,725	111,358	43,697	21,631	10,533	25,213
2000	228,374	13,906	115,776	41,507	20,231	10,785	26,169
2001	226,839	14,094	102,866	35,554	22,574	11,282	12,547
2002	208,207	13,147	94,029	26,394	22,963	10,957	15,020
2003	209,622	13,550	93,079	22,601	24,471	11,901	16,878
2004	211,230	13,718	92,905	19,623	26,360	12,943	17,645

Note. From *Law Yearbook of China* (1987–2005).

lawyers' practice. In the same year, the first national lawyers' unified exam was held. More than 29,000 people applied for the exam, but only 1,134 people (3.9%) passed the exam and received their licenses. The lawyers' exam has become a routine test since then. Held every 2 years at first, the frequency of the exam was increased to once a year after 1993. The number of applicants jumped from 111,000 in 1995 to 140,000 in 1998, then to 180,000 in 1999, and to more than 210,000 in 2000.[16] In January 2002, the All China Female Lawyers Association also was established, and it became

Table 3.8 Information on the Legal Aid System, 1997–2006

Year	Funding (Unit: 1 Million Yuan)	No. of Assisted Cases	No. of Organizations	No. of Workers
1997			133	
1998			446	
1999	27.8806	91,726	1,235	3,920
2000	19.4116	114,287	1,890	6,109
2001	52.0623	147,269	2,274	8,458
2002	84.4433	135,748	2,418	8,285
2003	164.5684	166,438	2,874	9,457
2004	245.7744	190,187	3,023	10,458
2005	280.523	253,665	3,129	11,377
2006	370	310,000	3,150	11,700

Note. 1997–2005 data from the *People's Daily*, May 12, 2006; 2006 data from the *People's Daily*, January 26, 2007.

a new organization for almost 30,000 female attorneys (20% of all lawyers) in the country.[17]

Lawyers' practices have become more diversified over the years. The number of enterprises that hired lawyers for yearly consulting services increased from 411 in 1982 to 276,097 in 2005. In 2005, lawyers provided legal services in 965,956 civil cases (a 117-fold increase from 1981), 354,229 criminal cases (a fourfold increase from 1981), 50,389 administrative litigations (a 2.5-fold increase from 1991), 36,361 litigations involving foreign affairs (a 50-fold increase from 1983), and 933,346 nonlitigious legal affairs (a 204-fold increase from 1981; see Table 3.11). Longitudinal data clearly show that lawyers became more and more active in various litigations, and their role in the legal system was definitely growing.[18]

Legal Study and Mass Education

After the new China was founded, legal higher education grew together with the general educational system in the 1950s with steady increases in teachers and students (see Table 3.12). The numbers of both teachers and students, however, were still very low during this period mainly due to a general acknowledgment of limited legal functions in the new socialist system. The growth was severely disrupted in the Cultural Revolution period. From 1966 to 1976, only two law-related departments existed in the whole

Table 3.9 Development of Law Firms and Lawyers

	Law Firms			Lawyers			
Year	Total	Cooperative	Partnerships	Total	Full-Time	Part-Time	Special Consultants
1979	685			2,200			
1980							
1981	2,023			8,571	6,213	2,358	
1982	2,350			12,114	7,859	3,530	
1983	2,472			15,471	8,774	5,770	
1984	2,773			20,090	10,262	9,828	
1985	3,131			31,629	13,411	18,218	
1986	3,198			21,546	14,500	7,046	601
1987	3,291			27,280	18,308	8,972	855
1988	3,473			31,410	21,051	10,359	1,002
1989	3,646			48,912	23,606	20,109	2,409
1990	3,716			47,461	23,727	10,652	2,614
1991	3,748	73		41,639	19,919	10,662	3,901
1992	4,176	198		45,666	22,124	12,391	3,975
1993	5,129	505		68,834	30,401	16,793	10,166
1994	6,619	1,193		83,619	40,730	20,171	9,637
1995	7,247	1,625		90,602	45,094	17,994	11,696
1996	8,265	2,655		100,198	47,879	20,243	15,376
1997	8,441	846	2,085	98,902	47,574	18,695	12,892
1998	8,946	955	2,448	101,220	51,008	17,958	10,966
1999	9,144			111,433	61,761	17,082	
2000	9,541			117,260	69,117	15,639	
2001	10,225			122,585	76,558	13,699	
2002	10,873			136,684	90,012	12,186	
2003	11,593			142,534	99,793	6,850	
2004	11,823			145,196	100,875	6,966	
2005	12,988			153,846	114,471	7,418	

Note. From *China Judicial Administration Yearbook* (1995–2000), *Law Yearbook of China* (1978–2005) and *Chinese Statistical Yearbook* (2005, 2006).

Table 3.10 Number of Foreign Law Firms and Hong Kong Law Firms Opened in Mainland China

	Foreign Law Firms			Hong Kong Law Firms		
Year	Beijing	Shanghai	Other Places	Beijing	Shanghai	Other Places
1992	4			1	3	3
1993	10	3	2	3	1	5
1995	6	4	1		1	2
1996	7	6		1		
1997		1				
1998	5	8	1	2		1
1999	6	8		14 (total)		
2000	4	5	1			
2001	3	5	1			
2002	5	11		4	4	5
2003	4	9		2	1	1
2004	9	15	2	3	1	4
2005	11	11	1	1	6	4
2006	2	5	1	1	1	2

Note. From *China Judicial Administration Yearbook* (1995–2000, 2003–2004); online news posted at *Chinanews.com*, October 23, 2002; the *News Express*; October 24, 2002; 2003–2006 data from www.legalinfo.gov.cn posted on August 15, 2006; September 14, 2006.

nation, with very few teachers and students. Only after 1978 did legal education finally gain a rebirth. In the next 10 years from 1978 to 1987, the number of law colleges and departments increased from 6 to 86; the number of teachers increased from 178 to 5,216; and the number of law graduates increased from 99 to 12,639 (see Table 3.12; see also discussions by Michelson, 1998a; Tan, 2000; J. Wang, 1988). These numbers continued to grow in the 1990s and in the new millennium. By 2006, more than 600 law programs were open nationwide with more than 200,000 students.[19]

Table 3.13 presents a similar trend for graduate law students. Numbers of both graduates and students at schools hovered around 100 in the 1950s, were severely downscaled in the 1960s, reemerged after 1978, and quickly developed in the 1980s to reach several thousands. Since 1995, 39 master programs have been established nationwide; these programs had admitted

Table 3.11 Professional Practice of Chinese Lawyers

Year	Enterprises With Permanent Legal Advisors	Civil Cases Involved	Criminal Cases Involved	Economic Dispute Cases Involved	Administrative Litigation Cases Involved	Nonlitigious Legal Affairs	Legal Cases Involving Foreign Affairs
1981		8,123	65,179			4,550	
1982	411	23,231	93,712			12,836	
1983	3,846	37,311	103,492	20,257		12,100	709
1984	15,349	31,956	163,476	55,313		20,194	1,997
1985	39,453	52,923	101,707			41,136	4,324
1986	43,184	162,999	136,837			41,185	4,375
1987	59,478	208,627	154,485			55,061	5,320
1988	88,108	265,326	170,194			71,618	8,412
1989	109,609	365,197	232,206			133,226	12,594
1990	111,899	330,672	252,344			110,139	9,980
1991	128,921	209,568	230,967	173,111	14,307	236,707	11,214
1992	151,501	214,321	219,739	182,021	16,061	277,030	14,719

Year							
1993	185,715	246,187	191,657	237,119	15,260	350,408	18,423
1994	203,320	264,854	208,806	276,720	16,283	403,544	26,718
1995	234,496	316,250	204,382	324,909	18,043	452,021	20,444
1996	223,043	353,840	245,877	360,224	19,360	435,483	27,730
1997	232,434	454,273	275,188	403,337	29,168	1,222,239	24,765
1998	235,676	526,633	296,668	414,229	35,865	851,433	21,618
1999	238,576	592,455	309,767	426,358	39,006	716,287	18,793
2000	247,160	640,610	317,108	438,672	41,785	770,087	30,531
2001	254,758	667,232	339,549	402,669	43,800	1,162,715	10,609
2002	265,362	767,628	335,267	381,164	43,703	827,057	26,788
2003	271,669	781,452	324,454	405,133	48,115	876,696	20,622
2004	282,361	853,897	332,688	357,326	50,778	904,516	37,728
2005	276,097	965,956	354,229	376,793	50,389	933,346	36,361

Note. From *Law Yearbook of China* (1987–2005), *China Judicial Administration Yearbook* (1995–2000, 2003–2004), and *China Statistical Yearbook* (2005, 2006).

Table 3.12 Legal Higher Education in China, 1949–1987

Year	Number of Colleges (Cs) and Departments (Ds)	Number of Teachers	Number of Graduates	Number of New Students	Number of Students in School
1949	53	542	4,015	297	7,338
1950	53	542	1,679	1,425	6,984
1951	36	647	1,363	888	4,225
1952	3 Cs & 10 Ds	450	1,403	1,271	3,830
1953	4 Cs & 4 Ds	268	977	1,271	3,908
1954	4 Cs & 6 Ds	408	1,897	2,180	4,017
1955	4 Cs & 6 Ds	519	962	2,087	4,801
1956	4 Cs & 6 Ds	796	409	2,824	7,108
1957	4 Cs & 6 Ds	752	385	1,691	8,245
1958	4 Cs & 4 Ds		1,531	898	7,114
1959	4 Cs & 4 Ds		1,826	1,248	5,674
1960	4 Cs & 4 Ds		2,217	1,694	5,271
1961	4 Cs & 4 Ds		1,366	1,320	6,126
1962	4 Cs & 4 Ds		802	460	3,796
1963	5 Cs & 4 Ds	793	613	959	3,571
1964	5 Cs & 4 Ds	948	836	1,243	3,725
1965	5 Cs & 4 Ds	924	857	1,298	4,144
1966	2 Ds		617		3,527
1967	2 Ds		884		2,643
1968	2 Ds		1,212		1,431

29,448 students by June 2004 and conferred a total of 8,848 master's degrees.[20] In addition to law programs, specialized procurators institutes and police academies were established and started growing slowly after the reform (see Table 3.14). At the same time, legal research and publications increased in the 1980s. From 1980 to 1991, 64 legal research organizations were established (compared to a total of five in all years before), eight law presses went into operation (compared to one in all the years before),

Table 3.12 (Continued)

Year	Number of Colleges (Cs) and Departments (Ds)	Number of Teachers	Number of Graduates	Number of New Students	Number of Students in School
1969	2 Ds		1,308		123
1970	2 Ds		123		
1971	2 Ds			80	80
1972	2 Ds		71		
1973	2 Ds			36	36
1974	2 Ds			293	329
1975	2 Ds		160	100	269
1976	2 Ds		49	179	410
1977	1 C & 2 Ds		294	256	576
1978	3 Cs & 3 Ds	178	99	995	1,299
1979	4 Cs & 6 Ds	688		2,041	3,315
1980	4 Cs & 14 Ds	1,015	109	2,838	6,029
1981	5 Cs & 23 Ds	1,227		3,751	9,944
1982	6 Cs & 28 Ds	1,743	1,238	4,982	14,635
1983	10 Cs & 25 Ds	2,078	3,113	6,923	18,286
1984	18 Cs & 43 Ds	2,766	3,103	9,509	25,237
1985	23 Cs & 48 Ds	4,027	5,367	16,164	36,129
1986	26 Cs & 54 Ds	4,977	7,329	13,526	43,178
1987	26 Cs & 60 Ds	5,216	12,639	13,139	42,034

Note. From *Law Yearbook of China* (1988, pp. 99–100, 1104–1106).

and 57 law newspapers and 72 law journals and newsletters initiated publication (compared to 4 and 23, respectively, in all the years before; see Table 3.15).

After the reinstatement and development of legal education and study, legal scholars and jurists gradually began to contribute to China's legal reform, using their unique positions.[21] In 1994, the CCPCC held its first internal legal lecture in an effort to help raise the CCPCC members' legal

Table 3.13 Graduate-Level Legal Education in China, 1949–1987

Year	Number of Graduates	Number of New Students	Number of Students in School
1949	32	16	26
1950	7	55	76
1951	13	96	175
1952	47	88	168
1953	80	50	121
1954		70	169
1955	47	73	189
1956	99		112
1957	82		5
1958	5		
1959		21	21
1960		11	27
1961		8	47
1962	14	15	53
1963	21	2	30
1964	6	8	25
1965	15		10
1969	10		
1979		80	122
1980		40	171
1981	78	185	358
1982	197	267	582
1983	91	594	1,137
1984	60	964	2,022
1985	480	1,563	3,073
1986	904	1,426	3,841
1987	1,294	1,469	3,951
Total	3,582	7,101	

Note. No new graduate students were accepted between 1965 and 1978.
From *Law Yearbook of China* (1988, pp. 1106–1107).

Table 3.14 Established Procuratorate Institutes
(Colleges) and Police Institutes, 1978–1991

Year	Procuratorate Institutes	Police Institutes
1978		1
1980		2
1981		2
1982		1
1983		3
1984		12
1985		5
1986		1
1987	1	
1988	15	2
1989	4	
1990	1	
1991	10	1

Note. Law Yearbook of China (1992, pp. 841–842).

awareness and to propose suggestions for the building of the legal system. Since then, the CCPCC legal lecture has been organized at least once a year, and by 2006, a total of 18 lectures had been organized (see Table 3.16). Following the CCPCC's lead, the NPC Standing Committee started holding its own legal lectures once every 2 months in 1998.[22] Many of these legal lectures were given by legal scholars in various fields.

To answer the call from high-level officials, legal education was quickly expanded to the masses. In July 1998, an intellectual property case tried by the First Intermediate Peoples' Court in Beijing was televised nationally for the first time. Since then, televised trials have been used from time to time as an effective means for legal education.[23] With the advance of Internet technology, legal Web sites were opened and online information systems became the latest means of mass legal communication and education.[24] In 2001, the MOJ established December 4 as the national legal education day and has tried to diversify its educational program each year since then.[25] Despite such efforts, China still has a long road to travel in its mass legal education, especially in rural areas. In 2006, a survey jointly organized by the *People's Daily* and China University of Political Science and Law showed that villagers in

Table 3.15 Legal Studies Organizations and Publications, 1949–1991

Year	Legal Study Organizations	Law Presses	Law Newspapers	Law Journals and Newsletters
1949			1	3
1950				1
1951			1	
1952	1			1
1954				1
1955				3
1956		1		2
1957			1	3
1958	2			
1960	1			
1972	1			
1976				1
1978				1
1979			1	7
1980	3	1	4	4
1981	3		7	4
1982	1		12	2
1983	2		7	4
1984	7		6	11
1985	7	2	10	14
1986	15	1	3	9
1987	7		3	8
1988	9		1	6
1989	5	4		3
1990	3		2	3
1991	2		2	4

Note. *Law Yearbook of China* (1992, pp. 843–849).

Table 3.16 Legal Lectures Organized by the Chinese Communist Party Central Committee

Number	Date	Topic
1	12/9/94	International trade legal system and General Agreement on Tariffs and Trade
2	1/20/95	Issues in building the legal system of the socialist market economy
3	2/8/96	Theoretical and practical issues in building the socialist legal system and the rule by law
4	12/9/96	The function of international laws in international relations
5	5/6/97	"One Country, Two Systems" and the Basic Law of Hong Kong
6	12/23/97	The advance of science and technology and the building of the legal system
7	12/14/98	The society security and the building of the legal system
8	6/11/99	Rural reform, development, and stability guaranteed and promoted by law and the legal system
9	11/26/99	State-owned enterprises reform and development guaranteed and promoted by law and the legal system
10	9/22/00	Legal guaranty of the development the western region and the acceleration of the development of the middle and western regions
11	7/11/01	Utilization of legal means to protect and accelerate the healthy development of IT industry
12	12/26/02	Implementation of the national Constitution and building *Xiaokang* society
13	9/29/03	"Running the country according to law" and building political civilization
14	4/26/04	Building the legal system and the socialist market economy
15	12/20/05	Reform on administration and improving economic legal system
16	5/26/06	Protection of international intellectual property rights and building PRC's intellectual property legal system
17	6/29/06	Running government scientifically, democratically, and legally
18	11/30/06	Study on how to build socialist democracy at local levels

Note. From The *People's Daily*, December 6, 2006.

four sampled provinces had very poor legal education indeed. For example, less than 15% of respondents knew the basics of the national Constitution, and 72.6% of respondents did not know the difference between governmental policies and laws.[26]

Legal Professionalism

In the process of building a legal system, a new term, *legal professionalism*, was proposed to answer the call for legal reform. Efforts were made (a) to designate the legal profession as a unique profession with its own rules and practices, (b) to specialize different players working within the legal profession, and (c) to elevate the legal system to a higher level and grant it a relatively autonomous status.[27]

Legal Autonomy and Practice as a Unique Profession

After the legal reform, Chinese scholars and the government quickly recognized a long-standing problem: Law and the legal system were not granted independent status, and its practice was always subject to influences of administrative policies and controls. Very often scholars studying Chinese law and the legal system concluded that Chinese law has a fundamentally instrumentalist nature (see, e.g., Corne, 1997; Potter, 1995, 1998). To change this nature, to establish an autonomous effective legal system became one goal of the legal reform. Specific rules (e.g., the Civil Procedural Law) were set up to provide that all courts are to "exercise judicial power independently and are not subject to interference by administrative organizations, public organizations or individuals" (cited in Potter, 1995, p. 74).

One measure to make the legal profession distinctive was to change the equipment and outfit of its major players. In May 2001, both judges and procurators' official uniforms were changed. The new uniform abandoned the old military style (e.g., the epaulet on the shoulder) and was designed in a dark-color, suit style consistent with international standards.[28] In 2002, the All China Lawyers Association enacted uniform dress codes for lawyers who appear in courts, and the new dress codes took effect in 2003.[29] With the new attire, players in the courtroom can be easily identified, and they appear more formal and part of a unique profession. In addition to the attire changes, many other things were introduced into the courtroom to formalize procedure and practice. In September 2001, judges at the people's court in Siming district (the Siming Court), Xiamen began to use gavels in the courtroom, and this practice received positive feedback from both judges and the audience. Based on the Siming Court's experience, the SPC granted the use of the gavel to courts at all levels on June 1, 2002.[30] In December 2001, another trial was held at the Siming Court in which witnesses were asked to take an oath before they testified, and this was the first attempt to introduce a witness oath-taking system in China.[31] Those changes in the courtroom seemed miniscule, but they all served the same purpose of formalizing court procedure and granting more power and authority (at least symbolically) to judges.

Quality Control of Legal Practitioners

The low education level of legal practitioners in general was always a deep concern for the advance of legal professionalism. In 1995, both the Judges Law and the Procurators Law went into effect, and one specific function of both laws was to raise the professional level of judges and procurators. For example, the Judges Law required that new judges must have either a law degree or a university degree with special legal knowledge. For acting judges who were army retirees without formal education, the new law required them to receive various training within a limited time (see discussions by Brown, 1997; Corne, 1997).

In addition, internal exams were held within the judicial and the procuratorial systems after 1995 to control the quality of judges and procurators. In 4 years from 1995 to 1999, more than 90,000 judges and 59,000 procurators took their exams (see Table 3.17). In January 2002, the Judges Law and the Procurators Law were revised, and the professional bars were again raised for new judges and procurators.[32] In the same year, the MOJ, the SPC, and the Supreme People's Procuratorate (SPP) decided to combine exams for judges, procurators, and lawyers into one national exam. This was a new effort to formalize and systemize the exam selection process. All who want to practice law have to pass the unified national exam. In March 2002, the first national law exam was held. More than 360,000 people took the exam, but less than 8% of them met the minimum score requirement.[33] In 2003, the number of exam takers fell to 170,000, but it gradually increased over

Table 3.17 Examinations for New Procurators, Assistant Procurators, Judges, and Assistant Judges, 1995–1999

	Exams for Judges (Every 2 Years)			*Exams for Procurators*		
Year	Number	Applicants	Exam Takers	Number	Applicants	Exam Takers
1995	1st exam		>30,000	1st exam	5,833	5,551
1996				2nd exam	13,228	12,571
1997	2nd exam		27,500			
1998				3rd exam	27,045	25,839
1999	3rd exam		33,000	4th exam		15,209

Note. From *Law Yearbook of China* (1996–2000).

the next 3 years, despite a very rigorous passing rate set up by the government (barely over 10% each year; see Table 3.18). Once exams became the standardized method of selection, they were also adopted in other domains within the legal system, such as the prison system[34] and the enterprise legal consulting service.[35]

In addition to the exam selection, the SPC tried to introduce an open selection system for the first time in March 1999, and called for applicants from the public to apply for some positions of senior judgeship.[36] On August 16, 2000, the SPC published the Rules for the Selections of Presiding Judges to standardize the open selection practice. From 2000 to February 2007, the SPC selected 22 judges from the public, many of whom were attorneys, law professors, and scholars.[37] Courts at lower levels quickly adopted this practice, and open competition became another effective way to improve the quality of judges.[38]

Even with such great efforts, the education level of legal practitioners in China is still not promising. By July 2002, official statistics reported that only 47% of lawyers, 29.9% of procurators, 24.9% of judges, and 22% of public notaries held university degrees.[39] These low percentages showed how serious the obstacle is. It will take many years for China to reach the goal set by both the Judges Law and the Procurators Law.

Internal Rules and Regulations

One step in the process of professionalization was to enact internal rules and regulations to govern practitioners. In November 2000, both the SPC and the SPP passed regulations to prohibit spouses and children of high officials in the judicial and procuratorial systems from providing paid legal services and conducting relevant businesses.[40] In March and April 2001, specific regulations on judges and procurators' withdrawals from trials because of

Table 3.18 Unified National Law Exam, 2002–2006

Year	Number of Applicants	Number of Actual Exam Takers	Number of Passers (% of Takers)
2002	360,000	310,000	24,800 (8%)
2003	197,000	170,000	19,500 (11%)
2004	195,000	179,000	20,000 (11%)
2005	244,000	219,000	31,664 (14%)
2006		278,000	

Note. Data over time from The *People's Daily*, www.acla.org.cn, and www.legalinfo.gov.cn.

potential conflicts of interest were enacted and implemented. The scope of this regulation went even beyond one's official term. For example, it provides that judges and procurators cannot represent clients in courts within 2 years after their official retirement or termination.[41] In October 2001, the SPC published the Professional Ethical Rules for Judges,[42] and it further introduced a practice of resignation at fault in November.[43] Both measures aimed to tighten regulations on judges' professional behaviors, and punishments were set to impose on violators. As reported, the total number of judicial workers who were punished due to such violations decreased from 2,512 in 1998 to 1,450 in 1999, 1,338 in 2000, and then to 1,080 in 2001.[44] In October 2005, the SPC enacted another regulation on judges' professional behavior and put it into practice to further strengthen its internal control.[45] Most recently in September 2006, the SPC announced the establishment of a formal press release system for national people's courts and asked lower level high and intermediate courts to follow this practice. This is another move to centralize courts' control.[46]

Regulations were gradually expanded to govern lawyers' practice as well. In 1991, a regulation on lawyers' service fees was enacted by the MOJ. The low standards set in this regulation, however, failed to keep up with the pace of economic development. In 1997, the regulation was officially abandoned. Pending a new one, many local governments (e.g., local ministries of justice) adopted their own regulations.[47] Despite great geographical variations, lawyers' fees in general are not low by any standard in China. For instance, the hourly fee in Chongqing city was set between 200 and 2,000 yuan in 2002. In contrast, the average annual per capita income in Chongqing city was only 27,166 yuan (2,263 yuan per month).[48] In 2002, to supplement its regular legal aid system, the government in Shenzhen city, Guangdong province, adopted a new rule to require all local licensed lawyers to provide free legal service in at least two cases each year as a part of the pro bono program.[49]

Internal Ranking

It is no secret that there is an official hierarchy within the judicial and the procuratorial systems. Because of the existence of such a hierarchy, it was argued that control of the superior over the subordinate limited the autonomy of lower level judges in ruling cases (see relevant discussion in Chapter 6). However, one new ranking system was put forward in March 2002. Based on this new system, judges would be ranked at four levels: Chief Justice (*shouxi dafaguan*), Justices (*dafaguan*), Senior Judges (*gaoji faguan*), and Judges (*faguan*), with a corresponding system for procurators.[50] The goal of the new system reportedly was to streamline the old system for better organization. Because the new ranking was essentially determined according to the old hierarchical system, the new practice is more likely going to strengthen, rather than change or weaken, the old hierarchy.

Rule of Law v. Rule by Law, and Moral Education

From the beginning of the legal reform, the Chinese government was determined to build an effective legal system based on law to avoid the same mistake of the rule of man during the Cultural Revolution period. As a matter of fact, early discussions among scholars focused primarily on the confrontation between the rule of law and the rule of man. The general agreement seemed to target excessive influence by powerful individuals, and to replace the rule of man with the rule of law (see Peerenboom, 1993; C. Wang & Zhang, 1992).[51] Over the years, the process of legal systemization and bureaucratization, as discussed earlier, seemed to support the fact that China was moving toward its goals.

Scholars studying Chinese political and legal systems abroad, however, raised doubts on China's practice of the rule of law. They proposed that China is practicing instead "the rule by law" (see such arguments by Epstein, 1992; Keith, 1994; see Peerenboom, 2002a, 2004, and Zheng, 1998, for their efforts to reconcile such conceptual differences). For example, as J. Chen (1999) argued, the Western notion of rule of law embraces a series of important concepts, such as supremacy of law, judicial independence, equality before the law, separation of powers, checks and balances, a parliamentary system, and protection of human rights. All those key concepts are still very inadequately developed in China. Keith (1994) also pointed out that the Chinese "judicial independence" (*shenpan duli*) refers to the elimination of the Communist Party's political influence in actual judicial decisions rather than the total elimination of the Party's influence over the general policy direction of the judicial process. In essence, China's judicial independence did not originate from the concept of separation of powers. Potter (1995, 1998) concluded in his study that the Chinese government's approach to law is fundamentally instrumentalist, and laws and regulations are enacted explicitly to achieve immediate policy objectives of the regime. Rather than a limit on the state power, law is a mechanism to exercise state power in China.

The Chinese government indeed made no intention to hide the guidance (as one form of control) of the CCP over the building of the legal system. The official definition of "ruling the country in accordance with the law" (*yifa zhiguo*) was codified as follows:

> Under *the lead of the Communist Party* and based on the Constitution and laws, the populace administer national affairs, economic, cultural, and social affairs via various means. It is to guarantee all national affairs to be accomplished according to laws, and to realize the systemization and legalization of the socialist democracy. The basic system and law will not be changed with changes of national leaders or changes of those leaders' personal opinions.[52]

Apparently, the focus was on restraint of individuals' excessive powers, not the lead of the Party in general, despite the confusion. In January 2001,

President Jiang Zemin proposed one more term "building the country based on moral education" (*yide zhiguo*), and called for a combination of both the "moral education"[53] and the rule of law. It was argued that moral value is another important component of the superstructure in addition to the legal system (based on the Marxian doctrine), and both moral education and the legal system are necessary for the advance of Chinese socialism.[54] The term "building the country based on moral education" was defined as follows: "guided by Marxism, Leninism, Mao's thought and Deng's theory, (it is) to build socialist moral-value system consistent with the development of the socialist market economy; to make the morality model automatically accepted by the populace."[55] The definition once again specified the guidance of the Party (in)directly in the process of moral education.

In sum, since the reforms in 1978, the Chinese legal system has been changing along with the economic system. The Chinese government made great efforts to (re)build the legal system. As a result, an organized system is emerging in China, although it still diverges greatly from the Western model of the rule of law. The divergence is due to many factors (e.g., culture), and to a large extent the Chinese political system seems to be limiting the development of the legal system. I focus next on the relation between the political system and the legal system.

CENTRALIZATION OF POWER VERSUS DECENTRALIZATION OF POWER

In his study, Weber (1984) paid close attention to Chinese traditions such as Confucianism and Taoism and tried to find something comparable to (or distinct from) the Western religious impact on the capitalist system. He concluded that the incentive for economic rationalization appeared only briefly in Chinese history during the Warring States period (475–221 B.C.) and never established its dominance afterward. Rather, patrimonialism and traditional clan (the kinship, or *Zu*) dominated Chinese society under the influence of Confucianism and strongly weakened the state's centralization of power and administration. As a result, no independent legal system (as well as specialized legal practitioners) had ever been built to serve the interests of capitalist enterprises in Chinese history.

After 1949 the new government tried to lead the nation into a communist society based on Marxian doctrines. To a large extent, this process was accomplished through the destruction of the old system as discussed in Chapter 2. The authoritative power of the central government had been tremendously increased, and this was seemingly consistent with Weber's study of China and his prediction of more bureaucratic control in socialist societies in general (see discussion by Giddens, 1971). This centralization of power, however, did not lead to the legal, formal rationality and the rise of modern capitalism as predicted by Weber. Rather, excessive power and control only led to an authoritarian government based on Mao's charisma and to a social disaster when the government motivated the whole nation to enter into political movements for class struggle.

After China kicked off its reforms in 1978, it looked like that the country's legal system had finally begun moving in the direction predicted by Weber. Nevertheless, scholars raised a new theory, the decentralization theory, to explain social and economic changes in China.

The Argument of Decentralization and Its Expansion

Decentralization theory was first proposed to explain economic development after the reform. With the decline of the planned economy, the central government placed increased reliance on the market and material incentives and granted more substantive decision-making power to local governments and individuals. Once local governments and individuals had a chance to thrive, China's economy quickly developed (see World Bank, 1988; S. Zhu, 1989). As a matter of fact, the decentralization measure was not new, and it had happened prior to the reform. The decentralization after 1978, however, was significantly distinct from previous measures in two respects. First, previous efforts toward administrative decentralization were pursued to improve the delivery and supervision of the planning system, but the decentralization after 1978 was undertaken to reach the lower levels of government to facilitate market reforms. Second, the decentralization process after 1978 went beyond the simple scope of granting administrative power to local governments, moved into economic domains, and benefited different levels of government and nongovernmental organizations and agents, such as individual households, enterprises, and financial institutions (World Bank, 1996).

When the economic reform deepened, some concerns were raised as to the side effects of the decentralization approach. First, although the decentralization resulted in economic development as expected, it also caused economic disparity among provinces. For instance, different policies were adopted in different geographical locations, and the decentralization was not evenly implemented in the whole nation. The result was a clear disparity (both economic and political) in different regions, and local protectionism (e.g., for resource competition) was emerging in more advanced provinces (Wang, Cheng, Yang, & Yang, 1995; World Bank, 1990). Second, and related to the first concern, some scholars showed concerns over political power competition and national stability in general (e.g., the rise of regional power replacing central power; S. Wang, 1995). In spite of such concerns, the decentralization theory received wide popularity.

Once the economic decentralization theory was entrenched, efforts were made to expand it into other domains. For example, in his study of the Chinese law-making process, M. S. Tanner (1999) pointed out an increasing acquisition of power and influence by various political organizations (e.g., the NPC), and argued that a further decentralization of (policymaking) power among "elite, bureaucratic, institutional and social groups" (p. 232) is necessary for a more open, consultative, and democratic legal and political system in the future.

In his study of the changing Chinese legal system, S. Zhu (1989) acknowledged that the success of economic reform was due to the decentralization of the planned economy, and the decentralization measure gave more power, both economically and politically, to the local governments. Judicially, there also were signs that local governments gained some leeway to substantiate general policies and laws from the central government (e.g., tremendous increase of local laws and regulations). Based on these observations, Zhu argued that the systematization of law was helped and enhanced by the decentralization of legislative power with the development of the economic reform, contrary to Weber's theory. This argument of decentralization of legislative power (e.g., law making) was later echoed by some other scholars as well (see, e.g., Lu & Miethe, 2007).

In sum, with the decline of the planned economy, the decentralization theory was raised primarily to explain economic development in China after the reform. Nevertheless, the theory was expanded to explain legal and political changes. Without discrediting its theoretical power in the economic domain, caution should be called with the expansion of the term, especially for understanding China's legalization. Such caution is substantiated by both theoretical and empirical observations with regard to the nature of the Chinese polity and its policy implications as argued later.

Theoretical Basis: Centralized Government Based on Totalitarianism?

For a long time, China was viewed as a nation under a totalitarian communist regime in which economic, political, and social decisions were controlled and made by a few powerful individuals. Such a totalitarian model lends support to the decentralization theory in which a dominating central government gradually loosens its control and grants more power to local governments and entities. Scholars studying Chinese political and economic systems, however, increasingly found this totalitarian model far from adequate (see e.g., general comments on the totalitarian model by Christiansen & Rai, 1996). For example, Solinger (1984a, 1984b, 1993) pointed out that within the communist regime, there had always been a "three-line struggle," where the bureaucratic, the radical, and the market represented three different models competing with each other. The policies adopted by the CCP were a product of continuous competition, grouping, and regrouping among these three models. This explained the swing of Chinese domestic policies in the prereform era (e.g., from economic reform attempts to class struggle). Only after 1978 did the reform model become the dominant one.

In Shue's (1988) study, she strongly critiqued the assumed totalitarian model under Mao's regime and argued that the cellular social structure (the "honeycomb polity" as she termed it) and the segmentation of rural political economy really confounded the "top-down" centralization attempts. In the interaction between the center and the local were the long-ignored local cadres (dating back to the *gentry*, an elite group in Chinese history). It was those local cadres who had to maintain the basic structure of the rural, to bear high political pressure, and to take risk of the socialist dictatorship. In practice, they produced a variety of defensive and aggressive localistic strategies to maintain their power. After the economic reform, the commodification of the rural economy had a dramatic impact on creating new social relations. Old communes (as the very basic economic mode) were changed or regrouped into companies (for rural industries) or relatively independent work teams (for agricultural production). The old power of local cadres was broken down, and economic elites emerged as a new force. In no way were economic, political, and social policies a one-way, top-down movement. They were, more accurately, multiple-way interactions, only getting more complex after the reform.

In her study of Chinese urban enterprises, Oi (1989) expanded Walder's (1986) clientelist bureaucracy model and suggested that clientelism existed in the economic production and political power struggle in rural areas as well. Criticizing the totalitarian model, Oi showed how rural peasants, as clients, always had to rely on the patrons (i.e., local cadres) to communicate with the state. In contrast to the totalitarian model, the clientelist model showed considerably more flexibility, subjectivity, and personal sentiment in the exercise of power and control. The economic reform shook the old structure but did not change the very basics.

Wank's (1999) ethnographic study in Xiamen in the late 1980s and mid-1990s showed that the revival of private business after the economic reform did not necessarily lead to the decline of patron–client ties. Rather it led to the emergence of a new commercialized form of clientelism. The new entrepreneurs and local governmental officials formed a special connection in the process of reform and found appropriate ways to bargain with the central state, taking advantage of their increasing autonomous economic power. It was mutual benefits among the entrepreneurs, the local governmental officials, and the central state that bonded all three together, regrouping and restrengthening clientelism in the new era.

In similar patterns, all these theoretical and empirical research showed that the long-assumed existence of a powerful, totalitarian central government was highly questionable, even in Mao's era. Policymaking and implementation were never a one-way, top-down imposition. Rather, there was a multiway and complex interaction. If these arguments were valid and accurate, the decentralization theory would have to be reconsidered on its basis, especially in political and legal domains.

Practical Implementation: Recentralization Along With Decentralization

A careful distinction should be made between economic power and other controls (e.g., administrative control) when evidence of policies from the central government is reviewed in the decentralization process. As noted earlier, economic decentralization caused some serious problems in its implementation. One way to curb those problems was a resurgent recentralization of *administrative control* from time to time.

First, as many scholars noticed, China's economy, by many measures (e.g., state enterprise share of total economic output), was more decentralized compared with other socialist countries even before the reform. This could be one important reason for the success of economic decentralization in China's reform (see such arguments in Shirk, 1994; Wank, 1999; World Bank, 1988). Even after economic power was granted to local governments and individuals, the administrative control of the state never faded away. Rather, it was transformed into different forms, consistent with the earlier discussion of local cadres' powers (see Butler, 1985; Solinger, 1995).

Second, the result of the economic decentralization process was not as decentralized as expected, that is, ensuring every player had a fair and equal chance and therefore a share of economic development, but rather, in an ironic way, as Solinger (1993) pointed out, through market incentives (e.g., by encouraging firms to invest in each other or buy each other out):

> state assets and market power are becoming even *more concentrated* than ever in the best and the biggest state enterprises, through the operation of policies that intentionally favor the fittest. Additional increments of power are also flowing to state-run bureaucratic offices, such as the materials departments, as their personnel are charged with supervising the disposal of the surplus supplies being traded outside the plan's pathways. (p. 144)

The state plan (due to the reserved administrative control) was transformed but still present: "Its existence is manifest in its old offices (even if they now hang out a new nameplate), in the habits it shaped, the patterns of association it fostered, and the *guanxi* developed between those who have lived by those habits and patterns" (Solinger, 1993, p. 197).

One example of such old habitual controls was the so-called administrative review and approval (ARA; *xingzheng shenpi*). The ARA was always used as a way to control key industrial and commercial projects. When it no longer met the requirement of the market economy, the Chinese government began to overhaul this practice. From December 2002 to May 2004, the State Council reviewed 1,795 projects and abolished ARA in 1,600 of these projects.[56] The lesson is that after decades of unequal treatment based on the planned economy, once the economic policy was opened to the market through decentralization, the result indeed seemed to be *unfair* to players in the game through claimed fair rules, especially in the early years of decentralization. It will take a long time for the weaker players to catch up and level the field.[57]

Third, facing problems caused by economic development in general (e.g., the increasing regional disparities) and by the overheated economy in particular (e.g., inflation), the central state adopted temporary recentralization measures from time to time. On the one hand, it became a necessary means of market adjustments; on the other hand, it reflected the complexity of the underlying dynamic (i.e., the reciprocal accountability relationship between the central government and lower levels of government), as opposed to a pure top-down hierarchy (World Bank, 1995). As pointed out, "the stop-go nature of decentralization in China is a reflection of the changing relationship and the accommodation of interests as between various factions within the central government itself, provincial governments from different regions, sub-provincial governments, enterprise managers, and households" (World Bank, 1995, p. 95; see also World Bank, 1988).

In short, China's unique social structure compounded the polity and policies adopted by the central government during the reform era. Evidence suggests that both economic and administrative policies and practices did not fully comply with the decentralization theory. Moreover, a distinction between macro- and microlevel controls is very useful here. During the reform, the central government gradually shifted its focus toward the macrolevel control as it left the microlevel control in the hands of local governments and business entities (see, e.g., World Bank, 1988). The decentralization theory overemphasized the micro process and ignored the macro control by the central government. In fact, the central government carefully controlled its pace in the reform process and implemented measures of both decentralization and recentralization of administrative as well as economic power.

Another Reading of the Economic Reform and Center–Local Relations

In their study of the impact of the economic reform on center–local political relations, some scholars adopted a different approach; that is, to study the economic reform in a power-struggle picture.

In her critique of the presumed totalitarian model, Shue (1988) argued that the reform policies adopted by Chinese leaders in the 1980s were exactly aimed to counter (and they had to conquer in this process) the local immobilism and primordial peasant localism based on the honeycomb structure. For a unified market economy to develop in the whole nation, reform needed to conquer two obstacles: the old cellular structure of rural life economically (independent and self-sufficient) and the subcultures of localism politically (subject to the influence of patrimonialism). As Shue pointed out, the power of local elites over local people in rural areas had been weakened after the reform, and the local elites had to adjust their means of control to the emergence of new economic elites. The result was a constant grouping and regrouping of local power relations in a process of answering the central state's calls. In such a reading, the reform, through adjusted power and control relations at the local government level, would give the central state more power as needed in the building of a unified and effective market economy.

Oi's (1989, 1999) studies also showed how the local clientelism managed to make changes and maintain power control after the reform when the local economic, political, and cultural structures became less homogenous. The political interests of local officials, instead of being at odds with local economic interests, became institutionally tied to them. With the decline of the old ideological and political structure, more changes and adjustments are necessary at the local level for further development of the whole nation.

Essentially, the question is how to adjust the center–local relations. With the development of a unified market, instead of dependent enterprises negotiating with local governments based on local rules, there is an increasing need for autonomous enterprises that are disciplined by the market and subject to general and systematic rules defined by central agencies. By liberating those enterprises from the control of local governments, the center can circumscribe local political influence and continue developing an integrated as well as efficient national economy (World Bank, 1990).

It should be noted that this process is not necessarily a win–lose situation, in which one party gains at the loss of another. Rather it could be a win–win case. Wank's (1999) study found that one paradox after the emergence of new mercantilism was that "it reflects the increasing autonomy of locales from the center while simultaneously stimulating the importance attached by local political and business elites to maintaining the larger political entity of China governed by the center" (p. 218). In other words, there is a strong interdependent relation between the center and the local. On the one hand, the local is making adjustments to keep its control, and one necessary step in this process is to keep its pace with the national economy (partially due to the innate nature of capitalist development). On the other hand, the center also needs strong local governments to maintain and implement its general policies to establish a unified market economy. To adjust new center–local relations within the market economy, the center must adopt a legitimate and effective means to restructure the old system. This new means is the process of legalization (see such an argument by L. C. Li, 2000).

CENTRALIZATION OF POWER, RATIONALITY AND LEGALIZATION

As discussed earlier, this study warned against the overemphasis of the decentralization theory in its application and raised questions about its expansion into other domains without careful distinctions. To gain a better understanding of China's legal reform, I turn to Weber's classical theory. Weber's analyses of rationality, bureaucratization, and centralization of power still shed light on the interaction of China's economic, political, and legal systems in the new era.

Rationality and Centralization of Power: A Revisit of Weber's Theoretical Framework

In Weber's (1988) comparative study, he tried to answer the question of how modern capitalism emerged in Western Europe but not in other civilizations. The answer, according to Weber, lay in the fact that a particular form of capitalism was necessary for economic development to take place, and this particular form appeared only in Western Europe. Significantly different from the mere pursuit of gains that existed everywhere in other civilizations, modern capitalistic activity became associated with the rational organization of formally free labor only in the West. Together with other factors, the availability of a religion-based ethic, namely the Protestant ethic, was crucial in the transformation of the spirit of modern capitalism.

Weber further observed that both the capitalist enterprise and the capitalist state shared a common character; that is, their authority relations were identical. Economically, capitalism centralized the ownership of the means of production. Most free laborers had nothing but their human capital and therefore had to follow the "established rules of the game." Politically, the means of administration and the means of violence were similarly concentrated in the hands of the centralized state. It was this centralization of power that connected both the economic and the political spheres (Inverarity, Lauderdale, & Feld, 1983). In contrast to Marx, Weber argued that the formal rational legal procedure did not emerge as a consequence of economic changes. Instead, the existence of rationality in the legal system was a precondition for the emergence of modern rational capitalism. The roots of formal rational law lay not in the economic base but in the centralization of power politically.

Without denying the importance of the economic factor, Weber focused on the process of rationalization and bureaucratization of the legal system (as well as other political administrations) in establishing the modern capitalist system. For Weber, "rationalized social practices are those rule-governed forms of social action which are calculated and calculable, based upon a self-reflexive knowledge of their aims and conditions, and oriented to achieving these ends by the most instrumentally appropriate means" (Garland, 1990, p. 179). The exact power of rationality in the legal proceeding lay in the predictability (of outcomes) and the calculability (of profits and losses), which served the interests of capitalist development. In other words, the operation of the legal system increased the degree of certainty with which the outcomes of economic activities could be calculated in advance (Weber, 1954). Correspondingly, the existence of an autonomous legal system and applicable legal rules (as well as legal staffs who know and follow the exact legal process) was crucial to the formal, rational legal decision making. It guaranteed effective functioning of the legal system.

On the other hand, the advance of bureaucratization was directly associated with the expansion of division of labor in various spheres of social life, and by no means was specialization limited to the economic sphere. Based on rationality, bureaucracy was essentially a way of organizing specialized scientific and technical knowledge for accomplishing technically defined goals. It was precisely this element of calculability that made bureaucratic administration capable of coping with the immense tasks of coordination necessary for modern capitalism. Their technical superiority such as precision, speed, consistency, availability of records, continuity, possibility of secrecy, unity, rigorous coordination, and minimization of friction and of expense for materials and personnel was the decisive reason for the success of bureaucratic organizations.[58]

It is clear that all those key terms such as centralization of power, rationality, and bureaucracy were closely related in Weber's legal and economic studies. One cannot treat them separately in either theoretical or empirical analyses.

China's Legalization and Centralization of Power

After the commencement of economic reform, China initiated its legal reform through systemization and bureaucratization as discussed earlier. To a large extent, this process signified a dramatic transition in economic, political, and social organizations.

In his study, Weber (1978) pointed out three types of power legitimacy in history: rational legal rules, traditional power, and charismatic personal authority. He himself paid much attention to the Chinese patrimonialism and traditional clan, *Zu*, both of which dominated the ancient society under the influence of Confucianism and strongly weakened the state's centralization of power and administration. After the new China was founded in 1949, to strengthen its political control the CCP intentionally weakened the power of the local clans under the name of "feudalist pernicious vestige." While Mao was building up his charismatic personal authority, he never eliminated all traditional virtues. Rather, he retained them but removed their association with Confucianism. By doing so, Mao was able to turn them into a means to increase his power and control under the so-called charismatic-ideological domination (Corne, 1997). More specifically, legitimate domination in Mao's era was a combination of both Mao's charismatic power (at the center) and the traditional power (at the local level; Rojek, 2001; J. Zhu, 1991). Mao's power and control reached its apex in the Cultural Revolution period but led the nation into a disaster.

Learning the lesson, Deng Xiaoping initiated legal reform and Jiang Zemin further established the rule of law in the Constitution. Facilitating economic reform, these moves should be viewed as attempts to relegitimize the authority and power of the center state in the process of political reform. Economically, the traditional rural structure has been gradually changing from independent, self-sufficient localities to an integrated entity dependent on effective functioning of the market (both domestic and international). Unified rules have been promulgated to free individual enterprises and households from excessive interference by local governments and guarantee their autonomous and equal status in the market system. As a matter of fact, a great number of laws, rules, and regulations enacted by the NPC, its Standing Committee, the State Council, and local people's congresses after 1978 were economically driven. For example, within the 5-year term of the 8th NPC (1992–1997), a total of 125 laws were passed, and 54 (43%) were directly related to the socialist market economy (J. Chen, 1999).

Politically, legalization also serves several key functions. First, it becomes an effective means to legitimize the governing of the central state. As recognized, law typically offers the illusion of fairness and equality because of the presumed equal access to legal institutions. As a result, law becomes one form of domination and control accepted as a legitimate means of management in general (Lauderdale & Cruit, 1993). Given the fact that both traditional and personal charismatic controls are waning sharply in the new era,[59] legalization has become an alternative to legitimize the power control of the state. Second, the process of legalization sets up legal boundaries for all governmental functions (both the center and, more important, the local[60]). This regulation and control of power abuse through laws and the legal system are indeed very important, although there have been questions about the effectiveness of such functions in the current Chinese legal system.

Third, the process of legalization has an important function of granting substantive rights to Chinese citizens within a modern system. This effort is to treat each citizen as a legally responsible subject or object both economically and politically. Through this process of individualization, local excessive and illegitimate controls (e.g., protectionism) would be challenged, and, as a result, the center state power would become the final supreme and legitimate authority. For example, in 1987 the Organic Law of the Villagers Committees of the People's Republic of China was put into trials in rural areas, and it was finalized in 1998. The new law aimed to assist villagers' self-governance in rural areas and to grant peasants rights in village elections.[61] One major move in this process was the use of village elections by peasants to counter the control of local cadres. In December 2001, 189 villagers at Cizhou, Hengxin village in Ma'anshan city, in Anhui province, called a general meeting to dismiss the head of the village from the office. Although the effort failed due to a lack of majority support after voting, it showed that villagers gained an increasing awareness of their legal rights, and the new election became a potential control on local power.[62]

In sum, there is ample evidence in the process of legalization to support the Chinese government's intent to use the legal weapon to restructure various organizations and strengthen its power and control in the new era. The centralization of power could well be a necessary condition for the building of rational legal as well as economic systems in contemporary Chinese society, and this is consistent with Weber's theory.

Back to the Decentralization Argument

Due to the close connection between economic power and administrative control, the term *decentralization* might be convenient but misleading in studying changing Chinese economic, political, and legal systems. After the reform, significant economic and administrative power was granted to local governments, individual enterprises, and households through various incentives under the socialist market economy. Nevertheless, the power of the center state was not necessarily weakened as a result.

When scholars raised the decentralization argument, one key issue was how to measure the centralization or decentralization of power, both quantitatively and qualitatively. In ancient feudal Chinese society, there was always a central government with authority and power, sometimes quite enormous (Frank, 1998). Nevertheless, the patrimonial and kinship control in local areas was substantial, countering the central government's power. The change after 1949 was both radical and complete when Mao managed to wield his power to balance the local patrimonialism. In comparison with these two, it is still unclear and questionable as to what extent the transformation and reformation of power structure after 1978 constituted a significant reduction in the function of the communist government. For example, as S. Zhu (1989) admitted, it was always necessary for local governments to implement general policies or laws from the central government in a specific way in the local area, even though they could enact more detailed practical rules and regulations locally. The (judicial) decentralization was not principally in conflict with, but complementary to, the legislative purpose of the central government.

In fact, the Chinese government was very careful with its authority and power control. The June 4 incident in 1989, in which numerous students and civilians protesting at Tiananmen Square were killed, was a good example for showing its tight control in an emergency (see Baum, 1994, for a detailed discussion of the June 4 event). Recently, the government once again showed its determination to crack down on potential challenges from traditional kinship when there were signs that the local *Zu*'s control resumed and grew in some places. It was officially declared that the control of *Zu* was a form of the rule by man based on private interests as a challenge to the authority of the official government.[63] Similarly, the most recent wave of the severe strike campaign since 2001 specifically targeted underworld organizations (*hei shehui*) because those organizations not only committed crimes locally, but also took part in economic and political activities (to facilitate their crimes) and constituted a serious challenge to governmental power.[64] All these examples showed that power control was still very tight in China, and the Chinese government was utilizing legal means to legitimize and strengthen its political control. In such an analysis, the argument of decentralization of power in the domain of political and legal control would be misleading, and there is a need to carefully redefine the scope of its use (see Baum & Shevchenko, 1999, for such an example).

CONCLUSION

In this chapter, I focused on a theoretical understanding of China's legalization process and its connection with political reform. In the new era, the Chinese government tried to respond to both economic and social changes and at the same time save its political and ideological control. One effective means adopted to achieve both ends was the legalization process under the label of the rule of law. So determined in nature, China's legalization always appeared to lag behind its economic reform (Gao & Song, 2001). Nevertheless, it has been carried out quickly through systemization and bureaucratization.

Analyzing the economic reform, some scholars proposed the decentralization theory to explain the process in which the local governments gained some power and discretion in handling economic affairs. The term was later expanded into administrative and judicial domains. My research called for caution in the use of such expansions, both theoretically and empirically. Indeed, the term *decentralization* has rarely been carefully defined. Overemphasis of decentralization misinterpreted the power relationship between the central government and the local, ignored macrolevel control by the government, and blurred important distinctions among economic, administrative, and legal controls. Conceptually, it would be more helpful to look at the issue as a continuum, rather than a dichotomy (decentralization vs. centralization), so that scholars, researchers, and practitioners can focus on specific measures adopted (e.g., which one is more salient and dominating) at different stages (pre-, inchoate, or advanced reform period) in different fields (economic, administrative, or legal).

Applying Weber's theory, I argued that the process of legalization should be explored within a broader scope as part of China's ongoing political reform. The Chinese government has adopted legal reform as a new means of legitimizing and maintaining its political control through the centralization of power in the new era (and this is supported by the best available evidence). Only in such a way could the audience gain a better understanding of the necessity of China's legal reform and its corresponding political implications.

Finally, there is always serious concern about the CCP's intervention during this legalization process. For example, as noticed, the Party still had various controls over lawmaking through means such as preapproval of draft laws, involvement by the Central Political-Legal Group, control over key appointments and meeting agendas, and heavy influence over legislative debate (M. S. Tanner, 1994). The most famous Four Cardinal Principles, namely, the socialist road, the dictatorship of the proletariat, the leadership of the Communist Party, and the Marxism-Leninism and Mao Zedong Thought (plus Deng's Theory and Jiang's "Three Represents" now), were also legally entrenched as fundamental bases of the communist government and China's legal system (Lo, 1995). These features of "Chinese characteristics" gained China's legal reform a reputation of the rule by law. In a way, the Party's intervention was inevitable, and it showed the exact inherent contradiction faced by the CCP; that is, at the same time to keep its one-party political control and to broaden and relegitimize its authority through the process of legalization. Despite such ambivalence, the Chinese government should have learned the lesson that according to Weber, all these interventions would damage the building of an autonomous and effective formal rational legal system.

4   Crime and Punishment in Transition

[handwritten annotation: 1997 Revised Criminal Law]

In the last two chapters, I examined both economic and political changes after 1978, which laid the foundation for the rebuilding of the Chinese legal system. In this chapter, I pay special attention to crime and punishment issues in the reform era and examine dramatic social and ideological changes in society.

Even though the legal system was rebuilt and strengthened after 1978, China suffered from an increasing crime rate. New crimes (e.g., economic crimes) and criminal groups (e.g., juveniles and underworld gangs) emerged and made up a significant part of the crime picture. Facing this problem, the Chinese government adopted a "severe strike campaign" approach to curb the ascending crime rates. In those campaigns, harsher punishments were imposed on criminals, usually at a faster pace and sometimes based on violations of normal procedures. The government always declared success after more criminals were arrested and sentenced. Based on official data and reports, I focus on the severe strike campaign, analyze how it was specifically planned and implemented, question the crime control effect of the campaign, and explore other functions served by the campaign. I suggest that we should study crime and punishment issues from a different perspective, through the impact of dramatic social and ideological changes after the reform. The roots of the crime problem lie in the deepened stratification of the society and the fading of communist ideological control prevalent in a process of social transition. Such an approach helps the audience understand the limitation of the anticrime campaign and shows that China's practice was not unique. Rather China's practice was consistent with the complex political power plays adopted in other nations.

RISING CRIME RATE IN THE NEW ERA

As a socialist nation, China had a low crime rate compared with other nations, and its successful crime control and low recidivism rate were often the focus of Western studies (see Bakken, 1991, 2000, 2005; Bracey, 1985, 1988; Dutton & Lee, 1993; Hobler, 1989; Rojek, 1989). China's crime rates nevertheless had been steadily climbing since the reform in the late 1970s.

Statistical Support of the Rising Crime Rate

First, there was little doubt that China's crime rate had been going up based on official longitudinal data. Table 4.1 lists the total number of criminal cases investigated by public security organizations and the rate of criminal cases per 100,000 people yearly from 1950 to 2005. It shows that China's criminal case rate was low after the new China was founded. It was around 50 cases per 100,000 people in the early 1950s, and even decreased to about 30 cases per 100,000 people in the late 1950s and early 1960s. This period of time often was portrayed as the golden time for China's crime control (see Bakken, 2000, for different numbers and his interpretation in Chapter 11). The trend clearly changed its direction in the late 1970s when the crime rate climbed to more than 70 cases per 100,000 people. The ascending momentum was stopped temporarily by several rounds of the severe strike campaign in the 1980s and 1990s (see Figure 4.1), but the crime rate in general still kept climbing, indeed very quickly, in the late 1980s and 1990s. The number reached 200 cases per 100,000 people in 1990 and was pushed back into the 100s in the 1990s, to some extent due to internal adjustments such as a new definition of theft in 1992 (for detailed information, see Curran, 1998; He, 2001; Xiang, 1999), but it soared again in the late 1990s, broke the 300 mark in 2001, and reached an all-time high of 363 cases per 100,000 people in 2004. When broken down by crime type, scholars confirmed that the crime rates of most violent crimes also increased over the years and aggravated the crime situation (see, e.g., Bakken, 2005).

Table 4.2 shows the total number of public prosecutions brought up by the People's Procuratorates from 1986 to 2005. It confirms the general trend in which the crime rate was increasing. Except for some decrease in the early 1990s (probably due to the redefinition of theft) and a slight dip in 2002, prosecutors brought up more and more public prosecutions over the years. By 2005, the total number of public prosecutions reached 654,871, more than double the number in 1986.

Youth and Juvenile Delinquency

Another major concern for the Chinese government was the severe youth and juvenile delinquency problem. Due to different age definitions of youth and juvenile groups in China, separate columns representing both groups are listed in Table 4.3. It shows that before the reform, youth and juvenile delinquency, as a percentage of total crimes, rose in the 1960s due to the endless class struggle, especially in the Cultural Revolution. The percentage fell back into the mid-30s near the end of the Cultural

Table 4.1 Number of Criminal Cases Investigated by the Public Security Branches

Year	Number of Cases	Per 100,000	Year	Number of Cases	Per 100,000	Year	Number of Cases	Per 100,000
1950	513,461	93.0	1973	535,820	60.1	1990	2,216,997	200.9
1951	332,741	59.1	1974	516,419	56.8	1991	2,365,709	209.4
1952	243,003	42.3	1975	475,423	51.4	1992[a]	1,582,659	138.6
1953	292,308	49.7	1976	488,813	52.2	1993	1,616,879	140.3
1954	392,229	65.1	1977	548,415	57.7	1994	1,660,734	142.9
1955	325,829	53.0	1978	535,698	55.7	1995	1,690,407	144.0
1956	180,075	28.7	1979	636,222	65.2	1996	1,600,716	135.1
1957	298,031	46.1	1980	757,104	76.7	1997	1,613,629	135.0
1958	211,068	32.0	1981	890,281	89.4	1998	1,986,068	159.1
1959	210,025	31.3	1982	748,476	73.7	1999	2,249,319	178.6
1960	222,734	33.6	1983	610,478	60.0	2000	3,637,307	287.3
1961	421,934	64.1	1984	514,369	49.9	2001	4,457,579	349.3
1962	324,639	48.2	1985	542,005	52.1	2002	4,336,712	337.6
1963	251,226	36.3	1986	547,115	51.9	2003	4,393,893	335.8
1964	215,352	30.5	1987	570,439	54.1	2004	4,718,122	363.0
1965	216,125	29.8	1988	827,594	77.4	2005	4,648,401	353.6
1972	402,573	46.2	1989	1,971,901	181.5			

Note. No accurate data are available during the period from 1966 to 1971 due to the Cultural Revolution. From *Law Yearbook of China* (1987–2005), B. He (2001), Deng & Cordilia (1999), and *China Statistical Yearbook* (2006).
[a]Based on a new definition of theft, the number of thefts (usually as a large percentage of total crimes) sharply dropped, causing the sharp decline of 1992 number here. See B. He (2001) and Xiang (1999).

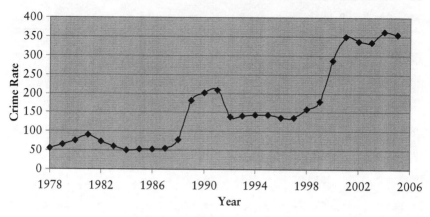

Figure 4.1 Crime rate per 100,000 population, 1978–2005.

Source: (1) *Law Yearbook of China* (1987-2005); (2) *China Statistical Yearbook* (2006).

Revolution. After the reform, however, youth delinquency regained its ascending momentum, and its percentage in the total crime quickly passed 40% and jumped into the 60% to 70% range in the 1980s. Moreover, juveniles under 18 became more involved in these crimes, with percentage of the total crime soaring to more than 20% in the 1980s from a very minimal 1.4% in 1977.

Table 4.4 presents more recent information, from 1988 to 2005, based on a different measurement. It shows that the percentage of youth and juvenile delinquents in the total number of prosecuted criminals was decreasing even though the number of prosecuted youth and juveniles was relatively stable, usually between 200,000 and 250,000 per year. This was explained by the ascending crime rate committed among older adults. On the other hand, Table 4.4 affirms the increasing problem for juveniles under 18. Their percentage in the total number of youth and juvenile delinquents decreased a little in the early 1990s but steadily increased in later years, passed 20% by the year 2002, and reached 28% by 2004. In 2005, the total number of prosecutions reached 285,801 and the percentage represented by juvenile under 18 jumped to 28.9%.

In short, troublesome youth and juvenile groups were always a major concern for the Chinese government. Over the years, severe crime problems involving both groups did not appear to be improving. In recent years, the lower percentage of youth and juvenile crime among total crimes was mainly due to increased crimes committed by older adults, not to the decrease of youth and juvenile delinquencies. The increasing number of crimes committed by juveniles under 18 also became major concern (for discussions on juvenile crimes in earlier years, see Keith, 1994, and Ngai, 1994).

Table 4.2 Total Public Prosecutions Brought up by the People's Procuratorates

Year	Total Prosecutions	Through Police Investigation	Through Self-Investigation
1986	257,219	220,324	36,895
1987	240,958	219,557	21,401
1988	262,896	244,553	18,343
1989	340,992	314,296	26,696
1990	385,903	356,111	29,792
1991	347,770	316,077	31,693
1992	330,604	305,161	25,443
1993	317,384	296,795	20,589
1994	385,271	353,121	32,150
1995	385,372	352,296	33,076
1996	481,520	445,507	36,013
1997	360,696	334,011	26,685
1998	403,145	380,445	22,700
1999	464,785	443,377	21,408
2000	480,119	456,376	23,743
2001	559,860	542,715	17,145
2002	527,354	512,540	14,814
2003	560,978	538,217	22,761
2004	612,790	586,960	25,830
2005	654,871	630,063	24,808

Note. From *Law Yearbook of China* (1987–2005) and *China Statistical Yearbook* (2006).

New Crimes and Criminal Groups

The worsening crime problem in China was also evident in the emergence of new crimes and criminal groups in the new era. The most noticeable example of new crimes was the emergence of economic crime. Before the reform, economic crime was not a big concern; however, it quickly jumped into people's view along with economic reform and development. Figure 4.2 shows the total number of economic crime cases accepted by the courts of

Table 4.3 Youth and Juvenile Delinquency as a Percentage of Total Crime, 1952–1991

Year	Youth Delinquency (14–25 Years Old)	Juvenile Delinquency (14–18 Years Old)
1952	20.2	
1955	22.0	
1956	18.0	
1957	32.3	
1961	30.0	
1964	30.0	
1965	35.0	
1966–74	40–50	
1975	37.0	
1977		1.4
1978		2.2
1979	47.6	3.3
1980	61.2	7.0
1981	64.0	13.3
1982	65.9	19.6
1983	67.0	18.0
1984	63.3	20.4
1985	71.3	23.8
1986	72.5	22.3
1987	74.4	21.6
1988	75.7	21.0
1989	74.1	19.9
1990	69.7	16.3
1991	65.0	14.6

Note. From Bakken (1995).

Table 4.4 Youth and Juvenile Delinquency, 1988–2005

Year	Total Prosecuted Youth and Juveniles	Percentage of Total Prosecuted Criminals	Juveniles Under 18	Percentage of Total Prosecuted Youth and Juveniles
1988	214,747	58.55	32,449	15.1
1989	293,435		42,766	14.6
1990	332,528	57.31	42,033	12.6
1991	268,206	52.88	33,392	12.5
1992	250,262	50.78	33,399	13.3
1993	228,311	50.74	32,408	14.2
1994	267,842	49.12	38,388	14.3
1995	247,391	45.54	35,832	14.5
1996	269,749	40.53	40,220	14.9
1997	199,212	37.85	30,446	15.3
1998	208,076	39.39	33,612	16.2
1999	221,153	36.71	40,014	18.1
2000	220,981	34.54	41,709	18.9
2001	253,465	33.96	49,883	19.7
2002	217,909	31.05	50,030	23.0
2003	231,715	31.2	58,870	25.4
2004	248,834	32.6	70,086	28.2
2005	285,801	33.9	82,692	28.9

Note. From *Law Yearbook of China* (1987–2005); 2005 data from the *China Statistical Yearbook* (2006).

the first instance from 1982 to 2004. In 1982, the number of accepted cases was 35,176, and it kept climbing until it reached 78,133 in 1986. After the official crackdown, the number decreased over the next 2 years but regained its ascending trend and reached an all-time high in 1990 with 88,184 cases, more than double the number in 1982. In the early 1990s, the number was sharply reduced mainly because of new case-registration criteria instituted in 1992 (Xiang, 1999), and it fluctuated afterward until it started another rising trend after 1997. At the same time, the nature of these economic crimes was getting worse. For example, by the late 1980s, there were only dozens of fraud cases in the nation with very few involving a value of more than 1 million yuan; however, by the late 1990s, the number jumped to more than 10,000 cases annually, and many cases involved a substantial value of more than 100 million yuan.[1] Around the turn of the new century, there was another reported surge of economic crimes. Cases investigated by the police increased from 52,000 in 1998 to 85,000 in 2001, and many cases involved huge monetary values, with some reaching billions of yuan.[2]

As a response, new laws and specialized branches were established to deal with economic crime (on the Chinese government's early reactions to economic crime in the 1980s, see Herb, 1988; Townsend, 1987). In 2001, economic crime was officially defined as "any commercial act under the market economy with an aim to gain illegal interests that violates national economic laws or regulations, severely disturbs economic order of the society and is subject to punishment under the criminal law."[3] Next, criminal charges of economic crime increased significantly. The 1979 Criminal Law included less than 20 official charges, but the number increased to more than 100 with the 1997 revised Criminal Law. In September 1998, the Ministry of Public Security (MPS) established a bureau of "economic crime investigation" to specifically combat economic crime.[4] Many criminals were punished under the new laws, and some were sentenced to death.[5]

Besides new crimes, new criminal groups also emerged. Table 4.5 shows the number of criminal gangs and gang members from 1979 to 1998. Both numbers increased after the reform and experienced a decrease only in the late 1990s after the government made a great effort to crack down. Although there was disagreement within Chinese academia, some scholars believed that these criminal gangs had gone through a transition from loose street gangs to more organized criminal groups modeled on traditional Chinese tongs (Gao & Song, 2001; B. He, 2001, 2003). Those traditional (and now

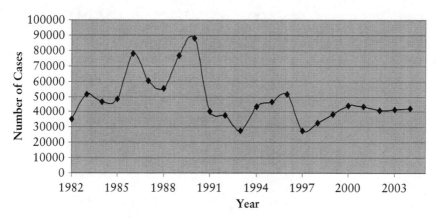

Figure 4.2 Economic cases accepted by the Courts of the First Instance, 1982–2004.

Source: Law Yearbook of China (1987–2005).

new) criminal organizations were often labeled underworld organizations (*hei shehui* in Chinese; the literal translation is "dark society"). By 2000, the government finally recognized this version of organized criminal gangs, and officially adopted the term "criminal gangs of underworld organizations." Based on the legal interpretation of the SPC, those organizations shared the following characteristics: (a) having a highly organized structure with rules and internal hierarchical divisions (e.g., leaders and followers); (b) carrying certain economic power with an ability to make economic profits through illegal means; (b) enjoying deep connections (e.g., through bribery, coercion, or both) with some governmental officials and the privilege of their protection and authoritative power; and (d) controlling fixed turf(s) within which organized crimes (e.g., extortion and violence) were conducted.[6] Since April 2001, the most recent round of the severe strike campaign has been targeting criminal gangs of underworld organizations. By the end of 2001, courts at all levels ruled on more than 300 cases involving such organizations, and more than 12,000 gang members were sentenced.[7]

In short, by any measure, there was a consensus that China was experiencing increased criminal activities in the reform era. How the government responded to this problem is the next question.

Table 4.5 Number of Criminal Gangs and Gang Members, 1979–1998

Year	Number of Criminal Gangs	Number of Criminal Gang Members
1979	> 3,400	
1983–1986	197,000	876,000
1986	30,476	114,452
1987	36,000	138,000
1988	57,229	213,554
1989	97,807	353,218
1990	100,527	368,885
1991	134,000	507,000
1992	> 120,000	> 460,000
1993	> 150,000	575,000
1994	> 150,000	> 570,000
1995	> 140,000	> 500,000
1996	136,225	> 670,000
1998	102,314	361,927

Note. From He (2001, 2003).

SEVERE STRIKE CAMPAIGN

In response to the rampant crime problem, the Chinese government initiated a special campaign against crimes. It was often labeled as a severe strike[8] campaign.

Three Rounds of Severe Strikes

In August 1983, the government launched the first round of "severe blows against serious criminal activities" to stop the crime wave of the early 1980s. Harsh and rapid punishments were actually adopted well before 1983, both by the central and local governments for the purpose of "swiftly and severely punishing criminals who jeopardize public security" (see Leng, 1982; H. M. Tanner, 1994a, 1994b, 1999). The crackdown was officially accepted, expanded, and intensified in 1983. The campaign targeted mainly "hooligan gang elements" guilty of gang fighting, harassment of women, rape, and other offensive behavior. The crackdown had an impact on almost every major crime because of its broad definition of the offense of "hooliganism." During the campaign, arrest and execution quotas were reportedly assigned to provinces and municipalities. By January 1984, the foreign press reported that the campaign might have resulted in 100,000 arrests and 5,000 to 10,000 executions (Woo, 1997). The campaign was extended into 1984. By the end of October, the Central Commission on Politics and Law reported that 1,027,000 criminals had been arrested on charges of homicide, arson, robbery, rape, and hooliganism; among them, 975,000 were prosecuted and 861,000 were sentenced (including 24,000 death sentences and death sentences with a 2-year reprieve). Moreover, 687,000 new prisoners entered labor reform, and 169,000 entered labor reeducation (data from H. M. Tanner, 1994b; compare with data presented by Seymour, 1988). This campaign, which officially ended in January 1987, resulted in the largest sweep of criminal offenders since the 1950 campaign against counterrevolutionaries.

In April 1996, the second round of the severe strike campaign was initiated. The primary focus of this round was to counter the proliferation of armed and violent crimes, including specific operations against prostitution-facilitating activities. During the first 2 months of its implementation, the campaign resulted in an estimated 1,000 executions, many involving gang members engaged in pimping and trafficking of women (Gil & Anderson, 1998; see also Stern, 1997). Although there is disagreement on the official ending date, this round of the campaign lasted about 10 to 12 months (Q. Zhang, 2002).

In April 2001, the Chinese government initiated the third round of the severe strike campaign, and it was planned to last until April 2003. As noted, criminal gangs of underworld organizations were officially declared as the main target. By the end of 2001, courts at all levels judged more than 300 cases involving such organizations, and more than 12,000 gang members were sentenced. The battle continued in 2002. In August, public security organizations made a call to crack down on both robbery and looting, and in November, the MPS planned a 1-year special action against crimes connected with cellular phones, bank cards, and motorcycles.[9] Both actions were aimed at continuing and intensifying the ongoing campaign. Table 4.6 shows the strength of both the 1996 and 2001 campaigns. Criminal judgments rendered by the people's courts at all levels increased tremendously from 545,162 in 1995 to 667,837 in 1996. Among 656,349 cases with criminal punishment in 1996, 287,537 cases (43%) resulted in sentences longer than 5 years, including death and life sentences. Similarly, from 2000 to 2001, the total criminal judgments increased sharply from 646,431 to 749,659, with 188,610 cases (25.2%) receiving sentences longer than 5 years.

Principles of the Campaign

Beginning with the first campaign, the crackdown had been called to "swiftly and severely punish criminals who jeopardize public security." First, criminals were punished more severely in the campaign (*cong zhong*). One extreme example was the practice of death sentences and executions in these campaigns. As noted by scholars, there were only 21 crimes in the 1979 Criminal Law punishable by death. More offenses, however, were added and implemented by further legislation in these campaigns. By 1997, the revised Criminal Law carried 53 articles dealing with death penalty crimes (see Leng, 1985; Monthy, 1998; Scobell, 1990; Tifft, 1985, for more information). During the first around of the campaign, more than 10,000 executions were reported in 3.5 years from 1983 to 1986 (M. S. Tanner, 2000). Based on data collected by Amnesty International, Table 4.7 shows the estimated number of death sentences and executions from 1994 to 2006. In both 1996 and 2001 when the second and third round of the severe strike campaign were initiated, the number of death sentences and executions increased significantly (e.g., doubled or tripled) compared with other years, a clear result of the harsh crackdowns. In August 2002, in an effort to extend the crackdown against robbery and looting, the High People's Court in Guangdong province suggested to its subordinate courts that death sentences could be rendered to offenders in the most dangerous and violent burglaries and robberies conducted on public transportation.[10] In spite of the severity principle, a distinction was made to distinguish campaign targets from nontargets, and the heightened punishment was to be rendered only to those targets. Literally, Article 5 of the 1997 Criminal Law stipulated that "the severity of punishments must be commensurate with the crime committed by an offender and the criminal responsibility he bears," and Article 61 stipulated that "when deciding the punishment of a criminal element, the sentence shall be imposed on the basis of the facts of the

Table 4.6 Criminal Judgments of the People's Courts, 1988–2004

Year	Total Judgments	Not Guilty	No Criminal Punishment Given	Cases With Criminal Punishments					
				Total Cases	Death to Lifetime	≥ 10 Years	5 to 10 Years	< 5 Years	Other
1988	368,790	2,039	5,325	361,426	32,079		81,454	201,753	46,140
1989	482,658	1,582	6,035	475,041	16,607	29,377	119,272	248,981	60,804
1990	582,184	1,912	7,250	573,022	23,899	42,530	148,909	283,053	74,631
1991	509,221	1,983	7,587	499,651	60,526		123,808	231,784	83,533
1992	495,364	2,547	8,040	484,777	57,172		114,252	226,251	87,102
1993	451,920	2,000	6,371	443,549	173,897			197,115	73,537
1994	547,435	2,153	7,680	537,602	208,267			244,156	85,179
1995	545,162	1,886	7,911	535,365	219,922			231,202	84,241
1996	667,837	2,281	9,207	656,349	287,537			270,893	97,919
1997	529,779	3,476	8,790	517,513	209,309			215,750	92,454
1998	533,793	5,494	9,414	518,885	149,142			249,139	120,604
1999	608,259	5,878	9,034	593,347	157,462			292,130	143,755
2000	646,431	6,617	9,770	630,044	163,422			307,849	158,773
2001	749,659	6,597	N/A	N/A	188,610			369,154	N/A
2002	493,500	4,935	11,266	690,506	160,324			345,351	184,831
2003	747,096	4,835	11,906	730,335	158,562			357,991	213,718
2004	767,951	2,292	12,345	753,314	146,237			363,012	244,065

Note. From *The Yearbook of the People's Courts* (1988–1992) and *Law Yearbook of China* (1987–2005).

Table 4.7 Number of Death Sentences and Executions, 1994–2006

Year	Death Sentences	Executions
1990s	27,120	18,000
1994	2,780	2,050
1995 (first half)	1,800	1,147
1996	6,000	3,500
1997	2,495	1,644
1998	1,657	1,067
1999	1,720	1,077
2000	1,511	1,000
2001	4,015	2,468
2002	1,921	1,060
2003	1,639	726
2004	6,000	3,400
2005	3,900	1,770
2006	2,790	1,010

Note. From *Annual Reports on China*, Amnesty International (1996–2007), Amnesty International (1996).

crime, the nature and circumstances of the crime, and the degree of harm to society, in accordance with the relevant stipulations of this law." The heightened punishment, therefore, should be used only against those who "gravely endangered society."[11] In reality, however, courts had great discretion to select campaign targets in their actual practice because of broad definitions of laws.

Second, in crime campaigns, criminal punishments usually were rendered faster, and this was the "swiftness" principle (*cong kuai*). The swift nature was first reflected in its speed of investigating cases and making arrests by law enforcement agencies (usually in a short period of time). Arguably, there was a legitimate reason for such a sweep. The police did not want to give breaks to criminals after the campaign was initiated. Sometimes when a quota was set, however, the police gained another incentive to make massive arrests in a short time to show their achievements.[12] Indeed, the event of a sweep became a near standard in crackdowns. For example, in a mere 5 days from October 27 to 31, 2002, public security forces in Beijing investigated and handled 2,095 criminal cases and 68 criminal gangs and arrested 1,088 suspects.[13] Second, during the crackdowns, cases were tried faster through the judicial process. Based on the 1979 Criminal Law and Criminal Procedure Law, all death sentence cases had to be reviewed by the SPC. To cooperate with the crackdown, however, the Standing Committee of the NPC in 1981 adopted resolutions to grant the right to approve the death penalty for murderers, robbers, rapists, bomb throwers, arsonists, and saboteurs to the High People's Courts of the provinces, autonomous regions, and municipalities (although the approval of the SPC was still required for death sentences passed on counterrevolutionaries and embezzlers; see discussions by Leng, 1982; Tifft, 1985). Similar decisions were made by the SPC in 1983 to answer the call of the severe strike campaign. In 1996 and 1997, the Criminal Procedure Law and the Criminal Law were revised respectively, and both laws (e.g., Article 48 in the Criminal Law and Article 199 in the Criminal Procedure Law) clearly stipulated that "death sentences and executions shall be reviewed and approved by the Supreme People's Court." In other words, there was still no legal basis for the granting of review rights to lower level courts. The SPC did not take the review rights back until 2007 (see Chapter 6), and the review by lower level courts was practiced nationally without being questioned during those campaigns.[14] Moreover, although the 1979 Criminal Procedure Law stipulated that the time limit for a death penalty appeal was 10 days, it was shortened to 3 days in the 1983 anticrime campaign, showing a willingness by the judicial branches to supersede procedural requirements in cases involving great public indignation (such incidents were noticed by Keith, 1994; Woo, 1997). In the 1996 anticrime campaign, three men in Jilin province were arrested for robbery on May 21 and executed on May 31. Their trial and sentencing by the trial court, review, and approval of death sentences as well as the appeal hearing by the appellant court all took place in 5 days between May 24 and 28 (Amnesty International, 1997).

Besides these two natures, different wording sometimes was proposed as basic principles of the crackdown, such as the order–accuracy–severity (*wen zhun hen*) principles. The order principle required that each campaign (or battles in each campaign) be carried out in plans and orders; the accuracy principle required that in each case, basic facts and evidence be clear and accurate; and the severity principle required a harsher punishment for criminals. In a sense, they were more detailed guiding rules, not contrary to the essential severity and swiftness principles.

Measures of the Campaign

During these anticrime campaigns, law enforcement and judicial branches frequently adopted some common means and measures to combat crimes. First, campaigns were usually organized by battles with different phases targeting specific crimes, labeled officially as *themes*. For example, the first 1983 campaign targeted hooligan gang members and their crimes such as gang fighting, harassment of women, and rape. In 1989[15] the sweep was aimed at the so-called six evils: prostitution; producing, selling, and spreading pornography; kidnapping women and children; planting, gathering, and trafficking drugs; gambling; and defrauding people by superstitious means. In 1996, the severe strike was to counter the proliferation of armed and violent crimes including specific operations against prostitution-facilitating activities. In 2001, criminal gangs of underworld organizations were officially declared as the new target. As a continuation of the 2-year campaign, the public security organizations in August 2002 made specific calls to crack down on robbery and looting. In November 2000, new moves were planned against crimes connected with cellular phones, bank cards, and motorcycles. Most recently, in February 2006, the Chinese Communist Central Political and Legal Committee (CCCPLC) called for another round of crackdowns (not declared as a new round of the campaign) on underworld organizations or groups with such a nature in rural areas.[16] Although specific crimes were targeted at different battles, all anticrime campaigns were indeed full-scale, comprehensive crackdowns, not limited to the named crimes. The plan of battle was more strategic in this sense.

Second, judicial branches very often used *mass trials* to achieve a deterrence effect. In those mass trials, criminals were exposed to a large audience, and their crimes were denounced, followed by public sentencing and executions in extreme cases (Trevaskes, 2003). In the 1983 campaign, 30 convicted murderers, arsonists, rapists, and robbers were reportedly sentenced to death in August in Beijing in a sports stadium as 60,000 spectators cheered the judge's announcement (cited in Johnson, 1986; Leng, 1985; Tifft, 1985). Some Japanese reporters touring Anhui province in December 1983 also reported similar executions in an open field where 10 men, bound and kneeling, were shot to death. An audience of more than 2,000 witnessed the event (cited in Tifft, 1985). In the 1990s, despite the SPC's warnings against publicly humiliating parades of soon-to-be executed criminals, such practices were still noticed (see Amnesty International, 2004; Trevaskes, 2003). The same approach was broadly extended and frequently used in the latest campaign. In September 2001, courts in Tianjin city held 11 mass trials in 7 days and sentenced 158 criminals in 94 cases in front of an audience of more than 2,000 people; similarly, 148 criminals in 84 cases were publicly sentenced in 5 days in Hainan province, and 1,677 criminals in 1,063 cases were sentenced in 4 days in Shandong province.[17] In the first 4 months of 2002, courts in Yunnan province held 60 mass trials and sentenced 615 criminals. Among those sentenced, 427 received terms of years in prison and 188 received life sentences or death sentences.[18] It should be noted that mass trials were not a particular product of the severe strike campaign. Theoretically, there was a deep connection between mass trials and the mass-line movement in Mao's era, and the mass trial was adopted well before the initiation of the crackdowns (Leng, 1982). The use of mass trial, however, was definitely intensified in those campaigns.

Success of Severe Strike Campaigns at What Price?

Despite harsh crackdowns, the effect of severe strike campaigns was unclear. In the short term, it looked like the campaigns were successful. For example, in the 1983 anticrime campaign, the national crime rate decreased 44.7% during the last 4 months of the year compared with the first 8 months (Johnson, 1986; Tifft, 1985). Similarly, public authorities in later campaigns also claimed high rates of arrests, convictions, and immediately reduced crime incidents as their achievements. As pointed out by H. M. Tanner (1994b), however, one problem with such success stories was that these campaigns, by targeting specific offenses, produced artificially high rates of such offenses in the hitting times, therefore making any data immediately after the crackdowns appear lower. In that case, the subsequent declines were equally artificial. Moreover, criminals would have known how to hide during the crackdown and wait until the sweep was over. In contrast, longitudinal data in postcrackdown years should be more persuasive in studies of the effect of the campaigns. Such data, however, did not support the claimed success of the anticrime campaigns. Figure 4.1 shows that before the 1983 campaign was initiated, the crime rate (measured by criminal cases per 100,000 people) had already been declining. At best, the 1983 campaign helped to reduce the crime rate to its lowest point in 1984. Then the crime rate resumed its momentum in the next 3 years and kept climbing quickly after 1987. As to the second campaign in 1996, the effect was even weaker. Again, the campaign was initiated when the crime rate was going down slightly (from 1995 to 1996), but it failed to contribute to the declining trend in 1997 when the crime rate was almost identical to that of 1996. The crime rate picked up its ascending momentum afterward. In a very similar fashion, the 2001 campaign was only able to reduce the crime rate artificially in the next 2 years, followed by an all-time high of 363 cases per 100,000 people in 2004. In short, longitudinal data cast serious doubts on the claimed success by the authorities, and more recent rounds of crackdowns tended to have a weakened impact on crime control.

In addition, there were costs to anticrime campaigns, some expected and some unexpected. First, certain procedural protections were discarded in the process of punishing criminals swiftly and severely.[19] Deprivation of these procedural protections (such as the death sentence review from the SPC and the shortened appeal time) greatly weakened defendants' (already very limited) rights, and made the alliance among the public security, the procuratorates, and the courts more political than legal. These violations of legal rules (such as the Criminal Law and the Criminal Procedure Law) had a bad effect on consistent interpretation and application of legal rules in a stable legal system in the long run. Second, as many scholars noted, in the 1983 anticrime campaign, decisions to severely punish criminals were retrospectively applied to offenses committed before the initiation of the crackdown, even though the 1979 Criminal Law clearly prohibited this type of retrospective application (see discussions by J. Chen, 1999; H. M. Tanner, 1994a, 1994b, 1999). Once again, legal rules were compromised and subject to political controls as a means. Such violations weakened the stability of the legal system, and its damaging effect went beyond the scope of the legal system (on the impact of such violations beyond the legal system, see Boxer, 1999). Prices paid in these campaigns might look small at first glance, but they have long-term, more serious effects.

CONTINUATION OF THE CAMPAIGN IN THE TRANSITIONAL ERA

If, as argued, the crime campaigns had little impact on crime control, the next logical questions that should be asked include these: Why does the Chinese government still favor such a practice? Does it have some positive effects? What is the fate of such a practice in the future? The answers can be explored at both micro and macro levels. At the micro level, the crime campaigns did serve other important functions beyond crime control and therefore provided some justification for their existence. At the macro level, however, the incompetence of the campaigns in crime control was closely related to dramatic social changes in China, and this seemed to cast doubt on its further practice.

Microlevel Analysis: Other Functions of the Campaign

Although the crime control effect of the severe strike campaign was questionable, the campaign did serve other important functions. First, as suggested by Durkheim (1983, 1984), one particular function of punishing criminals was to fulfill a societal need as a requirement of moral boundary and to strengthen the "conscience collective" among people. Even though "repressive punishment" had been gradually replaced by "restitutory sanctions" in more advanced society, it never totally disappeared and occurred over and over to serve its social purposes. As a matter of fact, repressive punishment had a long history in China. In Mao's era, perpetrators of the most serious crimes were often executed publicly "to assuage people's anger," and the justification was made on the grounds of retribution to "appease the masses" (for more information and discussion, see Scobell, 1990). Even after the reform, public education was always a goal in anticrime campaigns, and mass trials served such a purpose. In those trials, certain rituals were performed with an emphasis on retribution and repentance of those criminals (because repentance symbolized acceptance and confirmation of social boundaries), and in a sense it re-created social order (Trevaskes, 2003).

Further, mass media such as television, radio, billboard, blackboard, bulletin, and poster were all widely used to announce trials and executions (see Bakken, 1993; Tifft, 1985). Sometimes to increase the dramatic effect, condemned criminals with their heads shaven and bowed were paraded through the streets with large placards hung around their necks describing their crimes (Tifft, 1985). According to Durkheim's theory, all these public shows were to vilify criminals, separate them from the populace, and further strengthen the internal solidarity among the majority.

Second, although lacking in long-term effects, severe strike campaigns were used frequently to raise people's awareness of crimes and to gain public support for such crackdowns. As discussed earlier, public propaganda was widely used in each crackdown to mobilize the populace. In May 2002, it was reemphasized that severe strike campaigns should be accompanied by the "publicity of the campaign."[20] Indeed, the populace rarely questioned the effect of severe strike campaigns and showed wide support for crackdowns. Based on survey results, the authorities always cited the increasing satisfaction and support of the public as an achievement of severe strike campaigns.[21]

Third, the severe strike campaign was proposed as a special means to serve specific political functions beyond the scope of crime control. For example, in July 2002, Luo Gan, Secretary of the CCCPLC, suggested to all subordinate political and legal branches that the ongoing severe strike campaign (initiated in 2001) should be carried forward to "ensure a stable and good social environment for the forthcoming 16th Party's Congress."[22] This call showed how crime control and the legal system were both subject to political purposes as tools. Although nothing was surprising given the long recognized instrumental nature of the Chinese laws and legal system, there was tension (not necessarily clear to many politicians in China) between those who are dedicated to the building of a modern, independent legal system and these types of politically motivated legal movements (see discussion by Trevaskes, 2003). At this moment, the Chinese government is still showing its willingness to sacrifice the former for its political control.

Finally, the short-term severe strike campaign became an indispensable complement to decreasing traditional crime control means. Before the reform, relatively static and stable neighborhood communities and workplaces exerted tight control over people's lives. It was not only difficult to commit crimes but also difficult for a person to become a criminal because of his or her close connections with others (see V. H. Li, 1978, for a detailed discussion on law and social control before the reform). After the reform, the community-workplace-centered control approach started losing its effects, giving way to a more individual-based control approach. Facing increasing crime rates, comprehensive management (*zonghe zhili*) was implemented to improve the community-workplace-centered approach with the individual-based control strategy. As H. M. Tanner (1994b) pointed out, the term had its roots in a 1979 report on youth crime, in which it was stated that all-around efforts would have to be made to eliminate social factors at the root of the problem. Although the term *comprehensive management* was not used, the report concluded that "we must carry out the leadership of the Party committees, mobilize the entire Party, get the Party secretaries involved, depend on schools, factories, government organizations, the army, street, rural production brigade and other base-level organizations, and all social forces to strengthen the education of youth" (Tanner, 1994b, pp. 252–253). Later, the term "comprehensive management of public security" was first used officially in May 1981, and it was viewed as a more effective way to cure the crime problem.

In practice, it was difficult for the police to effectively follow the comprehensive management approach, although the number of police more than doubled from 400,000 in 1978 to more than 800,000 in the early 1990s (Wong, 1994). At first, rather than going out to work with communities and workplaces, the police were simply swamped with increased crimes and became increasingly reactive and less responsive to neighborhoods. Later they figured out that the reactive, wait-and-answer approach was not working well to meet the call to quench crimes. Then, the police force became more mobile and proactive. This time, on the one hand, the police were trying to rebuild the old connection with residential communities, and, on the other hand, they adopted severe strike campaigns nationwide to actively reach out (for a study of how police responded to new challenges in the new era, see Dutton, 2005; Fu, 1993; Situ & Liu, 1996; Wong, 2002). In the wake of public security organizations' struggle, private security guards became more and more popular. In 1984 the first private security guard company was established in Shekou, Guangdong province, and by 2006 the number of security guards nationwide reached 2.3 million.[23] As reported, the majority of these security guards were nonresidents, had very low education (less than high school), and received minimum training before they started working.[24] Their roles, however, expanded over the years. For example, in 2005 and 2006, they arrested 117,000 and 162,000 suspects, respectively, and provided more than 300,000 leads to the police.[25]

To some extent, there was a competition between the comprehensive management approach (community-centered) and the crackdown approach (individual-based). The former focused on the integration of individuals in the community and the prevention of crimes, whereas the latter focused on high-pressure blows and striking out bad people from the community. As Dutton and Lee (1993) argued, by practicing the severe strike campaign, the police had "abandoned comprehensive policing strategies and moved towards a form of policing that targets particular types of crime at the expense of instituting all round regimes of management and one effect of this is a shift from preventive to punitive policing" (p. 330). The Chinese government realized, however, that the crackdown could not stop crimes, and it had to come up with new measures to readjust the comprehensive management.[26] To answer such a call, the most recent move in October 2006 by the public security organizations was to establish police offices in neighborhoods to improve community policing. By the end of 2006, more than 133,000 such neighborhood offices were established and more than 220,000 police were stationed in communities as a result.[27] The effect of such efforts remains to be seen.

It should be pointed out that China's seemingly inconsistent legal practice was not unique. As Garland (2001) showed, in the last two decades, the practice of crime control in both the United Kingdom and in the United States exhibited two distinct patterns of action: an *adaptive strategy* stressing prevention and partnership and a *sovereign state strategy* stressing enhanced control and expressive punishment. Policymaking became a form of acting out that downplayed the complexities and long-term character of effective crime control in favor of the immediate gratifications of a more expressive alternative. All these different, seemingly inconsistent means were adopted in the new era to balance short-term political support and gains with long-term systematic stability and rationality. In this sense, China was not an exception in its strategic power control play, and its severe strike campaign served just such a function.

Macrolevel Analysis: Society in Transition

In his study, Durkheim (1983, 1984) suggested a connection between social and legal evolutions. As societies progressed from less to more advanced forms (e.g., deepened division of labor), from an all-encompassing religiosity to modern secularism, and from collectivism to individualism, the legal system would shift from a predominantly penal law with "repressive organized sanctions" to the prevalence of civil law, commercial law, procedural law, administrative, and constitutional law with "restitutory" sanctions. During this transition, the traditional conscience collective is fading away, and if society could not re-create a new moral boundary to cope with new changes, society would face an increasing degree of social dysfunctions as well as crimes (see Garland, 1990; Giddens, 1971; Hughes, 1995). To follow the Durkheimian approach, China's crime and punishment should be studied from a different perspective; that is, through the impact of dramatic social and ideological changes after the reform.

With economic development after the reform, the division of labor was increasingly diversified in China. As a result, China witnessed deepened social stratification. In the remainder of this chapter, I examine several key issues in this transition, including urbanization, migration, household registration and its reform, social inequality, unemployment, and ideological transformation.

Urbanization and Migration

Along with economic development, China increased its speed of urbanization. Table 4.8 shows the composition change of the Chinese population

Table 4.8 Composition of Chinese Population (Unit: 10,000)

Year	Total Population	Gender Composition			Urban vs. Rural Population		
		Male	Female	Ratio (F = 100)	Urban	Rural	% of Rural Residents
1950	55,196	28,669	26,527	108.1	6,169	49,027	88.8
1955	61,465	31,809	29,656	107.3	8,285	53,180	86.5
1960	66,207	34,283	31,924	107.4	13,073	53,134	80.3
1965	72,538	37,128	35,410	104.9	13,045	59,493	82.0
1970	82,992	42,686	40,306	105.9	14,424	68,568	82.6
1975	92,420	47,564	44,856	106.0	16,030	76,390	82.7
1978	96,259	49,567	46,692	106.2	17,245	79,014	82.1
1979	97,542	50,192	47,350	106.0	18,495	79,047	81.0
1980	98,705	50,785	47,920	106.0	19,140	79,565	80.6
1981	100,072	51,519	48,553	106.1	20,171	79,901	79.8
1982	101,654	52,352	49,302	106.2	21,480	80,174	78.9
1983	103,008	53,152	49,856	106.6	22,274	80,734	78.4
1984	104,357	53,848	50,509	106.6	24,017	80,340	77.0
1985	105,851	54,725	51,126	106.9	25,094	80,757	76.3
1986	107,507	55,581	51,926	106.2	26,366	81,141	75.5
1987	109,300	56,290	53,010	106.9	27,674	81,626	74.7
1988	111,026	57,201	53,825	106.9	28,661	82,365	74.2
1989	112,704	58,099	54,605	106.9	29,540	83,164	73.8

over the years. In 1950, China's total population was less than 552 million, and almost 89% of the population lived in rural areas. From 1960 to 1981, the total population increased from 662 million to 1 billion, but the percentage of rural residents stabilized at just around 80% mainly because of tight control of people's migration. In the 1980s and 1990s, China's urbanization finally took off. The percentage of rural residents decreased to 70% in 1997, and reached its lowest level of 56.1% by 2006. Note the accelerating speed of the decrease. It took 17 years (from 1981–1997) to drop the first 10 percentage points from 80% to 70%, and then it took only the next 5 years to drop another 10%. Despite such progress, scholars studying China's

Table 4.8 (Continued)

Year	Total Population	Gender Composition			Urban vs. Rural Population		
		Male	Female	Ratio (F = 100)	Urban	Rural	% of Rural Residents
1990	114,333	58,904	55,429	106.8	30,191	84,142	73.6
1991	115,823	59,466	56,357	106.8	30,543	85,280	73.6
1992	117,171	59,811	57,360	106.9	32,372	84,799	72.4
1993	118,517	60,472	58,045	106.9	33,351	85,166	71.9
1994	119,850	61,246	58,604	107.0	34,301	85,549	71.4
1995	121,121	61,808	59,313	107.0	35,174	85,947	71.0
1996	122,389	62,200	60,189	106.9	35,950	86,439	70.6
1997	123,626	63,131	60,495	106.8	36,989	86,637	70.1
1998	124,810	63,629	61,181	106.8	37,942	86,868	69.6
1999	125,909	64,189	61,720	106.8	38,892	87,017	69.1
2000	126,583	65,355	61,228	106.6	45,844	80,739	63.8
2001	127,627	65,672	61,955	106.0	48,064	79,563	62.3
2002	128,453	66,115	62,338	106.1	50,212	78,241	60.9
2003	129,227	66,556	62,671	106.2	52,376	76,851	59.5
2004	129,988	66,976	63,012	106.3	54,283	75,705	58.2
2005	130,756	67,375	63,381	106.3	56,212	74,544	57.0
2006	131,448	67,728	63,720	106.3	57,706	73,742	56.1

Note. From *China Statistical Yearbook* (2001, 2005, 2006), *Almanac of China's Population* (2001), *China Statistical Abstract* (2002), and 2006 data from the *People's Daily*, March 1, 2007.

urbanization pointed out that compared with China's industrialization level (already beyond 50% by 2002), the level of China's urbanization is still pretty low.[28] A goal was set in 2002 to increase the urbanization rate to 75% in the next 50 years.[29] Gradually, urbanization has become one driving force for China's economic development, and every 1% increase in urbanization reportedly brings on a 1% to 2% GDP increase correspondingly.[30]

When extra labor became free (from being bound to the land) after the reform, China witnessed waves of population migration from rural areas to the inner cities. Due to lack of accurate data, there was little record of the floating population in early years, especially in the 1980s. There is little question, though, that the number was growing very quickly. Based on Solinger's (1999) study, the average percentage of floaters (i.e., migrants) in the permanent residents of major cities (e.g., Beijing, Shanghai, Tianjin, and Guangzhou) increased from 12.6% in 1984 to 22.5% in 1987, and to 25.4% in 1994. In 1994, the floating population reached 3.3 million in Beijing and 3.31 million in Shanghai (T. Zhang, 2001). From 1993 to 1995, the estimated number of migrants nationwide ranged from 20 million to 110 million based on different reports and measurements (Solinger, 1999). Data from NBSC showed that the floating population reached 144 million in 2000 and further increased to 147 million by 2005.[31]

Based on data in the late 1980s and early 1990s, Solinger (1999) found that major export provinces, such as Sichuan, Anhui, Hunan, and Jiangxi, had low average amounts of cultivated land per capita, low agricultural output value, low rural net income, and low percentage of rural laborers in town and village enterprises. She argued that the reason peasants chose to leave was in large part a reaction to state policies that had so structured their home environment. In fact, disparate policies implemented by the central government in early years of the reform clearly favored coastal provinces and cities. Even after favorable policies were made available to all provinces in the 1990s, coastal provinces and cities still enjoyed their favorable locations and the residual advantages of early privileges. According to a report in October 2002, migrants still came primarily from highly dense inner provinces such as Sichuan (exporting 16.4% of total floating population), Anhui (10.2%), Hunan (10.2%), Jiangxi (8.7%), Henan (7.2%), and Hubei (6.6%), and moved to more advanced coastal cities and provinces such as Guangdong (receiving 35.5% of migrants), Zhejiang (8.7%), Shanghai (7.4%), Jiangsu (6%), and Beijing (5.8%).[32] The migration structure hardly changed after many years of reform. These migrants, dominantly young men, allegedly committed a disproportionate number of crimes in urban cities and became the new target for policing (see Curran, 1998; S. Feng, 2001; Friedmann, 2005; Ma, 2001). In 2006, official data showed that 41.2% of arrestees of the public security organizations were transient floaters.[33] An empirical study of legal dispositions in theft cases showed that the transients, compared to the local residents, tended to receive longer pretrial detentions, although their final sentencing dispositions did not appear to be harsher (H. Lu & Drass, 2002).

Household Registration and Its Reform

As urbanization and migration quickly developed, the arbitrary separation between the rural and the urban based on the old control system, the household registration (*hukou*) system, became an obstacle to both. The *hukou* system worked very well before the reform, consistent with the planned economy as discussed in Chapter 2; however, it is losing its effect in the reform era, especially on migrants. To control the new migrants in major cities, the MPS issued Provisional Regulations on the Management of Population Living Temporarily in the Cities in 1985. On the one hand, it was an implicit recognition of the migrants' status by granting them semilegal status in the cities; on the other hand, it was a continuation of the *hukou* system with a clear goal of regaining the lost control (see Mathaus, 1989; Solinger, 1999). In the same year, to strengthen the *hukou* system, the Standing Committee of the 6th NPC in its 12th meeting passed Regulations of Residents' Identification Cards, and after 1989 resident cards became mandatory for everyone over the age of 16. From 1985 to October 2002, a total of 1.14 billion resident cards were issued.[34]

Although the central government tried to keep the *hukou* system alive, both its effect and existence became increasingly questionable. First, as a product of the planned economy, it prohibits the process of urbanization. Second, it is contrary to the development of a market economy, which requires free flow of both capital and labor. Third, it leads to artificial separation (e.g., the rural vs. the urban) and fragmentation (e.g., different status based on political orientations) among citizens who are supposed to enjoy equal rights both economically and politically. Fourth, its control over migrants creates a negative effect on their lives in new locations and hinders their normal activities (e.g., consumption) through actual disparate treatment.[35] Finally, it no longer functions effectively as population control, especially for increasing migrants.[36] During the NPC's annual meeting in March 2002, Chen Lini, a representative from Guangdong province, proposed restoring citizens' migration right to the Constitution, which was taken out in 1975.[37] In fact, despite slow moves by the central government, neighborhood registration reform has already been initiated by some local governments, such as in Guangdong province,[38] Zhejiang province,[39] Jinan city in Shandong province,[40] and some districts in Beijing.[41] These local governments adopted measures to eliminate arbitrary separations between the rural and the urban and to include rural residents in the welfare security system enjoyed previously by urban residents only.

What is worth mentioning is the role played by economic factors in this process. In the early 1990s, some local governments already planned to sell urban residency to individuals who could afford the cost (such incidents were recorded by Solinger, 1999; Y. Yan, 1994). After the household registration reform was introduced at the turn of the new century, local governments in major import areas quickly set up economic standards targeting outside migrants who would like to get local permanent residency, in addition to their internal conversion of local rural residents. For example, in October 2001, the public security organizations in Beijing announced standards for private enterprise owners who would like to stay permanently in Beijing. A residency in eight inner districts (Dong Cheng, Xi Cheng, Chong Wen, Xun Wu, Chao Yang, Hai Dian, Feng Tai, and Shi Jingshen) requires that (a) the applicant has been the main manager or legal representative of a private enterprise in the last 3 years; (b) he or she owns a house[42] with legal title; (c) the private enterprise has paid more than 800,000 yuan tax every year or more than 3 million yuan in total in the last 3 years; and (d) the enterprise has hired more than 100 Beijing residents every year or has hired 90% of its employees from Beijing residents in the last 3 years. For a residency outside the eight inner districts, the first two requirements are the same, and the tax amount in (c) is reduced to 400,000 yuan every year in the last 3 years or 1.5 million yuan in total; and the number of Beijing employees in (d) is reduced to 50 every year in the last 3 years or 50% of the total employees. Moreover, once an applicant becomes a Beijing resident living outside of the eight inner districts, he or she cannot apply for residency in inner districts for the next 5 years.[43] In a similar fashion, the Shenzhen government announced that both enterprise legal representatives who paid more than 300,000 yuan tax for 3 years in a row and individuals who paid more than 80,000 yuan for 5 years in a row could apply for its permanent residency.[44] In Zhengzhou, the capital of Henan province, permanent residency is open to (a) individuals who buy new houses (with more than 56 square meters), (b) individuals who have run enterprises for more than 3 years and paid more than 30,000 yuan in taxes for 3 years or paid more than 100,000 yuan in any year, and (c) individuals who earned a doctoral degree.[45]

It seems that the *hukou* system will eventually come to an end with further reform,[46] and a new means of population control will arise. In 2002, the Standing Committee of the 9th NPC reviewed revisions of the 1985 resident identification cards regulations, and proposed replacing the resident identification cards with a system of national citizen identification cards. The new card (readable by computers) upgraded the old one and covers citizens from Hong Kong and Macao.[47] This transformation, however, will take time given China's population and relatively low level of urbanization.[48] A 2002 survey showed that in major cities such as Beijing, employers still made local residency a prerequisite for employment.[49] As argued by Solinger (1999), the market alone cannot supply a full-fledged or permanent solution to problems of citizenship for the transients. The central government has to take actions to guarantee citizens' migration rights as well as equal economic and political rights. This is necessary to avoid further artificial regional separation and divergence based on different local policies.

Social Inequality and Unemployment

With deepened social stratification, the problem of social inequality emerged in China. Table 4.9 shows the standard Gini coefficient[50] in China over the years. Although the numbers are incomplete, we can still see a pattern, in which the number actually decreased in the early years of the reform (due to quick development in rural areas) from .25 or higher in the 1970s to .21 and .22 in 1982 and 1983, respectively. Then the number started increasing after economic stratification aggravated, and reached .40 around the turn of the

Table 4.9 Gini Coefficient in China Over Time

Year	Gini Coefficient	Urban Coefficient	Rural Coefficient
1975	.25		
1978[a]		.16	.21/.28/.32
1979[a]			.26/.28
1980[a]			.25/.26
1981[a]			.21/.23
1982			.22
1983[a]			.22/.25
1984			.27
1985[a]	.28		.28/.30
1986			.31
1988	.382		
1990			.29
1995	.389		
2000[a]	.417	.32	.35
2001	.39		

Note. From Whyte & Parish (1984); Selden (1985, p. 211); Online news report posted at www.people.com.cn (August 20, 2001); World Bank (1992); The *People's Daily* (July 9, 2002); Khan et al. (1992).
[a]Different coefficients were reported based on different sources.

century, a strong indicator of income inequality. This pattern seems to hold both for rural income inequality[51] and inequality in general.

In addition, social inequality has become substantially diversified and shows discrepancies between the rural and the urban, among geographical locations, and within different occupations, besides other increasing gaps (e.g., Maurer-Fazio, Rawski, & Zhang, 1999, showed how gender wage gaps actually increased from the 1980s to the 1990s in China). First, inequality between the rural and urban is always an undeniable fact in China, to a large extent aggravated by state policies (e.g., the control of the *hukou* system). Table 4.10 shows per capita annual income of both urban and rural households over the years. By the time of the reform, per capita annual income of urban households was about 2.57 times that of rural households. Because of many privileges enjoyed by urban residents (e.g., welfare benefits), the actual inequality was even worse. In the first half of the 1980s, due to quick development in the rural areas, the ratio between urban and rural income decreased (to about 1.85 in 1985). Then, the gap increased again to 3.28 by 2006. Note in Table 4.10, different measures are used, when the annual net income of the rural household is compared with the disposable income of the urban household. The gap would be even bigger if the same measurements were adopted, and some estimates predict that the actual ratio would be close to five or six to one if all privileges enjoyed by urban residents were counted.[52]

Second, due to differential policies adopted by the central government, coastal provinces and cities enjoyed many more benefits after the reform. As a result, the already existing geographical disparity (among the eastern,

Table 4.10 Per Capita Annual Income and Engle Coefficient of Urban and Rural Households

Year	Per Capita Annual Net Income of Rural Households		Per Capita Annual Disposable Income of Urban Households		Engle Coefficient (%) of	
	Value (Yuan)	*Index (1978 = 100)*	*Value (Yuan)*	*Index (1978 = 100)*	*Rural Households*	*Urban Households*
1978	133.6	100.0	343.4	100.0	67.7	57.5
1979	160.2	119.2	387.0	112.7	64.0	57.2
1980	191.3	139.0	477.6	127.0	61.8	56.9
1981	223.4	160.4	491.9	127.6	59.9	56.7
1982	270.1	192.3	526.6	133.9	60.7	58.7
1983	309.8	219.6	564.0	140.6	59.4	59.2
1984	355.3	249.5	651.2	158.1	59.2	58.0
1985	397.6	268.9	739.1	160.4	57.8	53.3
1986	423.8	277.6	899.6	182.5	56.4	52.4
1987	462.6	292.0	1,002.2	186.9	55.8	53.5
1988	544.9	310.7	1,181.4	182.5	54.0	51.4
1989	601.5	305.7	1,375.7	182.8	54.8	54.4
1990	686.3	311.2	1,510.2	198.1	58.8	54.2
1991	708.6	317.4	1,700.6	212.4	57.6	53.8
1992	784.0	336.2	2,026.6	232.9	57.6	52.9

the middle, and the western regions) has been further widened, and poverty is mostly concentrated in the western region (for a special report on China's effort in reducing poverty, see World Bank, 1992). Data from the NBSC showed that the average per capita annual salary in Shanghai reached 17,910 yuan in 2001, but it was only 7,928 yuan in Anhui (a province in the middle region).[53] Moreover, both the regional disparity and the urban–rural disparity are related. In 1999, the urban–rural disparity ratio in the eastern region was 2.15, but the ratio in the western region reached 3.47.[54] It appears that the urban–rural disparity has a much bigger effect on the less developed western region.

Table 4.10 (Continued)

Year	Per Capita Annual Net Income of Rural Households		Per Capita Annual Disposable Income of Urban Households		Engle Coefficient (%) of	
	Value (Yuan)	Index (1978 = 100)	Value (Yuan)	Index (1978 = 100)	Rural Households	Urban Households
1993	921.6	346.9	2,577.4	255.1	58.1	50.1
1994	1,221.0	364.4	3,496.2	276.8	58.9	49.9
1995	1,577.7	383.6	4,283.0	290.3	58.6	49.9
1996	1,926.1	418.1	4,838.9	301.6	56.3	48.6
1997	2,090.1	437.3	5,160.3	311.9	55.1	46.4
1998	2,162.0	456.1	5,425.1	329.9	53.4	44.5
1999	2,210.3	473.5	5,854.0	360.6	52.6	41.9
2000	2,253.4	483.4	6,280.0	383.7	49.1	39.2
2001	2,366.4	503.7	6,859.6	416.3	47.7	37.9
2002	2,475.6	527.9	7,702.8	472.1	46.2	37.7
2003	2,622.2	550.6	8,472.2	514.6	45.6	37.1
2004	2,936.4	588.0	9,421.6	554.2	47.2	37.7
2005	3,254.9	624.5	10,439	607.4	45.5	36.7
2006	3,587		11,759		43	35.8

Note. From *China Statistical Yearbook* (2001, 2005, 2006); *China Statistical Abstract* (2002, 2005); Data posted at http://www.legalino.gov.cn (October 2, 2006); 2006 data from the *People's Daily* (March 1, 2007). Data collected in the *China Statistical Yearbook* over time sometimes do not match (due to revisions). The most recent data are used.

Third, the increasing division of labor widened the gap among various occupations (see H. Wang et al., 1995). Careers in foreign-related enterprises, Internet technology, and business management quickly became the hottest professions, whereas state-owned and collective enterprises seemed to have lost their competitiveness in the market economy.[55] In 1999, the annual salary gap between the highest paid and the lowest-paid profession reached 7,214 yuan, a 15.8-fold increase from 458 yuan in 1978.[56] One direct result of such stratification is the income gap among people (especially urban residents). A 2002 study separated urban residents into five groups based on their annual disposable income in 1999, and the highest income group received 12,084 yuan, 4.6 times the level of the lowest income group (2,617 yuan).[57] The occupational disparity is also related to the nature of one's work. In 1995, the Gini coefficient for workers in SOEs was .28, and it was .347 for workers in nonpublic enterprises.[58] It shows that once the number of workers in the SOEs is reduced, the income gap tends to increase.

Finally, the increasing unemployment rate in China aggravated social inequality. For a long time, the Chinese government refused to admit the existence of unemployment (*shiye*) in China (as a socialist nation). Rather, the term waiting for employment (*daiye*) was used until it was finally replaced by unemployment in 1999 (E. X. Gu, 2001). Table 4.11 shows the officially reported number of registered unemployed people in urban areas and the unemployment rate over the years. The numbers reported clearly underestimated the actual numbers. For example, according to E. X. Gu's (2001) study, the number of laid-off workers reached 11.5 million in 1997, compared to the reported 5.76 million shown in the table. The underestimation is indeed acknowledged by the government. In October 2002, Qiu Xiaohua, Deputy Commissioner of the NSBC, admitted that the number of unemployed would be around 8 million if international standards were adopted, and the unemployment rate would be 4% to 5%[59] (compared to 6.8 million and 3.6%, respectively, based on 2001 data). Despite the underreporting, Table 4.11 shows that both the number of unemployed and the unemployment rate have kept climbing since the mid-1980s. In recent years, the main source of the unemployed came from the restructuring of the SOEs. Although another nice name, *xiagang*, was given to workers laid off from the SOEs, the number of *xiagang* workers quickly increased and reached 4.43 million (more than 60% of all unemployed) based on official reports.[60] Facing increasing *xiagang* workers, the government tried to make two efforts. One was to call for reemployment, in which the government heavily relied on nonpublic sectors to absorb the laid-off workers. It was reported that from 1998 to September 2002, about 16.8 million *xiagang* workers were reemployed, and 68% of them found jobs in either private or individual enterprises.[61] The other move by the government was to provide basic welfare security benefits to the unemployed[62] and special breaks (e.g., tax cuts and loans) to encourage their reemployment.[63]

Table 4.11 Registered Unemployed in Urban Areas and Unemployment Rate

Year	Unemployed (in 10,000s)	Youth (in 10,000s)	Youth as Percentage of Unemployed	Unemployment Rate (%)
1952	376.6			13.2
1957	200.4			5.9
1978	530.0	249.1	47.0	5.3
1979	567.6	258.2	45.5	5.4
1980	541.5	382.5	70.6	4.9
1981	439.5	343.0	78.0	3.8
1982	379.4	293.8	77.4	3.2
1983	271.4	222.0	81.8	2.3
1984	235.7	195.9	83.1	1.9
1985	238.5	196.9	82.6	1.8
1986	264.4	209.3	79.2	2.0
1987	276.6	235.1	85.0	2.0
1988	296.2	245.3	82.5	2.0
1989	377.9	309.0	81.8	2.6
1990	383.2	312.7	81.6	2.5
1991	352.2	288.4	81.9	2.3
1992	363.9	299.8	83.2	2.3
1993	420.1	331.9	79.0	2.6
1994	476.4	301.0	63.2	2.8
1995	519.6	310.2	59.7	2.9
1996	552.8			3.0
1997	576.8			3.1
1998	571.0			3.1
1999	575			3.1
2000	595			3.1
2001	681			3.6
2002	770			4.0
2003	800			4.3
2004	827			4.2
2005	839			4.2

Note. From *China Statistical Yearbook* (1980–2006) and *China Statistical Abstract* (2002).

In short, due to deepened stratification, social inequality increased in China. The inequality was evident in various aspects, such as the urban–rural disparity, regional disparity, and occupational disparity. These disparities were aggravated by the increasing unemployment rate. The main factors that separate people into different social groups have shifted from primarily state policies in the prereform era to a mix of economic factors and state policies in the reform era. The impact of inequality goes well beyond the economic scope and enters into people's daily lives. For instance, a special therapeutic hospital opened in May 2002 in Nanjing city, Jiangsu province, provided services only to clients who had an annual salary of more than 100,000 yuan.[64]

Transformation of Ideology

When China underwent dramatic changes economically and socially, the old ideology control under Mao's era started waning, and the younger generations quickly took up new ideas, values, and lifestyles. I focus on the very basic unit of the society, the family, as an example.

Control of the family was always the focus of the state power (see, e.g., Yuan, 1995). In ancient traditional Chinese families, the normative value system was built on Confucian values, especially *li*, not laws. After the CCP came into power, Mao Zedong initiated the mass-line movement and bound families closely with neighborhood communities and workplaces. In the reform era, the transition from a planned economy to a market economy to a large extent weakened the control of communities and workplaces. Families gradually gained independent status as the basic unit involved in production, commercial transaction, and consumption (see Davis, 2000, for a discussion of urban consumption revolution in China). As a result, families began to challenge old controls both internally and externally. Internally, one indicator of the increased freedom is self-selected and initiated dissolution (divorce) and remarriage. Table 4.12 shows the number of marriages and divorces from 1985 to 2005. The number of remarriages and divorces increased steadily over the years, the divorce rate increased from 0.9% in 1985 to 2.5% in 2004,[65] and the number of first marriages continued decreasing from 1996 to 2002 before it increased slightly in 2003 and 2004. As reported, the traditional Chinese family is in transition to a modern one with more emphasis on the quality of the marriage and people's freedom to choose new lives.[66] Externally, for a long time, a couple needed an approval letter for their marriage (or divorce) from their workplace, village committee (for peasants), or local neighborhood committee, besides their proof of residency, personal ID, and medical examination certificates, even though there were no such requirements in the Marriage Law. People took such regulations for granted, and under the old control system, workplaces (or village committees in rural areas) did play a significant role (e.g.,

Table 4.12 Number of Marriages and Divorces, 1985–2005

Year	Registered Marriages			Divorces	
	Total Couples	First Marriages (Persons)	Remarriages (Persons)	Total Couples	Divorce Rate (%)
1985	8,290,588	16,076,337	504,839	457,938	0.9
1986	8,822,935	17,075,107	570,763	505,675	0.9
1987	9,247,372	17,880,856	613,888	581,484	1.1
1988	8,971,750	17,285,077	658,423	658,551	1.2
1989	9,351,915	17,959,680	744,150	752,914	1.3
1990	9,486,870	18,191,303	782,437	800,037	1.4
1991	9,509,849	18,203,226	816,472	829,449	1.4
1992	9,545,047	18,320,957	769,137	849,611	1.5
1993	9,121,622	17,470,092	773,152	909,195	1.5
1994	9,290,027	17,793,306	786,748	980,980	1.6
1995	9,297,061	17,760,657	833,465	1,055,196	1.8
1996	9,339,615	17,817,240	861,990	1,132,215	1.8
1997	9,090,571	17,259,504	921,638	1,197,759	1.9
1998	8,866,593	16,753,749	979,437	1,190,214	1.9
1999	8,799,079	16,593,593	1,004,565	1,201,541	1.9
2000	8,420,044	15,813,933	1,026,155	1,212,863	1.9
2001	8,050,000	14,817,000	1,125,000	1,250,000	2.0
2002	7,862,000	14,403,000	1,171,000	1,177,000	1.8
2003	8,114,000	14,839,000	1,231,000	1,331,000	2.1
2004	8,671,000	15,696,000	1,520,000	1,665,000	2.5
2005	8,231,000	14,830,000	1,631,000	1,785,000	

Note. Marriage and divorce numbers after 2001 were reported in units of 10,000 couples in the *China Statistical Yearbook*. After major revisions, the 2006 *Yearbook* reported much lower divorce rates, although the increasing trend over time did not change. The new, revised divorce rates were not recorded in this table. From *China Statistical Yearbook* (2001–2006).

to be the matchmaker and an insurer of a long-lasting marriage). When the role of the workplace gradually declined in the reform era, people began to separate their public lives from their private lives and challenge the idea of getting such approvals from the workplace. Indeed, the media supported the challenge and asked for abolishment of this practice.[67] In October 2003, the revised Regulations on Marriage Registration were implemented and officially abolished such a practice. Due to this boost, the total number of divorces climbed even more quickly and reached 1.33 million in 2003, 1.66 million in 2004, 1.78 million in 2005, and 1.91 million in 2006.[68]

Those changing features of families quickly drew attention from the government, including the legal branches. The first response was a defensive move. For example, some legal commentators in 1980 advised that "the increasing number of divorce cases is related to an invasion of capitalist thinking and a failure properly to understand freedom of divorce" (Palmer, 1996, p. 123). During the mid-1980s, Ren Jianxin, President of the SPC, revealed a generally ambivalent attitude by the authorities toward the freedom of divorce. He acknowledged that such developments marked a welcome step in the direction of freedom of marriage but worried that too many divorce petitions resulted from hasty marriages or from the meddling of third parties in the marriages of others. Similar concerns were extended to remarriage and the restoration of divorced couples (Palmer, 1996).

In April 2001, the revised Marriage Law took effect and aimed to readjust familial relationships in the new era. During its revision, many discussions and surveys were conducted to solicit public opinion on a number of issues such as the prohibition of polygamy, criminal penalties for a third party who meddles in other people's marriages, and prevention and punishment of domestic violence (including marital rape).[69] The new law indeed adopted many suggestions from the public and tried to balance moral issues with legal issues. For example, the new law does not impose criminal punishment on third parties, but it stipulates that "both couples should respect and be faithful to each other" (Article 4), and "the wronged spouse has a right to claim legal (civil) compensation from the wrongful spouse who practiced polygamy, illegal cohabitation, domestic violence, or desertion" (Article 46). The judicial system has been applying the new law in marriage-related cases since its enactment.[70]

In short, after the reform, people's ideology changed gradually along with the change of society as a whole. When society becomes more diversified, mobile, and economically driven, individuals, their relationships, and their basic unions (families) become more versatile, unstable, and economically (rather than politically) binding. The government clearly felt the pressure from losing ideological control. In the 1980s, a strong defensive stance was taken to defend old values (and the system) against Western "spiritual pollution." The Tiananmen event in 1989 to some extent signified the apex of such ideological crisis and challenge (for the impact of losing ideology on the Tiananmen event, see D. Zhao, 1997). In the 1990s, as a way to save the fading values, a series of calls was made to rebuild the nation's "spiritual civilization" (see discussions by Deng & Cordilia, 1999; Gil & Anderson, 1998). Realizing the different nature of new battles, the government turned to the legal system as a new means to readjust social relations (e.g., the new Marriage Law, the new ID system, and the changing *hukou* system). This could be the last resort to legitimate and regain social control in the new era (see Corne, 1997).

CONCLUSION

In this chapter, I tried to lay out social and ideological changes in China after the reform, paying special attention to crime and punishment issues. Statistics showed that China had been suffering from an increasing crime rate and the Chinese government adopted a severe strike campaign approach to curb the ascending crime rate. In those crime campaigns, harsher punishments were imposed at a faster pace and were sometimes based on violations of normal procedures. Although the high-pressure power play had some short-term effects, statistical data over time did not support the claims of success from the government. These campaigns had been kept alive nevertheless to serve other functions. Officials in China indeed consistently called for the continuation of such practices.[71]

From a comparative perspective, the practice of China's severe strike campaign confirmed the limitation of a get-tough policy adopted in many other nations dealing with complex crime issues. However, such intermittent practices became a necessary part of policymaking for political gains (e.g., to gain public support), and China was not an exception in its practice. As argued based on analyses at the macro level, the increased difficulty China faced with crime and punishment in general and the anticrime campaign practice in particular was rooted in social and ideological changes. Population migration, together with increasing urbanization and economic stratification, changed the old structure of the society and caused many social problems (e.g., social inequality and unemployment). The old communist ideological control was fading quickly, and people were struggling with new moral boundaries. In such a transitional process, anticrime campaign practices cannot be effective without addressing other complex social problems.

Facing the new challenge, the Chinese government was trying to (indeed had to) go through the transition and at the same time adjust and rejuvenate the old control system (e.g., the call for comprehensive management). As a result, China's transitional system, including the legal system and its practice, necessarily embodied both new and old elements. Interestingly, this was not a transition in which the new elements totally replaced the old ones.

Some scholars found that both formal (legal) and informal (nonlegal) social controls were expanded along with modernization, and their expansions depended on each other to some extent (see, e.g., Deng & Cordilia, 1999; H. Lu, 1998, 1999). These observations showed the complexity of social and legal studies in China and raised more challenges both theoretically and practically. The practice of the severe strike campaign and the call for rejuvenation of the old control system were exactly such examples.

5   China's Globalization

In this chapter, I focus on the process of China's increasing connection with other nations within the global system and analyze the impact of globalization on China's domestic legal, economic, and political systems. China's economic, political, and legal reforms in the new era were made possible through, or perhaps mandated as a result of, China's increasing integration into the global system. Although not without some significant problems, the Chinese government has paced its integration, managed its domestic reforms, and gradually learned to become a key player in the global marketplace. In the discussion that follows, I first present a theoretical framework of the world-economy system and then discuss China's reactions to globalization. Next, I analyze the impact of China's becoming a participant in the globalized marketplace, pay special attention to China's decision to join the World Trade Organization (WTO), and analyze the potential impact that being a major player in the WTO may have on China's further development. Finally, I examine how China's integration into the global system has led to political and legal transitions at home.

WORLD-ECONOMY AND CHINA'S
REACTIONS TO GLOBALIZATION

The World-Economy System and Globalization

Globalization as a process of world system change has drawn increasing attention from scholars working from diverse perspectives. Many of them have warned about the devastating effects that globalization can have on developing nations, such as high levels of income inequality, uneven development among different economic sectors, and ensuing conflicts (see, e.g., Bornschier & Chase-Dunn, 1985; Lauderdale & Toggia, 1999; Stiglitz, 2002). Scholars also have questioned the practices of transnational organizations and examined the dialectical nature of the ensuing global changes brought about by these organizations (see, e.g., Harris & Lauderdale, 2002). Although China experienced some of these negative impacts, globalization also led to economic growth and legal changes in China. The approach that the Chinese government has taken to the global marketplace can be understood in terms of an amalgam of modernization theory and more significantly the world systems theoretical perspective.

Initially proposed by theorists such as Hopkins and Wallerstein (1980) and extended by Frank (1998), the world-economy theory provides a critique of conventional modernization and development theory and a further expansion and revision of the Marxian political economy theory. The conventional modernization theory assumes a unilinear trajectory of economic development for each nation or society (which is the main unit of analysis). Modernization theorists compare different economic, political, and cultural dimensions of countries and attempt to answer questions such as these: Why have some countries started earlier or moved ahead in economic development while other countries have lagged behind? What are the reasons for the disparate levels of economic development throughout the world, and how can backward countries catch up to the more advanced societies? In response, world-economy theorists have strongly criticized the conventional modernization theory on a number of grounds. For example, they pointed out that (a) conventional modernization theory has a tendency to reify the nation-state as the sole unit of analysis; (b) conventional modernization theory is based on the assumption that all countries follow a similar path of (linear) growth; (c) conventional modernization theory disregards transnational structures of the world-economy; and (d) the method of explanation of conventional modernization theory is based on ahistorical ideal types of national development (see Hopkins & Wallerstein, 1980, 1982).

In contrast, the world-economy theory contends that the capitalist system (mode of production) is a worldwide system and not a sum of separate units. The concept of world-economy is carefully distinguished from the concept of international economy, which is based on the notion of separate national economies and the view that trade among them produces the sum of the international economy. The world-economy theoretical perspective assumes that the entire globe is operating within the framework of one singular systemwide division of labor (currently the capitalist world-economy). This world system contains an ongoing, extensive, and relatively complete social division of labor with an integrated set of production processes. These production processes are related to each other through a world market that has been created and instituted in complex ways. The world-economy is not new to the 20th century. Rather, it has been in existence in at least part of the globe for centuries, if not millennia. For instance, Wallerstein (1984) contended that it has existed since the 16th century. Frank and Gills (1993) further expanded the world-economy structure and argued that it existed much earlier (even before the emergence of the capitalist economy system). From a world-economy perspective, it is not the capitalist mode of production that has determined the world economic system; rather, the world system established its own rules long before the triumph of the capitalism (Frank, 1998).

The world-economy paradigm has made a significant impact on various aspects of the global political economy. To fully understand this perspective, it requires a revision of many key concepts in traditional Marxian theories. For example, the economic backwardness in some nations or societies (the so-called developing nations) is not attributable to these countries "starting late," but is itself a condition produced (and reproduced) in the course and as a result of the rise of capitalism (Hopkins & Wallerstein, 1982). Various modes of production, such as slavery, serfdom, and the socialist mode of economy (especially in the areas within the periphery of the system), rather than being viewed as separate modes that developed independently, are viewed as important forms of capitalist exploitation that have served the purpose of capitalism within the world-economy (Chase-Dunn, 1982). Further, states, which are reduced to a secondary role as part of the super-structure of capitalism in traditional Marxian theories, are considered to have a significant role now in the world system (Chase-Dunn, 1982).

Increasingly we have witnessed important features of the world system such as its geographical expansion (gradual inclusion of nations and societies into the world system), proletarianization (more and more people becoming wage laborers), commodification and commercialization of natural resources and human labor, mechanization and industrialization (more and more technology being integrated into productive processes), and the development of world economic and political organizations (e.g., the WTO; Hopkins & Wallerstein, 1982). It is this latter effect of the development of the world system—the expansion of global political and economic organizations—that appears to have had a significant impact on China in the past few decades.

China's Reactions to Globalization

China's reaction to globalization has evolved in relation to changes in the world system. After the new China was founded in 1949, the country's connection with the outside world, especially economically advanced Western nations, was very limited (mainly due to ideological confrontations during the Cold War). Domestically, the communist government called for economic self-reliance, and internationally it sought and provided both material and ideological support from and to other communist nations. Despite its limited connection with the rest of the world, China was still under the influence of the world system even during these days when China was forced (externally) to "close its door."

The door was reopened after the economic reform initiated in 1978. At that time, the Chinese government began to realize that economic self-reliance would not be enough to fuel China's economic development. Rather, China would have to reach out and seek connections with other nations. At that moment, China's understanding was more along the lines of conventional modernization theory. China's leaders openly acknowledged China's economic "backwardness" and set a goal of turning China into an economically developed nation by achieving what they called the "four modernizations": modernizations of industry, agriculture, national defense, and science and technology. They were determined to catch up to the Western developed nations and by necessity to broaden China's connections with them.

In the next 20 years, after China increased and deepened its engagement with other nations, the Chinese government definitely gained a better understanding of the impact of globalization. Nonetheless, developing a framework for China's reactions to globalization was challenging. Theoretically, the Chinese government's reactions to globalization embraced a broad scope of divergent theories, confusing and sometimes even self-conflicting. First, a component of conventional modernization theory was never lost in the official language. Viewing itself as a developing third-world nation, the Chinese government set a long-term goal of reaching the development level of more advanced developed nations. Second, the Chinese government now concedes that economic globalization is an irreversible historical trend. With more nations becoming involved in this global economic system, China cannot be omitted from this process. Although being an active participant in globalization has potential dangers, the Chinese government began to realize that China has to face the challenge and speed up its national economic development along with the expansion of the world-economy.[1] As Chinese Vice Premier Wen Jiabao stated in 2001, "Economic globalization is an irreversible trend, and the Chinese modernization has to be conducted within such a global context . . . globalization provides both challenges and opportunities . . . [the] Chinese government needs to adjust its administration . . . [and] increase international communication and cooperation."[2] This understanding, although built on conventional modernization theory, definitely moves closer to Wallerstein's world-economy system.

Third, Chinese leaders have also taken note of the antiglobalization movement and rhetorically blamed the unequal relations among nations on economic structures and ideologies imposed by Western nations.[3] Fourth and finally, orthodox Marxian theorists in China have explained globalization in Marxian terms and contended that globalization is essentially a result of global expansion of capital and commercialization. According to their arguments, it is the inherent contradictions of capitalism that dictate both the development and destruction associated with the process of globalization, and that are responsible for increased economic stratification, intensified class confrontation, and the intermittent economic crises.[4] All these analyses correspond to relevant theoretical discussions with regard to the development of the world-economy (Wallerstein, 1984) and the postmodernity (see, e.g., Harvey, 1990; Oliverio & Lauderdale, 2005) in Western thought.

In sum, Chinese leaders appear to incorporate different aspects of these theories in their approach to globalization, contrary to the general belief that the communist government dogmatically sticks to one ideological perspective. Their approach to globalization shows an acknowledgment of the complexity of the world-economy system and the vulgarization of the term globalization in general, and they have taken a selective approach (*selective adaptation*, to borrow Potter's [2001a, 2004] term) to the incorporation of the values associated with globalization based on their unique practical and particular concerns, as discussed next.

CHINA'S PRACTICE OF GLOBALIZATION

"Open Door" Policy, Foreign Trade, and Investment

Along with domestic reforms in 1978, the Chinese government established an "open door" policy as its first step toward rejoining the outside world. The first trial of this policy was the establishment of special economic zones (SEZs) as "windows" for international trade and foreign investment. In 1979, Shenzhen, Shantou, and Zhuhai in Guangdong province became the first three SEZs, and Xiamen in Fujiang province became the fourth SEZ in 1980. In those SEZs, measures of market operation were introduced, and enterprises were given special preferences (e.g., tax breaks and exemptions, land use privileges, and duty exemptions) to attract foreign capital and technologies. The trial project turned out to be very successful. In 1980, the foreign currency holdings of Guangdong and Fujiang rose to six times their 1979 levels (Gross, 1988). Seeing the fruitful outcome, the central government quickly granted similar preferences to Hainan Island[5] and 14 coastal cities[6] in 1984, to the entire coastal zone in 1988, to Shanghai in 1990, and to 21 additional (noncoastal) cities along the Yangtze River and in the northeast in 1992 (see Shirk, 1994; H. Wang, 1996; X. Yan, 1992).

Since the establishment of those SEZs, both foreign trade and investment have increased tremendously. Table 5.1 shows China's foreign trade information over the years. In 1950 the total value of China's imports and exports was a little over $1.1 billion U.S., less than 1% of total world trade. In the next decade, both imports and exports increased steadily along with the general increasing trend of the world, and throughout the 1950s, China's portion of the total world trade averaged more than 1%. The rate of increase in China's trade, however, was slowed down and disrupted during the Cultural Revolution period. From 1965 to 1976, although the total value of China's imports and exports more than doubled (from $4.2 billion U.S. to $13.4 billion U.S.), it did not keep up with the increasing pace of world trade in general (a 600% increase from $385 billion to $2.01 trillion). Indeed, China's share of total world trade decreased to less than 1% again.

Only after the "open door" policy was implemented did China's trade rejuvenate and increase at an unprecedented rate. From 1978 to 2003, China's trade increased at an average annual rate of 15%, its share of total world trade increased from less than 1% to more than 5%, and its national ranking in world trade (merchandise) jumped from 32nd in 1978 to 3rd in 2004 (after the United States and Germany).[7] With increased connections

Table 5.1 Total Value of China's Imports and Exports, and Its Share and Place in World Total (Unit: $100 Million)

Year	China's Total	Exports	Imports	World Total	Share of World Total (%)	Place
1950	11.35	5.52	5.83	1,234	0.91	
1955	31.45	14.12	17.33	1,922	1.64	
1960	38.09	18.56	19.53	2,651	1.44	
1965	42.45	22.28	20.17	3,846	1.10	
1970	45.86	22.60	23.26	6,434	0.71	
1975	147.51	72.64	74.87	17,792	0.83	
1976	134.33	68.55	65.78	20,104	0.67	
1977	148.04	75.90	72.14	22,976	0.64	30
1978	206.38	97.45	108.93	26,482	0.78	32
1979	293.33	136.58	156.75	33,339	0.88	
1980	381.40	181.20	200.20	40,411	0.94	
1981	440.20	220.10	220.10	40,124	1.10	22
1982	416.10	223.20	192.90	37,798	1.11	20
1983	436.20	222.30	213.90	36,843	1.18	20
1984	535.50	261.40	274.10	38,893	1.38	16
1985	696.00	273.50	422.50	39,306	1.76	11
1986	738.40	309.40	429.00	43,260	1.70	12
1987	826.50	394.40	432.10	50,505	1.63	17
1988	1,027.90	475.20	552.70	57,372	1.78	15

in the world system, China's foreign trade became more and more dependent on other nations. Take the Sino–U.S. trade as an example: In 1978 the total trade value between the two nations was less than $1 billion U.S., but it reached $97 billion U.S. in 2002, close to a 100-fold increase in 25 years. In 2004, the number topped $169.6 billion, and the United States surpassed Japan to become China's second largest trade partner (after only the expanded European Union [EU]).[8] Moreover, it was reported in 2002 that for every 1% increase in the U.S. economy, China's exports to the United States would increase by 10%.[9]

Table 5.1 *(Continued)*

Year	China's Total	Exports	Imports	World Total	Share of World Total (%)	Place
1989	1,116.80	525.40	591.40	61,561	1.77	15
1990	1,154.40	620.90	533.50	69,816	1.65	16
1991	1,357.00	719.10	637.90	69,817	1.96	15
1992	1,655.30	849.40	805.90	74,843	2.19	11
1993	1,957.00	917.40	1,039.60	74,635	2.62	11
1994	2,366.20	1,210.10	1,156.10	85,704	2.80	11
1995	2,808.60	1,487.80	1,320.80	100,607	2.80	11
1996	2,898.80	1,510.50	1,388.30	105,184	2.78	11
1997	3,251.60	1,827.90	1,423.70	109,803	3.00	10
1998	3,239.50	1,837.10	1,402.40	108,209	3.02	11
1999	3,606.30	1,949.30	1,657.00	111,782	3.14	9
2000	4,743.10	2,492.10	2,251.00	130,300	3.64	7
2001	5,097.70	2,661.60	2,436.10	126,012	4.05	6
2002	6,207.90	3,255.70	2,952.20			
2003	8,509.90	4,382.30	4,127.60			
2004	11,545.50	5,933.20	5,612.30			3
2005	14,219.10	7,619.50	6,599.50			
2006	17,606.90	9,690.80	7,916.10			

Note. From *Collection of Statistics of Foreign Economic Relations and Trade of China* (2001); *China Statistical Abstract* (2002); *Chinese Statistical Yearbook* (2005, 2006); The *People's Daily* (September 24, 2002; March 10, 2003; January 26, 2006; January 11, 2007; January 26, 2007); H. Wang (1996).

Foreign investment in China increased dramatically along with foreign trade. Table 5.2 shows the utilization of foreign capital by the Chinese government. After the reform, total foreign capital investment increased steadily throughout the 1980s until 1989, when the Tiananmen event scared off many investors. Foreign investment quickly bounced back in the 1990s, however, and only showed a decrease in the second half of the 1990s due to the influence of the financial crisis in Asia before it picked up new momentum in the new century.

Table 5.2 Utilization of Foreign Capital (Unit: $100 Million)

Year	Approved Contracts of Foreign Investment		Realized Foreign Capital Value
	Number of Projects	*Value of Foreign Capital*	
1979–1982	979	194.61	126.43
1983	522	34.30	19.81
1984	1,894	47.91	27.05
1985	3,145	98.67	44.62
1986	1,551	117.37	72.58
1987	2,289	121.36	84.52
1988	6,063	160.04	102.26
1989	5,909	114.79	100.59
1990	7,371	120.86	102.89
1991	13,086	195.83	115.54
1992	48,858	694.39	192.02
1993	83,595	1,232.73	389.59
1994	47,646	937.56	432.10
1995	37,184	1,032.05	481.33
1996	24,673	816.10	548.04
1997	21,138	610.58	608.25
1998	19,850	632.01	585.57
1999	17,022	520.09	526.59
2000	22,347	711.30	493.56
2001	26,140	719.8	496.80
2002	34,171	847.51	550.11
2003	41,081	1,169.01	561.40
2004	43,664	1,565.88	640.72
2005	44,001	1,925.93	638.05
2006			630.00

Note. From *Collection of Statistics of Foreign Economic Relations and Trade of China* (2001); *China Statistical Abstract* (2002); *Chinese Statistical Yearbook* (2005, 2006); Data in 2006 from the *People's Daily* (January 26, 2007).

Table 5.3 shows information on foreign direct investment (FDI), an important indicator of total foreign investment. In 1989, China's FDI was $3.4 billion U.S., 1.7% of the world total. From 1997 to 2000, China's FDI stabilized between $40 billion and $45 billion U.S., and its share in the world total fluctuated along with the increase of total FDI in the world. In the new millennium, due to a sluggish world economy, the total world FDI decreased quickly from $1.3 trillion in 2000 to $826 billion in 2001, $617 billion in 2002, and $558 billion in 2003. In contrast, as China became the new hot spot for investors, its FDI kept increasing between 2001 and 2005, and its share of the total world FDI increased from 2.9% in 2000 to over 9% by 2003, and then decreased a little in the next 2 years due to the resurgence in the world total. In 2002, China also replaced the United States as the largest FDI recipient in the world when FDI in the United States plummeted from $124 billion in 2001 to less than $50 billion.[10] In 26 years from 1979 to 2005, the total accumulated FDI in China reached $622.4 billion; China has been the largest FDI recipient among all developing countries since 1991 and was the third largest FDI recipient in 2005 (after only the United States and Great Britain).[11]

With the massive infusion of foreign capital, China also became a hot new market for the direct operation of foreign enterprises. By the end of 2005, approximately 470 of the top 500 transnational enterprises had come to China to invest in direct operations.[12] As an example, Motorola opened its first representative office in Beijing in 1987 and established Motorola (China) Electronics Ltd. in Tianjin in 1992. In the next 10 years, from 1992 to 2002, Motorola was the largest foreign investor in electronics in China. Its cumulative total sales reached $21 billion, the value of its exports reached $8.6 billion, and the cumulative tax it paid reached $2.2 billion. In 2001 alone, as the most profitable foreign company in China, Motorola pulled in $5.4 billion via its Chinese market, 13% of its total world sales.[13] By 2005, the number of Motorola employees in China exceeded 10,000; its total cumulative investment in China reached $3.6 billion; and its total sales in China in the same year reached $8.983 billion, 25.4% of its total global sales ($35.3 billion).[14] Over time, foreign invested enterprises (FIEs) have shown rigorous growth and become more and more involved in China's economy. Table 5.4 shows export and import data by various types of enterprises over 25 years. At the beginning of the reform period, the involvement of FIEs in both exports and imports was very minimal, accounting for less than 1% of the total values of imports and exports. However, the involvement of FIEs increased very quickly over the years, especially in the 1990s. At the turn of the new century, the share of FIEs in both exports and imports reached and then surpassed 50%. Clearly, FIEs are becoming more and more critical for China's foreign trade, and the success of foreign investment and international trade has become an important impetus for China's economic development.

Table 5.3 Foreign Direct Investment (Unit: $100 Million U.S.)

Year	1989	1997	1998	1999	2000	2001	2002	2003	2004	2005
World total	2,000	4,000	6,440	10,867.5	13,879.5	8,259.2	6,177.3	5,578.6	7,107.5	9,162.7
China's total	34	453	455.8	403.2	407.2	468.8	527.4	535.1	606.3	724.1
Share of world total (%)	1.7	11.3	7.1	3.7	2.9	5.7	8.5	9.6	8.5	7.9

Note. The most recent data were used in case of discrepancy over time. 1989–1998 data from the *People's Daily* (November 22, 2002); 1999–2005 data from UNCTAD (www.unctad.org), *World Investment Report* (2004–2006).

Transformation of Domestic and International Structures

In the process of globalization, China has made major adjustments in its socialist economic structure to meet the demands of the new international environment. First, as discussed in Chapter 2, new modes of production (i.e., various non-state-owned economic activities) have been gradually reintroduced into China's economic structure. These non-state-owned economic activities were targeted in the early years of the revolution to be eliminated from the socialist economy. After almost 30 years (1949–1978) in which they were restricted or eliminated, the resurgence of these economic activities has revived China's economy. In sharp contrast, SOEs have gradually lost their competitiveness in the new environment, and the Chinese government has been trying to find ways to reform them. One such proposal is to encourage the intervention of foreign capital in the transformation of SOEs.[15]

Second, the process of globalization has impacted the transition of China's planned economy into a market economy. After the reform launched in 1978, the government quickly adjusted the old planned economy, although it was reluctant to use the term market economy (see Chapter 2). By the end of 1980s, China definitely felt more pressure from the increased speed of globalization, and the government realized that the old planned economic structure could no longer accommodate the demands placed on it by the rapid developments in the world-economy. Rather, a quick transition to a market economy was considered to be necessary (see Wu, 1989–1990). In 1988, the government rejected the dichotomy that characterized socialism and capitalism in terms of a planned and market economy, and in 1993 the "socialist market economy" officially replaced the planned economy in the amended Constitution. Despite its Chinese socialist characteristics, the new market economy has furthered the transformation of China's economic structure and helped China to forge economic connections with other nations in the world system.

Third, China's role has been increasingly diversified with its integration into the world system. For instance, China now has a growing investment in other nations in addition to its absorption of huge amounts of foreign capital. As reported, as early as the mid-1990s, China had already become the largest outward investor among developing nations and the eighth leading supplier of outward investment among all nations (Lardy, 2002). From 1995 to 1999, China's average annual capital investment in Southeast Asian nations was $146 million, representing 7% of all foreign investment in those nations.[16] At the same time, exports from major nations in Southeast Asia to China increased more than 100% from 1990 to 2000, and the trade share of the Association of South East Asian Nations (ASEAN) with China increased from 5.8% in 1991 to 8.3% in 2000, and the ASEAN had become China's fourth largest trading partner by 2005.[17] In 2001, the total foreign investment of China's 12 largest SOEs reached $30 billion, an equivalent of the total foreign investment of all nations in Latin America during the same

Table 5.4 Exports and Imports by Type of Enterprises (Unit: $100 Million)

Year	Exports				Imports			
	Total	State-Owned Enterprises	Foreign-Invested Enterprises (FIEs)	Share of FIEs in Total (%)	Total	State-Owned Enterprises	Foreign-Invested Enterprises (FIEs)	Share of FIEs in Total (%)
1981	220.10	219.55	0.32	0.1	220.10	218.32	1.01	0.50
1982	223.20	222.45	0.53	0.2	192.90	188.89	2.76	1.40
1983	222.30	218.45	3.85	1.7	213.90	207.73	6.16	2.90
1984	261.40	259.47	1.93	0.7	274.10	262.24	11.79	4.30
1985	273.50	270.37	2.96	1.1	422.50	399.33	20.64	4.90
1986	309.40	292.64	5.86	1.89	429.00	402.56	24.24	5.65
1987	394.40	380.01	12.07	3.06	432.10	391.02	35.14	8.13
1988	475.20	449.04	24.61	5.18	552.70	485.48	58.82	10.64
1989	525.40	475.06	49.19	9.36	591.40	495.34	90.02	15.22
1990	620.90	541.40	78.13	12.58	533.50	404.68	123.02	23.06
1991	719.10	597.00	120.50	16.74	637.90	462.10	169.10	26.51
1992	849.40	674.50	173.60	20.44	805.90	526.10	263.90	32.75

Year								
1993	917.40	652.60	252.40	27.51	1,039.60	597.10	418.30	40.24
1994	1,210.10	847.60	347.10	28.68	1,156.10	602.90	529.30	45.78
1995	1,487.80	992.60	468.80	31.51	1,320.80	653.92	629.38	47.66
1996	1,510.50	860.60	615.06	40.72	1,388.30	591.63	756.00	54.46
1997	1,827.90	1,026.89	749.00	40.98	1,423.70	609.74	777.21	54.59
1998	1,837.10	967.85	809.86	44.07	1,402.40	599.30	767.17	54.70
1999	1,949.30	984.86	886.28	45.47	1,657.00	741.81	858.84	51.83
2000	2,492.10	1,164.50	1,194.90	47.93	2,251.00	989.20	1,172.70	52.10
2001	2,661.55	1,132.3	1,332.35	50.10	2,436.13	1,035.5	1,258.63	51.70
2002	3,255.69	1,228.6	1,699.37	52.20	2,952.16	1,144.9	1,602.86	54.29
2003	4,383.70	1,380.3	2,403.40	54.80	4,128.40	1,424.8	2,319.10	56.17
2004	5,933.59		3,386.06	57.43	5,613.81		3,245.57	57.81
2005	7,620.00		4,442.10	58.30	6,601.22		3,875.16	58.70
2006	9,690.80		5,638.35	58.18	7,916.14		4,726.16	59.70

Note. From *Collection of Statistics of Foreign Economic Relations and Trade of China* (2001); 2001–2006 data from "Invest in China" (www.fdi.gov.cn), Ministry of Commerce of the PRC.

year.[18] In 2003, Chinese enterprises invested over $33.2 billion U.S. in more than 160 nations and customs territories, and China became the fifth largest overall supplier of outward investment in the world.[19]

Nevertheless, from a world systems perspective, China still has peripheral status in the world economic system compared with the core nations, although there are signs that China is moving from the role of a peripheral player into a semiperipheral and semicore role. China has experienced some difficulty in its upward mobility within the world system due to the uneven class formation and distribution of political power and unequal exchange within the global economic structure (see Bornschier & Chase-Dunn, 1985; Harris & Lauderdale, 2002; Stiglitz, 2002). Take China's exports as an example. China's fastest growing exports have been labor-intensive manufactured goods such as textiles, apparel, footwear, and toys. Textiles exports rose from $2.54 billion in 1980 to $12.81 billion in 1998, and apparel exports soared from $1.48 billion to $27.1 billion during the same period. In 1998, the apparel share of China's total exports reached 15%, and the share of textile and apparel exports reached 20.93% of the total exports in 2000.[20] Moreover, most foreign investment in China is concentrated on processing and manufacturing, and it has caused an uneven development in these sectors of China's economy. For example, 59.7% of the imports of FIEs in 2005, with a total value of $231 billion U.S., were utilized in processing and manufacturing.[21] As scholars have argued, it typically takes a long time for major changes in the stratification of the world system to take place, and China's place within this system is no exception (see Arrighi, Hopkins, & Wallerstein, 1989; Chase-Dunn, 1982; Hopkins & Wallerstein, 1996; Wallerstein, 1984).

China as a New Member of the WTO

It took Chinese leaders more than two decades to deepen their understanding of globalization, and it took nearly as long—15 years exactly—for China to gain acceptance from the largest global organization, the WTO. In 1947, China signed the Final Act of Geneva to establish the General Agreement on Tariffs and Trade (GATT) along with other nations. Due partly to the revolutionary transition in China, however, the new government's integration into international trade established by this treaty was delayed. After the reform, the Chinese government reopened its bid to the GATT. In 1986, China formally applied for an official membership to the GATT, but gaining approval turned out to be more difficult than expected. In 1994, in preparation for the establishment of the WTO, China expressed its wish to join this new organization, but it failed to reach mutual agreements with other member nations. In 1997, China reopened its negotiations with WTO members for membership. It took another 4 years and numerous negotiations for China to clear the road to its membership in the largest world organization, but finally, in 2001, China became a formal member of the WTO.[22]

Entry into the WTO is a significant indicator of China's movement toward greater participation in the world system. As Lardy (1994) argued, China's integration in the global system was often underestimated before it gained participation in the WTO. By the early 1990s, although China did not appear to be more open as measured by its trade ratio (i.e., imports plus exports as a percentage of GNP), when measured in other ways (e.g., the magnitude of inward FDI, the importance of foreign-invested firms in generating export earnings, the ability of domestic firms to access parts and components from abroad, and the importance of the country as a source of outward FDI), China was already more integrated into the world economy than Japan, Taiwan, or South Korea were at comparable stages of their economic development. By some measures, China was more open than these economies even on a contemporaneous basis.

After its formal entry into the WTO, the first task for China was to further open its door to foreign trade, and one main issue was China's import tariff rate. Figure 5.1 shows changes in China's average import tariff rate over the years. In 1982, China's average import tariff was as high as 55.6%, and the percentage slowly decreased to the 40% range in the 1980s. Major changes took place in the next decade, especially in the second half of the 1990s. By 1994, the average tariff rate was still as high as 35.9%, but it was quickly lowered to 23% in 1996 and then to 17% in 1997. To answer the call from the WTO, the average tariff rate has been cut continuously in the new century and fell below 10% in 2005.

Second, as a member of the WTO, China likely will continue to open its domestic market and apply nondiscriminatory policies to foreign investors and enterprises. Take foreign financial institutions as an example. Foreign banks have expanded their presence in China along with the progress of China's reforms. In 1981, the first foreign banks were opened for business

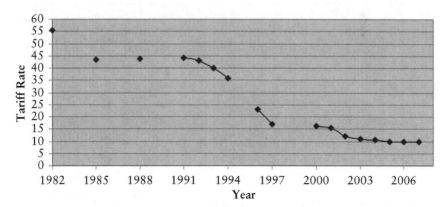

Figure 5.1 China's average import tariff rate (percentage), 1982–2007.

Source: (1) Lardy (2002, p. 34); (2) The *People's Daily*, January 22, 2007; December 23, 2002; (3) The *Beijing Youth Daily*, December 11, 2002.

in the SEZs on the southeast coast. By 1985, 17 foreign branch banks were operating in these areas. In the early 1990s China began to permit foreign banks to operate in Shanghai and a few other major cities. In 1999 it was announced that geographic restraints on foreign banks would be lifted gradually, and foreign banks could open branches in any city. On the eve of China's entry into the WTO, more than 150 foreign banks were operating in 23 cities (Lardy, 2002; see Table 5.5), and the number increased to 171 by 2004 (*Almanac of China's Finance and Banking*, 2004). In December 2001, foreign financial institutions were allowed to broaden their foreign exchange services to all enterprises and individuals and were permitted to conduct their Chinese currency business in Shanghai and Shenzhen (with more cities added in later years).[23] By 2005, all geographical restraints and business scope restrictions were lifted as China complied with the demands of its WTO membership.[24] In addition to financial institutions, China has been lifting restraints on other foreign businesses. In December 2001, foreign stock and securities institutions were allowed to conduct B-share transactions,[25] and by November 2002 the scope was further broadened to include almost all shares in China's stock market.[26] Similarly, the Chinese government began to allow foreign investors to participate in domestic trade, railway operation, and public facility construction.[27] All these appear to show that China is willing to work with more foreign investors and enterprises, and its connections with other nations have been both broadened and deepened.

Table 5.5 Foreign Bank Presence in China, 1991–2000

		Assets	
Year	Number of Institutions	RMB (Billions of Yuan)	Percentage of Total Financial Assets in China
1991	41/45	22.8	N/A
1992	73/79	30.5	N/A
1993	74/87	43.7	N/A
1994	92/99	102.1	0.9
1995	120/135	159.8	1.2
1996	131/147	248.6	1.6
1997	142/161	314.0	1.9
1998	142/161	283.0	1.7
1999	154/177	263.1	1.5
2000	154/177	287.3	1.5

Note. From Lardy (2002, p. 115).

Third, as a member of the WTO, China is obligated to follow a set of rules in the global trading system. Antidumping cases provide a critical example. For a long time, China paid little attention to and actually knew very little about dumping. Dumping, the selling of goods at an unreasonably low price to an importing country, is considered an unfair international trade practice based on price discrimination between the exporter's home market or a third country's market and the importing country's market. The so-harmed importing countries may trigger antidumping regulations based on internationally accepted practices and impose retaliatory punishments (e.g., high custom tariffs) on the exporting countries. As more nations became involved in the global trading system, they began to use antidumping regulations to protect their own products in the global market. In the 1990s, there were approximately 232 antidumping cases per year, and the number reached 251 in 2000 and 348 in 2001.[28] Economically developed nations (e.g., the United States, Canada, the EU countries) tend to initiate more antidumping cases, and China has become a main target in those cases because of its production of primarily low-cost, labor-intensive products. As early as the late 1980s, the EU initiated antidumping investigations into China's small television sets. In 1991, the EU imposed a 5-year 15.3% import tariff rate as a punishment on Chinese goods. In 1994, the EU further imposed a 28.8% tariff rate on large television sets made in China. By the end of 1998, a 44.6% retaliatory tariff was imposed on all China-made television sets, and as a result China's televisions were almost shut out of the European market.[29] In a similar fashion, 11 U.S. steel enterprises initiated antidumping accusations against China and 10 other nations in 2000,[30] and in 2002 the EU was working on some protective measures against China's textiles.[31] Between 1979 and October 2004, a total of 34 countries and customs territories initiated 669 investigations (including antidumping, subsidies, and safeguards measures) against China with a total value of $19 billion U.S.[32] According to the WTO data in Table 5.6, from 1995 to 2005, China was the top target in antidumping cases, leading in both the number of investigations and the number of measures imposed by other nations against China. The same pattern will likely continue in near future.

China tried to defend against these antidumping cases and to counterattack those accusations whenever possible. To answer the EU's challenge in the television case, Xiahua, a Chinese television enterprise, hired the law firm Van Bael & Bellis in Brussels to counterattack the antidumping accusation and submitted a review petition in 2000. After 2 years of negotiations, the EU reached agreements with Xiahua and six other Chinese TV enterprises in July 2002, and the Chinese TV enterprises reentered the European market after 4 years.[33] In 2002 alone, China initiated defenses in 48 out of a total of 58 antidumping investigations,[34] and there have been signs that the successful defense rate is increasing (Meng & Li, 2004). Despite such efforts, resorting to legal defense is still very intimidating to the majority of Chinese enterprises. A recent case stands out as such an example. In the summer

Table 5.6 Antidumping Cases Collected by the WTO

Item/Year	1995	1996	1997	1998	1999	2000	2001	2002	2003	2004	2005	2006 (January–June)
Cases initiated against China	20	43	33	28	40	43	53	51	52	49	56	32
Cases measured against China	26	16	33	24	20	29	30	37	40	43	40	15
Cases initiated by China	N/A	N/A	N/A	N/A	N/A	6	14	30	22	27	24	3
Cases measured by China	N/A	N/A	N/A	N/A	N/A	0	0	5	33	14	16	15

Note. Data from WTO antidumping statistics.

of 2005, the EU initiated an antidumping investigation on leather shoes made in China. In March 2006 the EU voted for a retaliatory tariff, and in October a 16.5% retaliatory tariff was formally imposed on all China-made leather shoes (as well as children's shoes) for a 2-year period. More than 1,200 Chinese enterprises are subject to this high tariff. Although there were numerous reports calling for a concerted effort among these enterprises to counter the accusation, only four of them filed an official appeal to the EU's decision by December when the appeal deadline ran out. The high cost of legal appeal, the complexity of the legal procedure, and unfamiliarity with WTO rules were all cited as reasons that stopped other enterprises from resorting to legal appeals.[35]

In addition to defending itself in these cases, the Chinese government also tried to use the same rules for its own benefit. Although not usually mentioned, China is also a victim of foreign dumping, and foreign dumping alone costs China 10 billion yuan ($1.2 billion U.S.) every year in losses (Shen, 1997). In 1997, the State Council promulgated the Anti-dumping and Countervailing Regulation of the People's Republic of China (ACR).[36] Although the new regulation has many problems, its passage indicates a learning process undertaken by the Chinese government during the process of its integration into the world system. From 1997 to the summer of 2005, Chinese enterprises initiated 39 antidumping investigations with a total value of over $6 billion U.S., and, if the WTO data presented earlier were used as a benchmark, such actions could have saved China more than 20 billion yuan (approximately $2.1 billion U.S.) over this time period.[37] In 2006, China initiated 10 new antidumping investigations and rendered nine final judgments on previous antidumping appeals.[38] In one such final decision, for example, the Ministry of Commerce imposed antidumping duties with rates as high as 61% on imported polyurethane originating from Japan, Singapore, South Korea, Taiwan, and the United States.[39] WTO data in Table 5.6 clearly show China's increasing effort in the new century in using antidumping rules against other nations, and China has become one of the reporting nations that top the list of antidumping initiations and measurement.

In sum, although China has had a slow start, its integration into the world system is accelerating. The Chinese government tried to control its opening process and strategically played the globalization card for its own benefit. To some extent, China's controlled globalization is necessary, as argued, for its healthy and steady development within the world system (Stiglitz, 2002). In the last decade, China reached out actively in the international arena and broadened its economic, political, and cultural communication with other nations worldwide. Membership in the WTO gives China a better platform for establishing connections with other nations. In November 2001, for example, China reached agreements with the ASEAN to establish a free-trade area (FTA) over the next 10 years, as the first step toward a larger East Asian free-trading zone. In the next 2 years, from 2002 to 2004, China–ASEAN bilateral trade increased by $50 billion U.S. The proposed

FTA would contain 1.7 billion consumers, a combined GDP of $2 trillion U.S., and $1.2 trillion U.S. of trade volume. It will be the most populous free trade zone in the world and one of the largest, along with the North American Free Trade Agreement and the EU.[40] Ideologically, China has kept a low profile in the world arena, and class struggle is no longer a priority for China's foreign policy as it was in the 1950s and 1960s. According to the globalization theory, China is becoming a part of and serving the capitalist economic system, although it still claims itself as a socialist nation.

IMPACT OF GLOBALIZATION ON CHINA'S LEGAL SYSTEM

Although China's globalization may be primarily a result of its economic needs, the impact of globalization on its domestic legal system has been important in China's political and legal development. As I argued in Chapter 3, China's legal reform is still an ongoing process, and I highlight here a few significant features in this process that reflect the influence of the globalization.

First, since 1978 significant legal changes have been made to serve economic development, including a series of Constitutional revisions. For example, the 1982 Constitution for the first time acknowledged nonpublic ownership activities as a "necessary and beneficial complement" to the socialist economy. In 1993, the amended Constitution established the market economy as the main economic mode at the socialist "preliminary stage." In the 1999 Constitution, nonpublic ownerships were established as "important components of the socialist market economy," and for the first time the Constitution guaranteed that "the People's Republic of China shall be governed according to law and shall be built into a socialist country based on the rule of law." It is expected that these Constitutional revisions (and new ones) will have a significant impact in the future.[41]

Consistent with constitutional revisions, major economic laws such as the Economic Contract Law and the Foreign Investment Law also have been created, amended, or revised several times to meet new economic needs.[42] Intellectual property law is an example. Mo's (1999a) research reveals that there were 4,044 registered trademarks in China prior to 1961, and more than half of them (2,035) were foreign-owned trademarks. The trademark registration and protection system was destroyed during the Cultural Revolution period and then resumed after the reform. In 1982, the Trademark Law was promulgated, and the Detailed Rules for the Implementation of the Trademark Law was published in 1988 (both were amended in the 1990s). Table 5.7 shows yearly foreign trademark registration information in China in the 1980s. Although the numbers fluctuate, note the rapid development of trademark registrations from less than 1,000 at the beginning of the reforms to several thousand each year in the second half of the 1980s. In 1993, the number surpassed 20,000, and it broke the 60,000 mark by 2004.[43]

Table 5.7 Foreign Trademark Registration in China

Year	Before 1978	1979	1980	1981	1982	1983	1984	1985	1986	1987	1988
Total registration	4,236	894	1,297	2,049	4,672	2,289	1,522	2,084	5,136	4,393	3,604

Note. From *Law Yearbook of China* (1988).

Correspondingly the total number of trademark registrations (including both foreign and domestic) increased to 132,000 in 1993 from about 20,000 in 1980. From 2000 to 2004, it increased at an amazing rate, adding about 100,000 more each year, and reaching 588,000 by 2004.[44]

There is a similar pattern in China's patent law. After the new China was founded, only six certificates of invention and four patents were issued through 1958 (Alford, 1995a). In 1984, the Patent Law was finally promulgated, and patent applications increased over the years. From April 1984 to the end of 2004, the total number of patent applications reached more than 2.2 million, including more than 410,000 foreign (nonresident) filings.[45] Data from the *2006 Patent Report* of the World Intellectual Property Organization (WIPO) showed that the total number of China's patent filings in 2004 (both resident and nonresident) ranked fourth in the world.[46] The most recent data from 2006 showed that a total of 573,000 applications were submitted and 268,000 of them were granted in China.[47] The new patent law, however, has many limitations, even after its 1992 revision, and there is a general reluctance to bring up such issues. From 1984 to 1992, Chinese patent officials reported fewer than 2,000 administrative actions and only 500 lawsuits (Alford, 1995a; see also F. Liu, 1987). With China's further integration into the global system, more effective measures probably will be taken to prevent violations of intellectual property rights.[48]

At the same time patent applications increased at home, China also increased its international patent applications based on the WIPO's Patent Cooperation Treaty. In 2002 China had only 784 international applications, but the number continued to grow and reached 3,910 by 2006 (ranked eighth in the world).[49]

Entry into the WTO brought another round of legal changes and adjustments domestically. Since 2001, in preparation and as a requirement for being a WTO member, China has been revising its domestic laws, regulations, and rules that were in conflict with WTO agreements and stipulations. This huge project involved many key governmental branches. For example, by March 2002, the Ministry of Foreign Trade and Economic Cooperation revised 51 and annulled 381 legal documents;[50] by May 2002, the SPC annulled a total of 120 legal interpretations to comply with WTO rules;[51] by December 2002, the State Council reviewed more than 2,300 regulations, annulled 830, and revised 325 of those regulations;[52] and in the same month, China's Customs finished its review of more than 3,000 regulations and documents and revised the Customs Law.[53]

At the same time, protection for intellectual properties was strengthened after China's accession of the WTO. From 2000 to 2004, the public security organizations cleared 5,305 intellectual property cases, and the procuratorates filed charges against 2,566 people.[54] From 2002 to 2006, people's courts accepted 54,321 intellectual property civil litigations, more than double the number of cases in the preceding 5 years (1997–2001) before China's entry into the WTO.[55]

Second, as China's economy has been further integrated into the global system, its legal system has become more open to other nations' legal practices and international standards. This process is evident in two key aspects. On the one hand, more laws are quickly enacted to deal with foreign-related affairs, and they cover a broad range from foreign investment and income tax to foreign trade. In August 2002, the SPC handed down decisions on issues related to international trade administrative litigations. For the first time, foreigners and organizations may bring up administrative litigations in the Chinese courts to counter wrongful governmental decisions.[56] These new broadened jurisdictions ensure foreigners' and foreign enterprises' legal rights in China, another strong indication of China's increasing compliance with international standards.

On the other hand, increasing legal communications (e.g., education, training and academic conferences) made between China and other nations and organizations have led to significant changes in China's domestic legal system. In recent years, a series of moves has been made on two reform agendas, one on the death penalty and the other on due process rights in criminal prosecutions. The adoption of lethal injection as a method of execution was the first step in death penalty reforms. Lethal injection was formally established in the 1996 Criminal Procedure Law as one means for execution. In September 2001, the SPC encouraged a full adoption of lethal injection executions nationwide, as it is believed that this practice is more "humane, scientific, and consistent with the requirement of a modern legal system."[57] Next, the SPC tightened its regulations and practices on all death penalty cases. In 2006, the SPC ordered that all death penalty cases adopt open trials in their appeals (*er'shen* in Chinese) after July 1, 2006, and the SPC further enacted detailed rules (e.g., for witness testimony) with regard to such open trials.[58] Furthermore, after years of discussions and preparations, the SPC finally took back the power to review and ratify all death penalty cases in 2007, ending a 26-year practice of allowing lower high courts to use such power (see discussion on lower level courts' review in Chapter 4). Numerous reports commented on this retrieval, and all emphasized the importance of taking death penalty cases seriously and treating human lives with high respect, although the consensus is that the practice of the death penalty will be continued in China.[59] Due to such reform efforts, the number of death sentences meted out by the courts in 2006, although not revealed, hit a record low in more than a decade based on an official report.[60] It was specifically mentioned that this "accords with the world's trend to gradually lighten penalties."[61]

The second reform agenda aimed to enhance defendants' due process rights in criminal prosecutions. First, take pretrial overdetention (*chaoqi jiya*) as an example. Since 2001, the people's procuratorates have identified overdetention as a key problem and made efforts to correct it. The number of official corrections (*jiuzheng*) on such overdetentions decreased from 64,254 in 2001 to 56,389 in 2002, to 25,181 in 2003 and further to 7,132 in

2004. The number of new reported overdetentions decreased each year from 66,196 in 2002 to 24,921 in 2003, 4,947 in 2004, 271 in 2005, and 233 in 2006.[62] In addition, China's judicial system also targeted such overdetentions and cleared 4,060 suspects in 2003, 7,658 suspects in 2004, and 2,432 in 2005 in those cases.[63] Second, some local legal branches started introducing key due process concepts modeled on Western nations. In October 2000, the People's Procuratorate in Shuncheng district in Fushun city, Liaoning province, began to grant "the right to remain silent" to most defendants in criminal cases. This right to remain silent (*chenmo quan*), sometimes called zero testimony (*ling kougong*), signifies a major change in China's criminal litigation practice because it requires a presumption of innocence rather than a presumption of guilt as in the traditional notion and practice.[64] After Fushun's first trial, people's procuratorates in several other cities in Liaoning province followed Fushun's lead,[65] although challenges quickly emerged and showed that this practice lacks effective support (e.g., meaningful lawyering practice and a plea-bargain system) in the Chinese legal system.[66] In November 2001, the People's Procuratorate in Zhuhai city, Gongdong province, enacted new pretrial criminal procedures in which criminal defendants will be notified of all their legal rights in written forms after they are arrested.[67] In March 2003, the Beijing First Intermediate People's Court implemented a new internal policy that required all criminal suspects be hooded in their transportation to the courthouse. It was aimed at protecting the suspects' identity and privacy.[68] In the last 2 years, audio- or videotaping during police interrogation were adopted by the courts, the procuratorates, and the public security organizations to prevent administrative misconduct.[69] All these are lessons learned from Western models with an aim to guarantee humanitarian treatments to defendants and due respect to their rights. Those trials are local with limited impact, but they showed new signs of the legal reform. Along with its globalization, China will (hopefully) provide more protection to Chinese citizens in its legalization process.[70]

Third, the globalization process, especially the entry into the WTO, has hastened China's political and legal reforms. Governmental control has taken on a new form, switching from imposed administrative policies to legitimate legal regulations. Entry and continued membership in the WTO requires a change in the government's role in the management of the national economy. A closed, authoritarian polity is gradually changing to a polity built on a more transparent, rational legal system. A successful transition in this direction is necessary both as an end and as a means in this process. The importance of this transition is well acknowledged by the Chinese government, and the goal is to replace administrative interventions with economic adjustments under the market economy and for all governmental functions to comply with legal rules and procedures.[71] The gradual abolition of administrative review and approval (ARA) (*xingzheng shenpi*) is a relevant example. For many years, ARA was used as an effective way to control key industrial and commercial projects; however, it does not meet the requirements of the market economy within the global economic system. The rescission of ARA took place first on foreign trade[72] and the banking system[73] as part of China's compliance with the WTO rules before it spread into other areas.[74] From December 2002 to May 2004, the State Council reviewed more than 1,795 projects and abolished ARA in more than 1,600 of these projects.[75] A successful transition in the reform era also requires a well-established and effective legal system on which the government may rely as argued in Chapter 3. China's entry into the WTO provided a stimulant to the legalization process. On the eve of China's entry into the WTO, both the court system[76] and Chinese lawyers[77] were called on to meet the new legal requirements after entry. In December 2002, the SPC published new legal interpretations with regard to both antidumping and antisubsidies cases. This assumption of China's rights and duties as a WTO member by the Chinese courts is viewed as an important step in the development of the Chinese legal system.[78]

Fourth and finally, as noticed by scholars, the Chinese courts were always viewed as heavily politicized. Politicization, as well as the low level of professionalism and local protectionism, has made the courts inadequate, if not incompetent, in addressing the legal concerns of foreign businesses. As a result, foreign disputants tried to avoid litigation if possible and turned to other forms of dispute resolution such as arbitration and mediation, in which they might have more control (see Brown & Rogers, 1997; Potter, 1995). Indeed, both foreign-related arbitration and mediation have made significant progress in China. When the China International Economic and Trade Arbitration Commission (CIETAC) was inaugurated in 1956, there were only 21 listed arbitrators (all Chinese nationals). Between 1959 and 1965, the Commission received only 27 cases. From 1967 to 1979, due to political turmoil of the Cultural Revolution, the CIETAC arbitrated merely 11 cases and mediated 60. Only after the reforms did the CIETAC regain its energy. The number of arbitrators increased to 65 in 1980, 71 in 1983, 291 (including 88 foreign nationals) in the mid-1990s, and 428 (including 147 foreign nationals) by the end of the 1990s (Mo, 1997, 1999b).

Table 5.8 shows arbitration cases ruled on by the CIETAC after 1986. The numbers increased from about 100 cases in the mid-1980s to more than 200 cases in the early 1990s, and broke the 800-case mark in 1995 after the Arbitration Law of People's Republic of China was enacted. The total monetary settlements involved in these cases also rose quickly from 300 million yuan in 1990 to 7.48 billion yuan in 2000 and further to 11.2 billion yuan in 2002. The 1995 Arbitration Law borrowed numerous international standards and signified a direct connection with the international arbitration system. From 1995 to 2000, 148 organizations were established nationwide to practice the new law.[79] Although arbitration and mediation turned out to be more meaningful to foreign businesses, these processes also have to deal with common problems such as evidence collection in discovery and difficulties associated with the enforcement of favorable results by the

Table 5.8 Number of Arbitration Cases Ruled on by CIETAC, 1986–2005

Year	Cases Petitioned	Cases Ruled	Total Value Involved (Unit: 100 Million Yuan)
1986		> 90	
1987		139	
1988	174		
1989	243	300	
1990	229	200	3
1991	274	205	
1992	267	236	
1993	486	294	
1994	829	574	27
1995	902	890	44
1996	778	797	41
1997	723	764	44.2
1998	678	736	61.15
1999	669	706	68.9
2000	633	738	74.8
2001	731	712	105.5
2002	684	694	112.83
2003	709	704	82.67
2004	850	700	71.6
2005	979	958	120.6

Note. From *Law Yearbook of China* (1987–2001); 2001–2005 data from annual work reports retrieved from the CIETAC Web site (http://www.cietac.org.cn/index.asp).

courts (see Brown & Rogers, 1997; Potter, 1995). The lesson for the Chinese government is at least twofold: On the one hand, a strong, more independent judicial system will be very important to China's further integration in the global economic system. On the other hand, while China still needs time to establish a full-scale legal system, other alternative forms of dispute resolution probably will continue to be strengthened and guaranteed.

CONCLUSION

In this chapter, I focused on the process of China's increasing connection with other nations within the global system. China's approach to globalization appears to follow a mixture of various theories, due to the complexity of the world-economy system itself and China's unique position as an emerging semiperipheral nation in this system. The complexity of China's engagement is evident not only domestically but also in China's practices and involvement in the global economic system. China's development to a large extent has been driven by the expansion of the world-economy system, and the Chinese government admitted that it has no choice but to join in this process of expansion. The question, in other words, is not whether China will be part of the system, but how China becomes part of the system. The Chinese government has tried to pace its integration, manage its domestic transitions, and monitor more precisely its increasing role in the system.

All these reactions to globalization are acknowledged by the Chinese government. In 2005, for example, Chinese President Hu Jintao stated in a speech delivered at the opening ceremony of the Fortune Global Forum held in China that:

> As China becomes more developed, its cooperation with the other countries and their corporations of various types is bound to increase in scale. China will keep opening up its market, find new ways of using foreign capital, improve on legislations and regulations for encouraging and protecting foreign investors, revamp foreign economic management, step up protection of intellectual property rights, and work still harder to help foreign investors and create an even better environment for trade and economic cooperation between China and the rest of the world.[80]

Despite the challenges, there is no doubt that China has become increasingly integrated into the world system. The Chinese government has gone through a transition from being pulled into the system passively to actively participating in it. China's admission to the WTO and efforts to establish free trade zones in Asia at the beginning of the new millennium are important examples of its gradual integration and its political strategy.

The entry of China into the WTO provides another impetus for internal reforms and China's global economic involvement. The old method of administrative control of the economy is no longer seen as effective and legitimate in the new era. Rather, a transition to a more open polity based on an effective, relatively independent legal system has become another necessity for China's increasing inclusion in the world system. Entry into the WTO, in this sense, provides both opportunities and challenges. The opportunities lie in the fact that the Chinese government may gain a new way to relegitimate its political and legal control through successful transitions, but the challenges lie in the fact that further integration into the global system may risk the CCP's ideology at home. The ways in which the Chinese government undergoes these domestic political and legal transitions along with its global integration process will be important in the new era.

6 China's Current Court System
Procedures, Role Players, and Main Issues

In previous chapters, I discussed changes that happened in China at the economic, political, legal, and social levels in the reform era and further extended China's domestic reforms into the global system. In this chapter, I focus on China's current court system based on my field research. Even though my empirical observations were conducted at the micro level, all major changes described previously at the macro level are reflected in the judicial system.

As one main branch of the legal system, China's court system has been growing along with the legal process. In fact, compared with the procuratorate and the public security systems, the court system has been the most active player in recent years, especially since the second half of the 1990s. Court reform has become a very popular slogan and many new regulations have been put forward to answer new calls. For instance, in 1998, the SPC published regulations to change the traditional "inquisitorial" trial model to the "adversarial" model in civil cases (see Reichel, 2005, for discussions on each model and comparison between them). In 1999, the SPC published An Outline of the Reform of the People's Courts in the Next Five Years (*renmin fayuan wunian gaige gangyao* in Chinese), and it became an important guideline for the court reform. In March 1999, the SPC published regulations to guarantee open trials to the public. Next, it established Regulations on Rules of Evidence in Civil Litigations (*zuigao renmin fayuan guanyu minshi susong zhengju de ruogan guiding*) in 2001, and evidential rules in administrative litigations in 2002. All these moves signaled a continuing effort by the judicial system in the process of legal reform. Domestically, Chinese scholars began to pay attention to the court reform (see, e.g., Su-li, 2000; L. Wang, 2001), and there is a clear need for such studies.

I laid out my study setting and court access and discussed cases I observed in Chapter 1. In this chapter, I first describe current court procedures. Then I focus on major players in the courtroom and analyze their different functions in dynamic interactions. Next I discuss major issues and problems I observed in the current court system in its daily functions. Finally I try to put court reforms back into the general framework of my analyses and draw some conclusions.

CURRENT COURT PROCEDURES

Internal Court System and Judge Panels

In terms of court structure, there are more similarities than differences among all courts I observed. Within each court, there are different divisions (*ting*), such as the criminal, the civil (sometimes the economic as another separate from the civil), and the administrative litigation divisions. There are chief (and deputy chief) judges who work as the administrative leaders within each division, and they are officially subordinate to the president (and vice presidents) of the court (*yuanzhang*). The hierarchy of the court is obvious and indeed has a very important function, as I discuss later.

There are two types of trial procedures. At the district courts, one presiding judge is allowed to try simple cases by himself or herself, applying a simplified or summary trial procedure (*jianyi chengxu*). All other cases are tried by a judge (collegial) panel (*heyi ting*) consisting of three judges[1] through a normal trial procedure (*putong chengxu*). According to the official rules, all three presiding judges, often working together for a reasonably long time, should try, discuss, and rule cases together, and each judge supposedly has an equal say in the final decision. As a practical matter, however, one judge usually acts as the leading judge (*shenpang zhang*) during the trial and is responsible for the trial procedure (i.e., announcing the opening, asking questions, and controlling the procedure). Governed by internal official rules,[2] the most prestigious judge in the judge panel (e.g., the chief judge if she or he is in the panel) usually sits as the leading judge. The other two presiding judges (*shenpang yuan*) can ask questions and help clarify issues during a trial. In addition, there is usually one charging judge within the panel (not necessarily the leading judge) who is primarily responsible for the case judgment. When the panel discusses the final judgment, the charging judge summarizes the case and proposes a solution first. With this expectation, the charging judge should spend the most time studying the case. Although not in any official book, this practice becomes an official way of subdividing the heavy caseload among three judges.

Besides professional judges, lay people could serve in a judge panel as a practice of the people's assessor system (*renmin peishenyuan*) in China.[3] Often referred to as a Chinese version of the jury system, the people's assessor system is officially established as part of the court system. It is designed to (a) increase the involvement of lay people in the legal system, (b) show that the system is indeed made by and serves the populace, and (c) serve an educational purpose among the populace. People's assessors are usually recommended by their workplace and selected by the courts (see Wang & Zhang, 1997). I witnessed the actual participation of people's assessors at both the Chengdu court and the Hai Dian court. The number of people's assessors in the judge panel varied between one and two, and it was not clear when they would participate in trials (because it is not mandatory). Based on laws, people's assessors should have the same duty and power as professional judges. In cases I observed, however, no people's assessors worked as a leading judge (probably due to their lack of prestige), and it is unlikely that they served as a charging one either (due to their lack of legal knowledge). Indeed, there is a big question mark with regard to their actual role in the trial.

Trial Procedures

Based on civil and criminal procedure laws, all cases are tried in the courts of the first instance either through a simplified procedure or a normal procedure. After a case is filed, it will be examined and categorized into one of the two types based on the complexity of the case (e.g., the facts and the litigation request). Although there are many differences between the two on paper, as a practical matter, I did not see major differences in trials with regard to the procedure. The simplified trial usually saved time in each phase of the procedure due to the simplicity of the case, and in practice most presiding judges in simplified trials still went through each step of the normal procedure.[4]

In the courtroom, the judges' table is in the center, and there is another table for the secretary, sometimes placed a few steps away in front of the judge's table (as in the courtrooms in Chengdu) and sometimes right besides the judges' table (as in the courtrooms in Beijing[5]). The plaintiff (or the prosecutor in criminal cases) sits to the right of the judges and the defendant (or defense attorney in criminal cases) sits on the left side.[6] In criminal cases, the defendant has to either stand (in Chengdu) or sit (in Beijing) in the center facing the semicircle made by the judges' table and other parties' tables (see Figure 6.1).

Once all parties of the case (usually two, but sometimes more with various third parties) appear in the courtroom, the secretary is responsible for checking the identities of each party and making sure that attorneys, if available, have the right documentation for their representation. The secretary then gives the file to the leading judge, who announces the opening of the trial.

The first task for the leading judge is to introduce the judge panel and the secretary, check with all parties to determine if there is any conflict of interest between the parties and the trial personnel, and inform the parties that they have a legal right to ask for personnel withdrawals and changes (*huibi*) if necessary.

The substance of the trial is divided into three phases: court investigation, court argument, and final closing argument. In each phase, parties take turns presenting in court. In the investigation phase, the plaintiff goes first to read the complaint, countered by the defendant's answer. Next, the plaintiff submits all evidence to support his or her case, and the defendant has a chance to cross-examine the plaintiff's evidence. Then, the defendant submits evidence to support the defense and allow the plaintiff to cross-examine. If there is a question with regard to the evidence submitted by one party, the

Figure 6.1 Courtroom setup at the Chengdu Court.

Illustration: (far center) the judges' table with the leading judge's seat in the middle; (near center) the secretary's table; (right) the defendant's table; (left) the plaintiff/prosecutor's table.

court will make a decision whether the evidence will be admitted. Sometimes, when the court cannot make a decision immediately, the leading judge usually says: "X party has a different opinion about the evidence submitted by Y party, and the argument by X is . . . the court cannot make a decision now, and we (judges) will study the case and evidence after today's trial and decide whether the evidence is admissible in the final judgment."

After all parties submit evidence, the trial enters the argument phase. Again, both sides take turns to express their opinions. Ideally, parties in the investigation phase shall make no legal arguments (except to buttress the admissibility of the evidence) but simply submit evidence. It is at the argument phase that they should make strong and logical legal arguments. In real practice, the two phases are often mixed (inevitably to some extent). The court usually shows little patience for parties' redundancy and cuts off their repeated arguments by saying, "Alright, you have expressed your points. Please move on and make only *new* arguments."

The final closing argument is very formalistic (and boring to some extent). Again, the court usually does not allow simple repetition of arguments already made. In fact, what the court wants to hear is if the parties still hold on to their litigation requests (after their arguments). It is sufficient for either party to simply say, "We insist on our litigation requests, and ask the court to rule in our favor." Compared with the closing argument in the U.S. system, this is in no way a phase in which a party tries best to impress the court.

In criminal cases, once the presiding judge announces the opening of the case, the prosecutor leads the prosecution by reading the official indictment (*qisu shu*). The judge checks with the defendant and the defense attorney (if available) to see if they have any questions about the indictment. Next, in the investigation phase, the prosecutor presents evidence to support the case, and supposedly the defendant and the defense attorney have a chance to cross-examine. Then, it is the defendant and the defense attorney's turn to present evidence, followed by the prosecutor's cross-examination. Similarly, both sides take turns arguing their case in the argument phase and in the final closing argument.

PLAYERS IN THE COURTROOM

Secretaries (*shuji yuan*)

Secretaries have an important role in the courtroom as well as outside of the courtroom. Usually, there is one secretary in a trial, but sometimes more secretaries are necessary for a long and complex trial so that they can take breaks. At the Qing Yang court, a secretary usually works with one or a group of judges, so that the "judge(s) and secretary" group is relatively stable over a period of time. Although I did not have a chance to talk to judges and secretaries in other courts, I found the same "judge and secretary" combination as well. This relatively stable relationship between the judge(s) and the secretary might be necessary for cooperative and efficient teamwork.

In terms of gender composition, there were 35 female secretaries to 17 male secretaries if one simply counts the numbers in the case summary tables. The numbers might be distorted because sometimes I observed several cases from the same "judge and secretary" group. It is safe, however, to conclude that in general there are more female secretaries than male secretaries. Most secretaries are very young, probably in their 20s. One secretary I talked to at the Qing Yang court in Chengdu was a law school graduate who started working just 2 years earlier. Doing secretarial work is a way to gain practical experience in the legal system, and as a common practice, many current judges started their careers as secretaries. This "from a secretary to a judge" selection system is changing, however, due to the call for legal professionalization (see Chapter 3). Today, the court no longer recruits judges from among secretaries.[7]

Before the trial, a secretary is responsible for preparing all paperwork, a function very similar to clerks in the U.S. system. In the courtroom, a secretary checks the identities of all parties and attorneys and then lets the judge know that everything is ready. During the trial, a secretary takes lengthy notes and tracks down important information for the trial, a function that makes the secretary more like a stenographer in U.S. courts. At courts in Chengdu, secretaries took notes by hand, but they were working directly on computers in Beijing. The computer note taking apparently is easier for making changes and saving information; however, it caused some trouble as well. First, the noise of the computer note taking bothered me as an observer. I was surprised that judges and other parties accepted it (they probably had to). Second, with hand note taking, as soon as the trial is over, the secretary can immediately give the papers to all parties and ask them to review and sign them. With computerized note taking, the secretary has to print the document first and then ask all parties to review and sign it. This one additional step (i.e., printing) could be difficult, especially when there is another case waiting for trial immediately after the finished one. Indeed, in a few instances at the Hai Dian court, the secretaries asked the parties to wait outside the courtroom, and they were printing the documents after the next trial had already begun! The justification is efficiency and convenience on the assumption that (probably) no party wanted to come back and spend another day at the court. The potential price, though, is accuracy. Neither the parties nor the secretary have a chance to review the record carefully before they add their signature.

Secretaries seem to have broad discretion in deciding what notes they are taking at trials, because they are not able to take down everything. In several cases, I found that the secretaries were not recording anything for a relatively long period of time, and their minds were apparently somewhere else. When I talked to a judge, he told me that he would usually go over the case with the secretary after the trial to make sure that the secretary had put down all the important things. Sometimes during the trial, judges specifically ask the secretary to write down certain things (or on the parties' requests). A trial record so dictated, very different from that of the U.S. system, is a product of a partial trial process and reflects the combined work of the secretary and the judges' recollection and understanding. Interestingly, I did see that in one case (45), the secretary asked some (good) questions of the parties. However, this is rare.

Judges

Compared with secretaries, the gender ratio for judges is pretty even. In the cases I observed, there were 63 male judges and 66 female judges.[8] Judges' ages varied broadly, from early 30s (or even younger) to mid-50s, based on my judgment. It is not uncommon for many young judges to work at the intermediate level courts.

Judges at different levels wear different uniforms. Judges at the district courts wear a dark-color, police-like uniform with a judicial badge on the jacket. Judges at the intermediate courts wear a long black judicial robe, very similar to the judge's robe in the United States. In fact, the judicial robe uniform was adopted not very long ago (see Chapter 3).

In the judge panel, there is an official hierarchy (the leading judges vs. other presiding judges), as well as a hierarchy of case assignments (the charging judge vs. other two judges). The leading judge sits in the middle of the judge table and leads the trial by going through each step and asking questions. It is usually not difficult to figure out who is the charging judge, because she or he is more actively involved in the trial: reading files, asking questions, and taking notes (remember that she or he is primarily responsible for the case in hand).

Different from judges in the United States, judges in China serve several different functions. First, presiding judges are supposed to know the law and make technical rulings if necessary (e.g., the admissibility of evidence). This is the function that U.S. judges have in the court system. Second, presiding judges more often have to summarize true legal issues from long, complex, and often conflicting stories told by both parties. It is very common that after one party rambles a long time, a judge interrupts and says, "OK, so basically you are arguing on three points, first, . . . second, . . . and third, . . . am I right? Do I miss something?" It is amazing that judges are so acute and quickly catch the keys of the case. It definitely requires experience, a sound mind, and an ability to summarize complex stories and turn them into legal issues suitable for a judgment. This is the job that usually should be done by parties' attorneys. Due to the lack of attorneys or insufficient lawyering skills, however, Chinese presiding judges often have to assume part of this job. Third, without jurors, presiding judges also have to evaluate factual evidence and eventually come to a final decision. Here, the judges play a role similar to that of a jury in the U.S. system. Fourth, near the end of each civil case, presiding judges always check with both parties to see if there is a chance for reconciliation (settlement). In fact, reconciliation is often preferred and pushed by the presiding judges. At this moment, judges are acting as mediators. Finally, during some cases or during conversations right after a trial, judges use a tone to admonish parties as a way of conducting moral education (as Merry pointed out in her research (1990), this is also common in U.S. trial courts). In short, Chinese presiding judges carry out multiple functions in the courtroom, which often combine the work done by judges, jurors, lawyers, and mediators in the U.S. court system.

People's Assessors

I witnessed the actual participation of one people's assessor at the Chengdu court, and six more at the Hai Dian court in Beijing. Among these seven assessors, two were men, and the other five were women. They were not wearing uniforms (they probably did not have them). Instead, they simply wore their usual clothes, like lay people.

According to official rules, people's assessors should have the same duty and power as professional judges, and their votes should carry equal weight in a final decision. Their actual performance, however, hardly matches such an expectation. In cases I observed, none of the people's assessors served as a leading judge (due to their lack of prestige). In one trial at the Chengdu court (22), the two professional judges always exchanged opinions with each other, but not with the people's assessor. Throughout the trial, the female assessor did not even ask one question. Similar situations happened in two trials at the Hai Dian court (47, 48), except that the female professional judge did ask both female assessors if they had questions for the defendant—and the answer was "No." Interestingly, in another case (50), two male people's assessors showed great interest in the case (an assault case). Both took some notes and asked good questions to clarify issues. I am not sure how much of a role gender played in these cases.

It is not clear how well prepared those assessors were for their trials. Based on their reactions, they probably knew nothing about the case beforehand. Due to my limited access, I could not follow up on their performance in the final ruling stage. However, they would be unlikely to serve as the charging judges and they would probably rely on the legal expertise of the professional judges (see Cohen, 1997). Although the actual role of people's assessors is questionable in reality, there is no sign of abolishing the practice. Rather, calls have been recently made to strengthen it.[9]

Prosecutors

A total of 18 male prosecutors and 8 female prosecutors showed up in 22 criminal cases. It appears that there are more male prosecutors in general. The age range was quite broad, from young inexperienced prosecutors (probably in their late 20s) to mature and experienced ones (probably in their late 40s). It was not uncommon for two prosecutors to show up for a trial, with the older, experienced one leading the prosecution and the younger prosecutor doing nothing but listening (acting like an intern).

There is no intention to hide the close connection between the prosecutor and the trial personnel. Often before the trial, prosecutors would chat with either judges or secretaries in front of the defendant and the defense attorneys. It is well known that the *Gong*, *Jian* and *Fa* (police, procuracy, and court) are one big family, and the prosecutor has at least an equal, if not higher ranking in comparison with the court.[10] Indeed, prosecutors seem to enjoy their privileges at trial. One day at the Chengdu court, what I observed confirmed what I heard: When the judges were entering the courtroom, every single party stood up ("all rise") except the male prosecutor, who stayed in his chair and stared at the defendant! This is to show an equal status between the court and the procuratorate.

Another privilege enjoyed by the prosecutor is total domination in presenting evidence and questioning of the defendants.[11] Usually, no one interrupts (or dares to interrupt) the presentation of the prosecution, but the prosecutor may interrupt the defendant's presentation and ask various questions at any time. At one trial (13), the defendant raised the issue that he was beaten by the police and therefore had signed the confession testimony. "Do you have evidence?" the judge asked. "No," answered the defendant. Immediately, the prosecutor jumped up and announced, "We have done a thorough investigation throughout the process and found no indication of any violation of laws and rules." The court did not say anything further.

It is not clear how well the prosecutors were prepared for trials, and in some cases the prosecutors did not appear to know about the case until shortly before the trial. Sometimes, they even had problems presenting, including reading the documents clearly (e.g., they could not recognize the handwriting in the police report), a clear sign that they did not have much preparation. In one case (44) at the Beijing First Court, the prosecutor and the defense attorney started chatting before the trial. The prosecutor told the defense attorney that he had "only three testimonies," so it was not a "big case" at all. Further, he could not explain why this simple case had to go through a normal procedure rather than a simplified procedure. All these gave me the impression that he was saying this is not a strong case. As soon as the trial began, however, he presented the case vehemently and concluded in his closing argument, "This is a clear case, and the evidence is strong and undisputable," even though it was not difficult to point out discrepancies among the three testimonies. I was really troubled by this prosecutor's behavior. His final statement did sound like a routine closing argument, but given what he was discussing before the trial, I found his argument not only flawed but also unethical.

Parties in Civil Cases

Parties involved in civil cases were very diverse, from husbands and wives in divorce cases, to common citizens in personal injury cases, to private companies in commercial conflicts, and to governmental agencies (e.g., police department) in administrative litigations. People are no longer afraid of going to court. Rather, they intentionally take advantage of the court system to safeguard their legal rights and gain personal or business interests.

Legal representation is becoming more common in litigations. In the cases I observed, legal representation either through attorneys or through another citizen[12] was utilized in 34 cases, and self-representation was utilized in other 15 cases (and 5 more were unclear on representation). Whether the party hires an attorney is very much related to the stake in the case. One judge, dealing mainly with divorce cases at the Qing Yang court in Chengdu, told me that not many people had attorneys in his court simply because "It's not worthwhile. You know, hiring an attorney is still pretty expensive, and in small cases like this (a divorce case), people just don't hire attorneys."

Parties' legal knowledge also varies greatly. People with legal representation appear to be more knowledgeable. This is so probably because (a) their lawyers or legal representatives do a good job keeping them well informed of the legal issues and procedures at court; and (b) parties who can afford legal representations such as private companies are usually more educated and sometimes are old customers in the legal system.

Parties' attitudes and reactions toward the court system are really a mixture. On the one hand, they come to court and rely on the expertise and more important the authority of the court to solve their problems. On the other hand, sometimes (especially when they cannot square their own notions of justice with the court rulings) they show frustration, anxiety, dismay, or even anger toward the court. Even in the courtroom, as I discuss later, parties often did not treat the court seriously enough and had a difficult time accepting systematic legal rules. It is fair to say that parties care more about the results than the procedures that they have to go through.

Defendants in Criminal Cases

In the 22 criminal cases I observed, there were 45 male defendants and only 4 female defendants. Apparently gender still plays a dominant role. All 4 women were very young, probably in their early to mid-20s. Two were involved with 6 male codefendants in a robbery case (38), and, based on their sentences[13] (compared with their male partners), their crime participation was relatively minor. Another woman was charged with blackmail (*lesuo*) because of her sexual involvement with a male (10). The last female defendant was charged with assault against her father's girlfriend (50). Therefore, the traditional sex role still has a major function in these cases.

All male defendants were quite young too, with most in their 20s and only a few in their 30s and 40s. Their crimes varied greatly, including robbery, theft, assault, embezzlement, selling obscene materials, drug use and trafficking, kidnapping, and murder. Seventeen out of 49 defendants had at least one defense attorney in the courtroom, and this percentage (35%) is not too low, given China's legal history and current situation (see H. Lu & Miethe, 2002), even though the attorneys' representation in the courtroom was weak and far from adequate based on my judgment.

The education level of these defendants was extremely low, with very few exceptions (in cases more like white-collar crimes). On several occasions the defendants announced their names incorrectly, could not spell them correctly, and got their birth dates wrong. In one trial (10) at the Qing Yang court, apparently the defendant did not understand what the leading judge said about his right to request trial personnel changes (withdrawal) in case of a conflict of interest. The judge finally said, "Do you have an opinion about the fact that we are trying this case?" The defendant still had no reaction. "Do you want to change judges?" "No, no." This time, the defendant understood.

All defendants were shackled, wore prisoner's uniforms, and were transported from the prison to the courthouse. Once the trial begins, all shackles are supposed to be taken off. However, at both courts in Chengdu, there were cases in which defendants went through the trial with their handcuffs on.[14] In one case, the prosecutor obviously did not notice it, and when he asked the defendant to show how long the defendant's knife was, the defendant (hands cuffed behind) could only say, "My hands are cuffed."

When there were multiple defendants, as a protective move, the security guards often asked the defendants to squat down in the corner of the room, waiting for their call from the court. Sometimes there was a chair reserved for the defendant in the center, facing the judges. However, once the trial began, the defendant had to stand up and continue standing until the trial was over as a way to show the authority of the court.

Most defendants were very cooperative with the prosecutors and the court. They quickly admitted their crimes and put up no defense. The best they could do was to ask for lenience (Cohen, 1997). Some of them were indeed well prepared with their closing statements. In one trial (47) at the Hai Dian court, a male defendant stood up and bowed toward both the judges and the prosecutor, and said, "Respectful leading judge, presiding judges, secretary, prosecutors, I know that I've committed this crime, . . . however, this is my first offense, . . . I hope that the respectful judges could give me another chance to be a 'new man' . . . with a lighter sentence." Certainly there were defendants who dared to play hardball and tried defensive moves such as questioning evidence presented by the prosecutor, recanting confessions made at the police station, or completely denying any involvement in the charged crimes. It is not clear how effective their defense was in those cases, especially given the fact that the defendants could rarely produce evidence to support their testimony.

Attorneys

Fifty-four attorneys (including 19 criminal defense attorneys) showed up in the courtroom to help parties with their legal representations. Among them, 38 were men, 10 were women, and there were 6 more whose gender I failed to track down.[15] Most attorneys are in their 30s or 40s. It is unknown how parties solicited their attorneys, but it is interesting to see law offices located just outside the court building (in both Chengdu and Beijing). The underlying message seems to be this: If you need an attorney, we are right here fighting for you.

Most attorneys had appropriate attire, such as suits, for court appearances. Some did not take clothing seriously, however, and looked just like lay people (i.e., did not look like lawyers). One day at the Hai Dian court, the judge started checking the defense attorneys' identities (a job usually done by the secretary) right before the trial and found the younger assistant did not have a license. As a result, the judge denied his representation. After the trial, I talked with three young law school graduates who also observed this case, and we all suspected that the judge's unusual questioning had something to do with the informal dress of the attorney and his assistant.[16]

The quality of the lawyers' representations varied greatly. I observed very good lawyering skills and representation on both sides in some cases and also almost silent representation by attorneys in a few cases. It did not appear that gender was a determining factor. Most female attorneys did a good job at the courtroom, and the worst work was done by male attorneys, in fact. The best representation was found in an intellectual property case (a patent violation) (43) at the Beijing First Court. Attorneys on both sides did a great job, making arguments, clarifying technical issues to the court, and attacking the other side's weaknesses. Everything was well organized, and the trial went very smoothly. This high quality might have something to do with the nature of the case as well as the high educational levels of the attorneys and parties (legal agents of big computer companies). In civil cases, it was not uncommon that the parties sometimes seemed to forget the function of their attorneys, lost their temper, and tried to make arguments themselves.

Compared with civil cases, representation in criminal cases was more difficult. In the cases I observed, no single defense attorney presented new evidence favorable to the defendant. The best they did was to point out discrepancies in the prosecutor's evidence and ask for sentencing lenience based on various pleas, such as first offense, young age, little culpability, and good behavior at the workplace (see discussion by Clark & Feinerman, 1996). There are definitely practical reasons for such poor defenses. As a private party against the state, the defense attorney usually suffers from time pressure (late notice of the trial or late appointment in the case) and finds it very difficult to talk to witnesses, establish new evidence, and sometimes even meet and talk with the defendant privately in prison (M. Gu, 1999).[17]

Good representation requires legal skills as well as preparation. In some cases, it was obvious that the attorneys did not prepare the case very well. One Friday morning in a criminal case (44) at the Beijing First Court, the defense attorney was talking to the prosecutor before the trial. He admitted that he did not get notice for the trial and all relevant files until Monday evening. It is hard to conceive that he could develop his defense in 3 days. In another criminal case (51) at the Hai Dian court, the defense attorney kept explaining in his defense that the defendant's behavior in the second theft was "voluntarily discontinued"[18] because the defendant returned the stolen VCR before he was questioned as a suspect at the police station where he confessed. The impatient judge finally suggested, "Is the defendant's behavior (confession) qualified as a 'self-surrender'?" Apparently not anticipating and prepared for this question, the defense attorney did not elaborate on this point before the trial was closed.

In a criminal case (13) at the Qing Yang court, two young male attorneys tried to play hardball. Seeing the prosecutor bullying the defendant by asking tricky questions, one attorney immediately made an objection: "I object, your honor. The prosecutor's question is not appropriate." The leading judge was very surprised and quickly answered, "Sit down, it's not time for you to speak." Later on, the young attorney interrupted the prosecutor's questioning two more times and tried to make counterpoints. The last time, the leading judge said, "It is not your time to speak . . . I assume this is not your first trial. You have to wait for your turn to speak!" I was amazed by the confrontation and wondered how much impact U.S. movies had on this young attorney. Moreover, the attorney specifically asked the defendant, "Has someone beaten you in the police department?" "Yes, several times," answered the defendant. Seeing no evidence, the leading judge said, "You have to get your own evidence (to prove you were beaten)." And the prosecutor immediately announced that he found no violations of laws and rules during the investigation. This is the only case in which a brave young attorney tried to challenge authority. Although the challenge did not seem to make a difference, it was still surprising.

Security Guards

Security guards, literally called court police (*fajing*), have a function in all criminal cases and sometimes in civil cases as well. They wear uniforms and hats and are responsible for court order and taking care of defendants in criminal cases. Usually, they take the defendants into the courtroom and take off their handcuffs once the trial begins. Sometimes, they "help" the defendant to stand in an appropriate manner, for instance, by saying "Put down your hands" in a harsh tone. As soon as the trial is over, they put the handcuffs back on and lead the defendants out of the courtroom.

They have a duty to the audience as well. It is common practice in the courtroom for the security guards to ask the audience not to sit in the front row, and they do not allow relatives of the defendant to give the defendant anything during or after the trial. In one trial (45) at the Beijing First Court, they also helped a very old man to the restroom and escorted several members of the audience out of the courtroom under the leading judge's order because of their inappropriate behavior (making noises). It seems that their duty is a simple one, but necessary to maintain the order and authority of a court.

ISSUES IN THE CURRENT COURT SYSTEM

During my observation, I noticed several major issues in the daily function of the court system. Those issues include the lack of authority of the court, insufficient evidential rules, judicial mediation as a formal function, disregard for procedural justice, internal review system, and the discrepancy between law and justice.

Court as a State Machine: Lack of Authority

When I was talking to a female attorney in Beijing and asked her what her first impression of the court system was, she thought a while and said, "Lack of authority as a court, and they (judges) did not treat it seriously enough."

I was surprised and asked for examples. She said, "While I was in court, I did not feel the dignity of a court. The judges, for instance, did not button up their clothes in the same way: some buttoned two, and others three." By then I was not sure exactly what she meant, and even wondered whether the way she felt was due to the fact that she, as a female, paid too much attention to the judges' attire.

As soon as I started my court observations, however, I immediately noticed the serious problem she mentioned; that is, even though the court is a state machine, most people do not treat the court system seriously. This phenomenon is very common, and it is shown in different forms by almost every player in the court system. Various examples follow.

Parties in Civil Cases

Both plaintiffs and defendants in civil cases occasionally show their disrespect to judges in the courtroom. In one case, a plaintiff left the court and went out to spit without asking for permission. In another case, one plaintiff left the courtroom for reasons unknown without asking for permission. In one appeal sentencing (4), the appellant who lost the appeal insisted on leaving his personal complaint (rather than a simple signature) on the court verdict. Even when the secretary and the judges told him that he could not do that, he kept saying, "No, that's your rule, but not mine." Eventually, he put down his complaint as he wished. In several cases, the defendants answered cellular phones while the trial was going on.

Audience

Nothing is better for the parties than a supportive audience at trials. Things, however, are sometimes out of control. In several administrative litigation cases, supporters not only exchanged opinions loudly with each other and laughed at stupid comments made by the opponent party, but openly made suggestions to the plaintiff in a whispered but clear voice. Some even stood up from their seats and sent notes to the plaintiff. In one case, the leading judge had to declare a recess to calm down the audience.

In criminal cases, relatives were eager to help out. In one case, when the leading judge asked the defendant where he got the knife before he stabbed the victim, one woman sitting in the audience whispered to the defendant, "(happened to) find on road." In another case, the defendant's mother immediately corrected her son's mistake without the court's permission when the defendant incorrectly answered the question about his birthday.

Things such as answering cellular phones and reading newspapers at trials were not uncommon, even when the court clearly ordered the audience not to do so. In one case, an audience member stood up, moved to the window, and opened it to breathe fresh air for a couple of minutes. It gave no impression that he thought this was a courtroom with a trial going on.

Security Guards

The first courtroom at the Qing Yang court is located on the first floor, with one door in the center facing west and a back door at the north end. It was quite common for the security guards to let other defendants go through the back door while a trial was going on. It appeared that everyone felt comfortable with the frequent disruption. In addition, security guards often talked loudly outside the back door, disregarding the ongoing trial. Inside the courtroom, security guards usually sat in the first row of the audience seats, and it was not uncommon to see them stretching out and yawning as if they were not part of the trial.

Secretary

It was usual to see secretaries put on their uniforms in front of the parties right before the trial began. Sometimes, their cellular phones rang, and they checked messages while the trial was going on.

Prosecutors

Because of their privileges, the prosecutors sometimes could behave differently. As pointed out, one day at the Chengdu court, when the judges entered the courtroom, the prosecutor did not bother to stand up. In another case, the prosecutor took off his uniform when he felt warm during the trial.

Unexpected Others

Besides the regular players, the same problem might arise from unexpected people as well. During one trial at the Chengdu court, one court staff member entered the courtroom, went to a presiding judge, left something on the judge's table, said "I'm taking off," and then left. In the same trial, one legal intern's cellular phone rang, and she made a phone call despite the ongoing trial.

Judges

One would expect judges to take a different role as the representatives of the court system. Unfortunately, their behavior did not appear to be better. First, some judges did not pay much attention to potential issues of conflict of interest before and after the trial. One day at the Chengdu court, while waiting for the defendant, the leading judge borrowed the plaintiff's cellular phone to call the defendant. In another trial at the Qing Yang court, the defendant gave a cigarette to the presiding judge immediately after the trial, and the judge simply took it. Second, in the courtroom, it is not uncommon for judges to put on their uniform in front of waiting parties at the last minute before the trial. During one trial at the Qing Yang court, one presiding judge left the courtroom twice after someone called him to the door. It was also common for presiding judges to exchange opinions among themselves while one party was still making an argument, paying no attention to the party. I also witnessed one presiding judge yawning and reading a newspaper in one trial at the Qing Yang court, and he immediately left the courtroom after the parties finished their closing arguments, but before the leading judge announced the adjournment. Similarly in another case at the Beijing First Court, one presiding judge was yawning and closed her eyes for a couple of minutes. On another day at the Hai Dian court, while one party was making his statement, the sole presiding judge was examining his hand and told the secretary, "It's got a thorn, and does not feel good."

Good Examples

The only good examples were attorneys and defendants in criminal cases. Attorneys are caught with their cellular phones ringing sometimes, but in most cases it appears that they simply forgot to turn the phone off. In general, they know the court procedure and follow it well.

As the most powerless party of all, criminal defendants always showed their respect to the court and to all other parties (e.g., secretaries, prosecutors) as well. Even those who played hardball in court (e.g., totally denying the charges) followed all rules closely. Keep in mind that all players in the courtroom, including judges, prosecutors, and security guards, could "teach" them how to behave properly. Their powerlessness makes them the most obedient party in the courtroom.

Throughout these examples, it is clear that most parties in the courtroom do not treat the court with a high level of dignity and sincere respect. This clearly damages the court's image and its authority. There are a number of reasons for this problem. First, the poor courtroom facilities may create trouble for trials. For instance, the 1st courtroom at the Qing Yang court is used as a passway to transport criminal defendants. In some small courtrooms, there is no block between the parties and the audience so that the supportive audience can easily talk to or pass notes to one party. Second, the use of high-tech communication equipment (e.g., cellular phones) sometimes caused trouble in court. Third, existing official laws and rules do not grant dignity and enough power to the court. Theoretically, it makes no sense to ask a prosecutor to act both as a person presenting a case (a subordinate to judges) and as a supervising official (a superior to judges). This is the reason prosecutors do not stand up when judges enter the courtroom. Fourth, internal official rules sometimes lead to unexpected problems in the court system. Having one charging judge taken main responsibility in one case makes sense because it subdivides the workload. However, I saw one side effect of this in the courtroom: If a judge is not responsible for the case, she or he might be reading a newspaper or taking care of other business even though she or he has to be present. Finally and more important, people still lack a strong notion of the dignity of law. For thousands of years in the Chinese tradition, law and the legal system were secondary to moral education, and people did not want to go to court. Only in the last decade did people start going to court more frequently. Law and the legal system are establishing their authority and professionalism (see Chapter 3), but they still have a long way to go. People's notion of the legal system now is a mixture of hope, question, sometimes distrust, and dismay (especially after failed contacts). All these feelings make people go to the court and rely on the system with certain reservations.[19] If people see the lack of sincerity and seriousness by the court staff (e.g., judges and secretaries), their reaction is going to be negative as well. Lack of dignity and authority is a common problem based on my observation, and it is a serious one. With further systematization of the legal system, it will improve. Nevertheless, people (especially court staff) have to learn how to treat the system seriously with respect and dignity.

Rule of Evidence: Problem With Hearsay

In 1998, there was a huge change in evidence rules. Replacing the old practice in which the court had the responsibility of collecting and presenting evidence, the new rule shifted the burden of proof to the party who brings up the issue in court. The slogan now is "the person who brings up the issue presents evidence" (*shui zhuzhang, shui jiuzheng*). The impact is enormous. One judge, who had worked at the Qing Yang court for 14 years, pointed out this change as a major one in the litigation process: "In the past, judges used to spend a lot of time and energy in collecting evidence. Now we don't worry about 'running and breaking our legs (*pao duan tui*)' any more."

Except for a few evidential rules specified in civil cases, criminal procedures, and administrative litigation laws, however, there is no unified rule of evidence. Many cases I observed were not difficult in nature; nevertheless both sides produced messy evidence. One main problem is the hearsay issue.

The problem with hearsay lies in its lack of trustworthiness, mainly because of the absence of the witness at trial who is claimed to have made the testimony. In the absence of the witness, the opposing party has no way to cross-examine the witness. In the U.S. legal system, hearsay evidence is generally not admissible (with various exceptions), and a witness usually shows up or is deposed to show up at court to buttress his or her testimony. In contrast, a witness's testimony, usually a written report, is admissible at court subject to judges' discretion in China.

In cases I observed, not a single party called a witness at court, and this caused many practical problems. In civil cases, very often after one party presents a piece of evidence, the opposing party raises many questions, such as the relevancy of the evidence and, more important, the trustworthiness of the evidence. In practice, judges either make a quick decision if possible (usually after a brief discussion among themselves), or declare that they have to study more after the trial and will decide the admissibility of the evidence when they make a final ruling. In a few cases, near the end of the trial, the leading judge came back to the evidence issue and declared the final decision based on suggestions of other presiding judges who apparently finished their homework during the trial.

I was so amazed by the process that I tried to clarify this issue with judges. The official answer was that judges have to make decisions based on three criteria: the legality of the evidence, the relevancy test, and the trustworthiness of the evidence. The first two seem simple, but still cause confusion sometimes. For instance, in one case, the presiding judges ruled that one piece of evidence submitted by the defendant was not admissible because it was not relevant to the case. When I brought the example to judges in the research group at the Qing Yang court, one judge agreed with the ruling but another judge questioned it. The most difficult issue is certainly the trustworthiness test. I was told that judges should make their decisions based on other evidence in the case; for example, is there other corroborating evidence to buttress the argued evidence? It seems that this is the best they can do, and the balancing (all evidence) test is usually called a "totality test" in the U.S. system for determining the admissibility of hearsay evidence.

Hearsay evidence is most devastating in criminal cases. In these trials, a prosecutor reads the testimony at hand, such as a police report, a victim's report, or witnesses' and experts' testimony in the evidence presentation phase. The prosecutor is often allowed to read several testimonies in a row before the defendant can question them. Without a pencil and a notebook to jot down key issues (remember sometimes the defendant's hands are cuffed), it is quite a test of the defendant's memory! The impression is that both judges and prosecutors do not expect the defendant to raise questions at all. In a few cases, the prosecutor said, "The next testimony is very similar to the first one, to save time, I'll just summarize it." How could a defendant question the details of the testimony if the defendant does not hear it?

Without the appearance of witnesses, all defendants are deprived of the right of cross-examination. The best they (and the defense attorneys) can do is to point out the discrepancies in the testimony or to deny the untrue part and tell another version. In one case (37) at the Beijing First Court, a female defense attorney did a great job pointing out major differences in two testimonies (from two codefendants), but I could not tell how much weight the presiding judges would assign to her arguments because she could not produce any new evidence to exonerate the defendant.

Most defendants did not realize, apparently, that they had the right of cross-examination. In one case (44) at the Beijing First Court, this issue came up. The defendant was charged with both drug use and selling. He admitted that he used drugs with others at home, but denied that he had sold drugs to others. The prosecutor presented testimony from three witnesses.

The defendant countered that he never knew the first witness (a woman), and he used drugs with the other two, but never sold drugs to them. When all evidence was submitted, the leading judge asked the defendant (as is routine), "Do you have new evidence to submit or new witness to call?" The defendant said, "I want to question the three witnesses, and I want to ask them (questions) face to face." (He was asking for the right of cross-examination, I thought.) However, the judge did not answer the request, but simply repeated his own question (and raised his tone): "Do you have *new* evidence or witnesses?" "No," the defendant answered. The case moved on. This was a sad ending to me, but dramatic.

When I raised this issue, judges in the research group confirmed that it is an old problem, and witnesses are not willing to show up at the court for numerous reasons, such as lack of compensation for travel, fear of retaliation by the defendants, the traditional notion of avoiding courts (trouble) as much as possible, and lack of mandatory power by the court to depose the witness. The appearance of the witness not only gives the opposing party a fair chance to examine the trustworthiness of the testimony, but also makes the trial much easier by reducing sloppy evidence. Moreover, it decreases the possibility of anyone committing perjury against a party, and it works as an extra safeguard against the police's violation of legal procedures.[20] In recent years, efforts have been made to encourage the appearance of witnesses in court. For example, police officers and investigators started testifying in court,[21] and some local courts enacted rules to ensure compensation (e.g., travel expenses) for witnesses' appearance.[22] On April 1, 2002, the Regulations on Rules of Evidence in Civil Litigations published by the SPC went into effect, encouraging the appearance of witnesses in court.[23] Despite such efforts, it was reported in 2006 that in some local courts, less than 1% of witnesses who should have testified at trial testified![24]

Formality Versus Informality: Mediation as a Necessary Part in the Court System

It would be better to start with my first court experience as an example. It was early on a Monday morning. The case (1), a divorce case, had already begun when I entered the courtroom. The husband and the wife, both very young, were not sitting in the reserved seats for the plaintiff and the defendant. Rather, the husband and his relatives sat on the right side (from the judge's position) of the audience seats, and the wife and her relatives on the left side. In the center, the secretary was taking notes. The judge, not sitting behind his table, was standing beside the secretary. The issue by then was not divorce, but division of assets. Without a property list, the judge simply went over each important item that both sides argued for. The judge intended to give the wife an old TV, but the husband held a different opinion, saying, "I want fairness." The judge cited the Marriage Law first: "It (the law) requires that in divorce cases, women and children should be accorded special care to some extent." Then he continued, "X, you as a big man, why do you fuss about it? . . . I know that it is not because of the TV. It is just that you cannot vent the air . . . Think about it. Be rational. The marriage is over now, and we are here to solve problems, not to argue." (It was interesting to notice that his voice went up and down very effectively.) He paused a while and tried more, "X, is it OK? (We) don't want to quit because of this, right? Talk to your relatives, (and) let's get it over." Under such pressure, the husband finally agreed. The trial moved on to another issue. The husband borrowed some money from friends for his sick father while he and his wife were still together, and he wanted to know if the borrowed money was counted as "common debt" that should be shared by the wife legally. The judge explained, "In principle, you borrowed the money while you were in marriage, and the female party should have a shared obligation to pay it. However, your marriage is too short (they had been married for only a few months)." The husband was not satisfied and asked again, "Is it (borrowed money) 'common debt' based on law?" The judge repeated his explanation and concluded this time, "Because your marriage is so short, it doesn't count as 'common debt.'" After that, the rest of trial went pretty smoothly. Finally, the judge conducted a moral education in his closing: "OK, this is it. Finally, I do have a few words . . . First, I hope both sides do not show anger at each other. You choose a divorce voluntarily . . . Second, parents of both sides shall not scold the child. A divorce is common today, and they are still very young. It is likely that they will find more suitable partners in the future. So, be understanding. On the other hand, you, as children, should understand your parents . . . and wish you both find suitable partners in future."

In this case, the judge clearly went outside of the legal boundary in solving problems and used a bit of everything such as the manhood principle, the persuasion of the relatives, the willingness of both sides to get things over, and psychological tactics to "vent the air" of both sides and to focus on "real issues." Without case law in hand, the judge explained the "common debt" issue in a way that made it acceptable to both parties (on the basis that the husband had to take it as law). Finally, the moral education clearly went beyond his legal duty and was aimed at solving social problems with the help of his legal position.[25] To a large extent, the nature of the case, a divorce case, made the judicial mediation more convincing and effective.

Gradually, I found that judicial mediation is involved in every single civil case, and it is indeed a formal part of the trial process.[26] Usually immediately after the trial, the leading judge will say, "Now, as a routine, based on the principle of voluntariness, the court is seeking any possibility of reconciliation between two parties. Plaintiff, do you prefer reconciliation? Defendant, how about you?" If there is a positive answer, the judges will try hard to push both sides to reach an agreement, and the pressure applied by judges sometimes has a great impact. In one administrative litigation case (3) at the Chengdu court, the plaintiff was suing a local police department for an arm injury caused by the police. At the end of the trial, the plaintiff turned down the mediation offer by the court and requested a court ruling and an apology from the police department. After the trial, the leading judge approached the plaintiff and pushed more: "As my personal advice, if you were cooled down (by the time the physical confrontation happened), it (the result) would not have been like this. It is legal (for the police) to ask for your ID. Mediation is the best way (to solve the problem). You are going to need their (the police's) help in future. 140,000 yuan (what the plaintiff requested) is too much. The police department has already paid you 28,000 yuan, and that's not a small number. (Let's) focus on the true issue here, alright? What do you say?" The plaintiff finally changed his mind and said "OK." Eventually the parties failed to agree on the amount on that day (I do not know what happened next). In this example, mediation went on even if the official trial was ended. The leading judge went very far trying to push the plaintiff, and she probably did not realize that she violated the basic principles of a fair trial. She expressed her personal opinions about the case (e.g., the police search was legal, the plaintiff was partially responsible, and the requested 140,000 yuan was not acceptable) before the judge panel reached an official ruling.

Despite of a number of potential problems in its practice (see, e.g., Peerenboom, 2002a), the advantage of mediation is obvious. Because an agreement is reached by both parties, there is little possibility for an appeal. Mediation saves parties' time and energy and reduces the court's workload (e.g., the court no longer needs to worry about confusing evidence and how to reach a ruling). It is clear that in some cases, both parties were perfectly ready for mediation even before the trial. However, they would still prefer doing it in the courtroom. One day in another divorce case (6), a couple entered the courtroom, and both felt uncomfortable with the formality of the trial process. Indeed they joked about it with the judge and got a amicable divorce with no arguments at all (the husband left all property to the wife). The judge was a bit surprised too, and told them, "It (an amicable divorce without any argument) is very rare like you." When I asked the judge afterward why the couple did not go through a normal administrative divorce process, the judge explained, "It is easier to get a divorce here. As soon as a divorce is ruled, it becomes effective immediately. There is no hassle here. You have to go through many steps if you go to the civil administrative organizations."[27]

In one loan conflict case (5) at the Chengdu court, the defendant (an attorney representing a company) did not deny a loan had occurred, but asked for an extended time to pay it off. Both parties immediately worked on how to come up with a viable payment plan. All (female) judges were very active, suggesting payment methods and calculating numbers. As soon as both parties reached a tentative result, the leading judge asked the attorney to call and finalize the payment with his client over his cellular phone. Obviously, she wanted to get it done right away. In mediations like this, the court is acting as a catalyst, and it is the court's authority and legal protection that the parties are seeking in their mediation.

Based on my observation, however, most cases in courts failed to reach an agreement. When judges see clearly that there is no way both parties can reach reconciliation, they would say, "Because the divergence (between two parties) is too large, this court is not going to try mediation at this moment." Apparently, in most cases parties fight all the way through the trial, and if there is a possibility of reconciliation, fewer cases would arise in the first place.

One final word about reconciliation is the complete lack of it (plea bargaining) in criminal cases. Consistent with the practice of the civil legal tradition, the notion is that any settlement between the prosecutor and the defendant (*kongbian jiaoyi*) is against the principle of justice in China. After I gave a talk at the Chengdu court, a heated discussion arose on this issue. A vice president of the court clearly expressed his dissatisfaction with the idea of "making a deal with the devils." In most of the criminal cases I observed, defendants plainly admitted their guilt and put up no defense. The effect is that all parties have to go through the trial even if the result is predetermined. One day at the Hai Dian court, as soon as a trial was over, the female prosecutor said, "There is no need at all for trials like this," and then left. It seems that if a settlement practice were introduced into the criminal system, it would save the time and energy of the parties involved and allow the court to focus on more controversial cases.

Substantive Versus Procedural Justice

For a long time, the Chinese legal system has been criticized as one without a guaranty for individuals' human rights. One such a focus is on the lack of necessary procedural protections. This issue has a close connection with another issue discussed earlier, the lack of dignity and sincerity in court. I witnessed many instances of them; most of them were minor issues but had bad implications. For instance, at the Hai Dian court, due to the capacity of the small rooms, it was very common for several defendants in different cases to be seated on the same bench and go through the trials one by one. Sometimes multiple defendants were tried at the same time in the same room, and apparently the court did not consider the issue of conflicts of interest between codefendants. In a sentencing (38) at the Beijing First Court, the impatient judge did not want to wait for a late defense attorney and announced the sentences anyway. In several cases, the judges were obviously in a hurry and blatantly interrupted parties' statements by saying, "Do you have a new argument? We have to save time."

To save time, what prosecutors usually do in criminal cases is to summarize the testimony rather than read them verbatim. Sometimes, judges do not even bother to show or turn the testimony over to the defendants and defense attorneys for cross-examination. In several cases, defendants brought up the "old issue" that they were beaten physically at the police station for a confession. No one, however, could produce any physical evidence in court.[28]

The most dramatic instance happened at the Hai Dian court. It was a Wednesday afternoon. Three criminal cases (51, 52, 53) were tried in the same courtroom, and all three defendants were seated on the same bench. The first case ended around 2:45, and the female prosecutor charging the first case left. All other parties were waiting for the next male prosecutor, who was delayed by another case next door. One female professional judge and two female people's assessors made up the judge panel. After about 10 minutes, one people's assessor asked the professional judge, "Could we try it ourselves?" To my surprise, the judge answered, "Alright, let's begin." She took the file from the prosecutor's desk, announced the opening of the case, and started reading the indictment. I was shocked. What would the case be when the presiding judge is also acting as the prosecutor? Is she going to go for a conviction or rule the case evenhandedly? A few minutes later, the male prosecutor showed up. He smiled to the judge and said, "Let me read it. I read faster." Then he took over the file and finished the case more quickly indeed by summarizing most of the testimony.

Violations of fair trial procedures (especially in criminal cases) are numerous and in various forms. No party seemed to take them seriously. The main justification is that these violations have nothing to do with substantive issues. In fact, in more than 90% of the cases I observed, the defendants plainly admitted their guilt and put up no defense except a plea for lenience. In other words, these procedural errors are harmless, and eventually there will be a conviction. This notion is consistent with Chinese legal tradition, which puts more emphasis on substantive justice than procedural justice. However, some legal scholars in China have started criticizing this dichotomy and arguing for more protection on procedural justice.[29] At the current stage, the court and the prosecution are playing the same card, and the only check from defense attorneys is not fully guaranteed by laws. It is going to take a long time to make substantial changes[30] and to realize the error in the following scenario: Again at the Hai Dian court, the secretary asked the defendants before the trial, "Do you admit (your guilt)?" "Yes, yes," the defendants answered.

Judge Panel and Internal Review System

Except in cases applying simplified procedures, a judge panel is required for all other cases. The main reason for using a judge panel is based on the belief that "two (or even three) heads are better than one." Absent empirical research on actual differences between the one-judge trial and the judge panel trial, some legal scholars in China compared the judge panel system in China with the single-judge system in other nations (see, e.g., Su-li, 2000; L. Wang, 2001). The comparison showed that the single-judge system is not necessarily less efficient, and it does not necessarily produce more mistakes.

My own observations tend to show that the judge panel may not actually be working as a panel as planned. I have discussed the internal division of labor among three judges. It was common to see that only one judge was following and reading the single copy of the file, and the other judges had no copies in hand. Without extra copies, how could the other two judges follow the parties' statements? I also witnessed judges reading a newspaper, working on another case, or taking a nap at trials. All these instances not only point to the mediocre quality of judges, but they also show that the judge panel may be only a formality (as noticed recently by Y. Li, 2002). Without access to see how the panel makes its final decisions, I cannot draw further conclusions.

There is one more function of the judge panel, though. Because the decision is made collectively, everyone is responsible for mistakes. This collective nature reduces the burden on each judge's shoulders and gives the panel more bargaining power with their superiors if necessary. This is consistent with the internal court review system. It is well known, and admitted by judges I talked with, that inside the court system, there is a hierarchy not only administratively but also professionally. Administratively, each superior level of judges enjoys power over their subordinates. Professionally, the judge panel has to report any major decision or difficult cases (e.g., when the panel has major divergent opinions) to the chief judge of the department; the chief judge then reports to the charging president of the Court (*zhuguan yuanzhang*), who reports the case to the Adjudication Committee of the Court (*shenpan weiyuanhui*). It is very likely that the final ruling in these cases was made not by the judge panel, but by a higher level review group, and this is called "the trial judges not rule, the ruling judges not try (the case)" (*shenzhe bupan, panzhe bushen*; C. Wang & Zhang, 1997; Woo, 2000). Sometimes, due to the influence of the higher authorities, a predetermined verdict has been reached even before the official trial starts, and this problem is recognized as "verdict first, trial second" (*xian pan hou shen*; Clark & Feinerman, 1996; Lubman, 1999; H. Tanner, 1994b; C. Wang & Zhang, 1997; Woo, 1999).

In an interview, one male attorney, Mr. Li, who used to work at the Chengdu court, related to me a case in which he was sitting as the leading judge. It was a business dispute case between an investor from Hong Kong and a local partner. The business was very successful, but the local partner concealed the profit and did not give the investor his share. Somehow the investor found out the truth, sued the partner in court, and asked the court to freeze the assets and save all potential evidence. The partner, now a famous business company in the local area, began to seek various extralegal means (e.g., looking for "connections" in courts and other administrative organizations) to delay and influence the case ruling. In addition, the legal representative of the local company was elected as a representative in the NPC, and the pressure from his activities was increased. On the other side, the investor was working on favorable "connections" as well, petitioning the government of Sichuan province through an Overseas Investors' Association, and asked for the protection of his interests. From 1996 to 1999, the case was tried three times, and was reported to the president of the Court, to the adjudication committee of the Chengdu court, and to the adjudication committee of the Sichuan High Court. As Mr. Li summarized, "The final result is no longer important here, but you can see clearly that seeking for extra means (*goudui* in Sichuan dialect) has such an impact on the final outcome, the court is not independent, and the presiding judges in the panel have no final ruling power."

In his research, Su-li (2000) took on different arguments and pointed out that most judges believe that the existence of the adjudication committee does not affect the way they rule cases, and the adjudication committee brings more benefits than costs in practice. According to those judges interviewed by Su-li, the adjudication committee first may help reduce bribery and corruption. The logic is that the briber may be able to buy one or two judges, but it will be difficult to get to all members of the committee. Second, the committee has a role in standardizing the court rulings and raising the quality of judges (cf. discussions by Brown, 1997; J. Chen, 1999). Third, the committee may help judges defend potential persuaders and the collective nature gives them more bargaining power. In my interview, Mr. Li pointed out that the internal review system (the hierarchical control) could be a price that has to be paid when the court system as a whole is competing for its own independence from controls by other (national) administrative branches. In other words, the internal organization is necessary if the organization as a whole wants to compete effectively with other outside organizations. If those observations are accurate, the internal review system will exist for an extended time, even if the court is taking measures to reduce the hierarchical control and review.[31]

Law Versus Justice

In her court studies, Merry (1990) found a disjunction between the law as it is in the legal system and the notions of justice in court-goers' minds. People who initiate court services have problems, not cases. They have to learn how to translate their problems into practicable legal doctrines in cases at trials. Unfortunately, this is not always easy due to the bureaucratic nature of the legal system.

Formalistically, judges often have to listen patiently to confusing stories told by both parties and summarize their problems as legal issues. I did witness some cases in which high-quality attorneys did an excellent job, and the trial went very smoothly. More often, however, judges have to shoulder part of the attorneys' functions in the courtroom.

Substantively, some parties who have problems simply cannot convert them into a legal language. In one appeal (20), the appellant, a businesswoman, sought to reverse the trial court's decision and sued her attorney for overcharging in his representation. Apparently, she hired the attorney in a loan dispute, signed a contract, and agreed to pay the attorney 15% of the recovered property. The attorney asked the trial court to freeze some properties (machine engines) during the money collection process, and eventually these engines were collected as recovered property for the money owed. Unfortunately, the value of the machine engines quickly depreciated due to market changes. Seeing the depreciation, the lady refused to pay her attorney. In the district court, the lady lost her case, and she lost again at the Chengdu court in the appeal. In her closing argument, she argued, "I have lost both money (because of the depreciation) and the case, and it doesn't feel that's the right way." However, she could not win legal support for this unfortunate result.

Similarly, in another appellate case (45) at the Beijing First Court, about 90 families in a village sued the village committee and land contractors for coaxing them into contracts in which the villagers sold their land at an unfairly low price. It was quite a scene to see villagers from 90 families swarm into one big hall and argue for their land rights. They did not hire attorneys, but tried their best, with difficulty, to point out how the village committee and land contractors avoided required procedures (e.g., convening a general meeting in the village) and coaxed them into contracts. The appellate court had a very tough time simply getting excited villagers organized in the courtroom, and the leading judge had to ask security guards to escort several troublemakers out of the courtroom to restore order. I do not know the final ruling in the case, but it is very likely that the appellate court will uphold the trial court's decision on the basis that these villagers agreed to sign the contracts. This is the effect of the law. Poor peasants may well have been coaxed into unfair contracts, but they still might have lost their legal battle in court.

Sometimes the legal argument turned into a moral argument. In one case (23) at the Chengdu court, a young man was suing his former workplace, a shoe factory, for legal compensation. He used to work as a security guard and got injured when he was trying to break up a fight. Both parties went through arbitration, but the plaintiff was not satisfied with the arbitration result and brought the factory to court. An old man (a lay citizen) was representing the plaintiff, and a young female attorney was representing the factory. Both knew each other well by then, and they even chatted a little before the trial. During the trial, the female attorney asked the appellate court to throw out the plaintiff's request for the injury subsidy. Apparently, at the district court, the judges asked the plaintiff whether he was requesting the lost wages or the injury subsidy, and the plaintiff chose the lost wages. Immediately, the female attorney asked the secretary to put it down in the record. Now, technically, as the female attorney insisted, the injury subsidy was a new issue that could not be brought up at the appellate court. The presiding judges were very reluctant to throw out the request (because it possibly would come back, and they would rather handle it once). However, their effort to persuade the female attorney failed, and they had to take a break to discuss how to handle it. During the short recess, the old man was very angry, and scolded the female attorney for being unethical: "You have to uphold justice. I have practiced law for more than 10 years, and I have never done anything like this." He further elaborated on how sad and difficult a situation the plaintiff had been in (e.g., no money to go to the hospital), and emphasized again, "Being a lawyer needs to have a sense of justice." Unfortunately, after the break, the judges had to agree with the defense attorney and throw out the new request. The old man's moral argument could not change legal technical rules.

Finally, the legal weapon is never an elixir, and sometimes it simply cannot "cure" the problems people have. The saddest case (32) happened at the Qing Yang court. A 21-year-old woman died in a traffic accident, and her parents were suing the defendant (either the driver or a company that hired the driver; this was unclear from the trial) for compensation. It seemed that most parties, including the judges, the defendant, and the legal representative of the parents, knew very well that the result could only be a matter of compensation, and they wanted to move on to the mediation stage. The heartbroken mother did not fully understand what mediation was and burst into tears. The judges showed little patience and kept asking the plaintiff, "Do you agree? Yes or no? Be straight." Under such pressure, the father gave permission for mediation, and the legal representative went up to the defendant and they started working on numbers (i.e., money). The mother was left aside, crying and talking about her daughter first to the judges (no response) and then to me (the only audience). I was speechless and sympathetic, but unable to offer any help.

CONCLUSION AND IMPLICATIONS

In this chapter, I focused on the current court system based on my field research. My court experience was extremely fascinating, and it was indeed a learning process. I tried to explain what I observed and learned, such as the court structure, active players, and some main issues that I had been thinking about. Although I presented each element individually, these elements were intertwined in a dynamic way. For example, the current court structure (both external and internal) limits the functions of major players and leads to some of the major issues discussed.

There are a number of implications for current court reforms, which would be better understood within the general structure as laid out in previous chapters. First, court reform becomes a major part of the legalization process. Through means such as professionalization, the court system has been gaining more power and prestige in society. An increasing number of people go to court to fight for their individual rights and interests. It is foreseeable that the role of the court will keep growing in the future. How to adjust the roles of different players inside the court system as well as the relationship of the court with other branches in the legal system is an important question. For instance, the privileged status of the prosecutor in the courtroom definitely needs to be adjusted to grant and guarantee more authority to judges and meaningfully protect legal rights for parties (e.g., defendants in criminal cases).

Second, the legalization process has to be studied in a broader context, as part of political reform. Political and financial restraints on the court system from both the local government and the central government inhibit the judicial independence of the court and the normal functioning of its daily work (see, e.g., discussions by Brown, 1997; Lubman, 2000). The CCP is trying to use legalization as a means to regain and relegitimize its authority and power in the new era and to save its one-party political control at the same time. Once this is understood, it becomes easier to grasp the limitations of the current court reforms (e.g., the internal review system).

Third, the development of the court system definitely bears certain Chinese characteristics due to the influence of Chinese traditions, such as the combination of adjudication and mediation (Lubman, 1999). Those Chinese characteristics do not necessarily work against effective functioning of the court system, and they are sometimes called domestic resources (*bentu ziyuan*). How to treat those domestic resources in the building of the court system is another question, especially when the court system is absorbing foreign elements (see works by Chinese domestic scholars such as Huang, 2000; Su-li, 2000).This brings us to the fourth and final point, the connection with the global system. The connection of the Chinese legal system with other nations' systems has definitely increased along with China's integration into the global system. The most recent prominent example is China's acceptance into the WTO in 2001 and its impact on the domestic legal system (see Chapter 5). China is adjusting its laws to international standards, and it is also learning technical lessons from other nations (e.g., general rules of evidence,[32] civil pretrial procedures,[33] and a unified civil code[34]). With further integration into the global system, how China's domestic legal system responds to international standards and absorbs foreign elements is another interesting question worthy of further study.

7 Conclusion

This research has studied the changing Chinese legal system through analyses of China's political economy over time. It has focused on the rebuilding and the functions of the legal system both conceptually and substantively in the new era within the context of the global system. In this concluding chapter, I summarize my substantive chapters first and try to put them into a systematic framework. Then I draw some implications and highlight potential contributions for future studies. More specifically, I discuss the nature of China's socialist market economy, the role of China's legalization, and its functions within the scope of political reform.

SUMMARY OF SUBSTANTIVE CHAPTERS

In Figure 7.1, I integrate Chapters 2 through 6 into a conceptual framework. It is those interactions among different systems (e.g., economic, legal, political) at different levels (macro vs. micro, local vs. national vs. global) that guided my research and organized my discussions. I started with the change of the economic base in China in Chapter 2. Since 1978, dramatic changes have been made to improve productive forces and adjust new economic relations. Various nonpublic economic activities reemerged, and the market economy gradually replaced the planned economy. Although the economic base has been dramatically changed, the Chinese government still claims that China is a socialist country through a series of reinterpretations of Marxism. It is these reinterpretations that incorporated those new changes that were unthinkable in the old days.

Along with economic changes, legal and political reforms were carried out in the new era, a topic that I addressed in Chapter 3. The Chinese government has been making efforts toward legalization through means such as systemization and professionalization. As I argued, however, China's legal reform should be studied within a larger picture (i.e., the ongoing political reform). Legalization becomes a new means for the Chinese government to regain and relegitimize its power and authority in the new era.

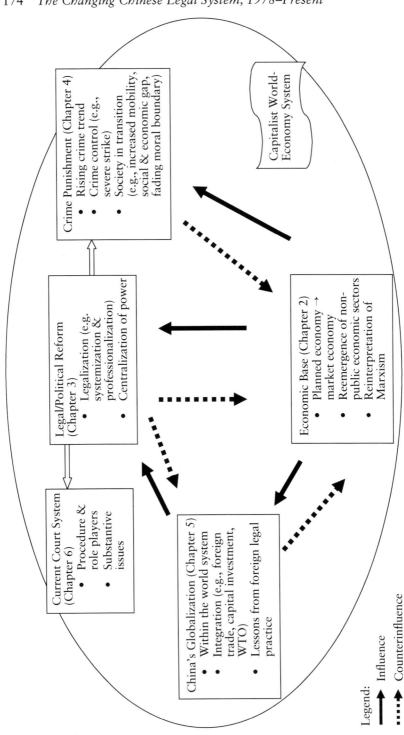

Legend:

⬆ Influence

⇒ Counterinfluence

Figure 7.1 China's legalization within the global system: A conceptual framework.

In Chapter 4, I focused on one main function of the legal system, crime control and punishment. Despite its strengthened legal system, China still suffered from rising crime in the new era. To curb the ascending crime trend, the Chinese government took various actions, including the severe strike campaign as the most salient one, to control and punish crimes. The effects of these approaches, however, are highly questionable in the current transitional era when Chinese society has experienced increased mobility, social and economic inequality, and fading traditional moral values.

In Chapter 5, I examined China's economic, political, and legal reforms from a global perspective. The process of China's integration in globalization has been increased along with the development of the global system in general. China's integration is evident by its increased foreign trade and foreign capital investment and its entry into the WTO in 2001. Based on the world-economy theory, China is increasingly becoming part of the capitalist world economic system despite its ostensibly socialist nature.

Finally in Chapter 6, I focused on one main branch of the legal system, the judicial system, and reported my field research. In the reform era, the role of the court system has been expanded significantly. For example, the total number of cases accepted by the courts of the first instance increased from less than half a million in 1978 to more than 5.5 million by 1999 (see Chapter 3). To respond to the increasing need, court reform has become very popular. My court observations suggest that the major changes described in previous chapters at the macro level are all reflected in the current judicial system. The court system is moving toward systemization and seeking more power and relative independence both internally and externally. Traditional influences, such as preferences for mediation (over litigation) and substantive justice (over procedural justice) and the lack of respect (from the masses) and guaranteed power (from the national political structure), however, still have major influences on the building and daily operation of the current judicial system.

IMPLICATIONS AND CONTRIBUTIONS OF THIS RESEARCH

Nature of China's Socialist Market Economy

In 1949 China declared itself a socialist nation along with other socialist allies. Consistent with orthodox Marxism, the Chinese government tried to convert the old economic structure into a socialist one based on public ownership under a planned economy in the following decades. The socialist practices by these allied nations, however, struggled, and the struggles led to various reforms (both economically and politically) in the 1980s and 1990s, and even to the demise of a number of socialist governments (e.g., the former Soviet Union and a number of Eastern European nations).

In such a context, China seemed to have made a 180-degree turn after its economic reform in 1978. Nonpublic modes of production were revived and thrived in the next 25 years, while the stagnating SOEs struggled to keep their dominance. Various means of capital accumulation, production, and management were borrowed from capitalist nations, and in 1993 the socialist market economy formally replaced the old planned economy. Given those dramatic changes in China and the setback of socialist nations within the global context, an obvious question arises about the fate of China's socialist practice, especially the nature of the new market economy.

For a long time, based on orthodox Marxism, Chinese people believed that there would be, as a historical transitional period, a linear (or spiral but eventually linear in nature) development from capitalism to socialism and eventually to communism (see Figure 7.2(1)). Although there were different understandings about particular characteristics and functions of the Asiatic mode of production (e.g., China's economic mode) within the scope of Marxism, there was a consensus among scholars (and politicians) in China on the eventual triumph of communism (see Z. Hu, 1989; Lin, 1989; Y. Wang, 1989; D. Wu, 1989). After the economic reform, the CCP proposed a new stage, the preliminary stage, for China's socialism in 1987. This new interpretation allowed China to move backward (e.g., taking advantage of capitalistic means of production) and paved the way for the establishment of China's market economy (see Figure 7.2(2)).

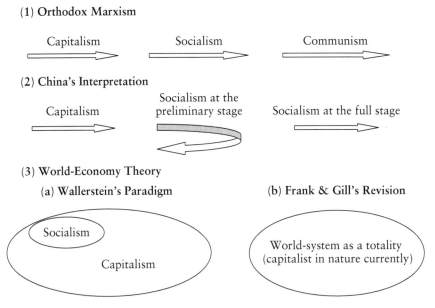

Figure 7.2 Capitalism vs. socialism.

As a matter of fact, the term socialist market economy was not created solely by the Chinese government. Seeing the failure of communist models all over the world, scholars already had started to study the impact of introducing market incentives into socialist economies in the 1990s (see Bardhan & Roemer, 1993; Boswell & Chase-Dunn, 2000; Ollman & Schweichart, 1998; Roemer, 1994, 1996; Schweichart, Lawler, Ticktin, & Ollman, 1998). China's practice as well as reforms in other nations indeed provided sources for scholars' analyses.

Theoretically, scholars hold divergent opinions about the feasibility of so-called market socialism. One key issue is how to assess the changing definition of socialism (or what makes socialism different from capitalism). For a long time, public ownership, planned economy, and collective production (for social use rather than profit) were believed to be key characteristics of a socialist economy. The adoption of a market economy, nevertheless, blurred the traditional boundaries between socialist nations and capitalist nations. For example, when proposing his idea about the practice of market socialism, Roemer (1993) backed off from adamantly stressing public ownership and put more emphasis on institutional guarantee of the equal distribution of aggregate profits.

In China, we see a pattern after the reform. First, the domination of public ownership gave way to nonpublic economic activities. The share of the SOEs had been shrinking in many aspects such as number of enterprises, number of the employed, gross output values, and average wages for workers. In some major cities, nonpublic ownership laborers already outnumbered workers in public sectors. Reforms were touted to keep the quality (rather than quantity) advantage of public ownership in the socialist market economy, although no specific answer was provided as to how to maintain the advantage. Second, the market economy already had triumphed over the planned economy. After dropping the distinction between socialism and capitalism with regard to the utilization of the market economy, the Chinese government quickly employed market advantages. Although the residual of central planning (e.g., the ARA practice) is still lingering, the government has made it clear that further reforms will remove such controls. Third, along with the economic reform, capitalistic concepts such as private property, exploitation, and alienation reemerged in China. For example, unearned income that does not come from one's labor is now justified and encouraged. As a result, Chinese society has been increasingly commercialized (Davis, 2000). Finally, Chinese society has been stratified economically since the reform. Income inequality has increased between different occupations, and it has been aggravated by political, disparate treatments based on geographical locations and arbitrary separation between the urban and the rural. All these factors led to changes in people's social status in the new market economy. In short, the pattern emerging after the reform appears to indicate that China is moving away from the long assumed socialist model and toward a capitalist model.

Despite the CCP's reinterpretations of Marxism, two major factors probably were underestimated. First, proposers and practitioners of market socialism did not take sufficient account of the logic and force of the market (with innate capitalist characteristics). The presumably controllable market may well turn out to be uncontrollable under the blueprint of market socialism and therefore change the nature of the system (see, e.g., such arguments by Ollman in Schweichart et al., 1998). Second, and more important, the power of the global capitalist system was underestimated. Scholars studying the world economy have long warned of the danger that socialist economies are likely to be transitional to capitalism under the influence of the global system (see, e.g., Frank, 1980). Under the influence of the worldwide system, various modes of production, including the socialist mode of economy (especially in the periphery areas), become important forms of capitalist exploitation and indeed serve the capitalist world-economy (Chase-Dunn, 1982, 1989; Hopkins & Wallerstein, 1982; see Figure 7.2(3)). Frank and Gills (1993) further expanded the world-economy structure and argued that it existed even before the emergence of the capitalist economic system. It is the world system as a totality with the nature of the capitalist system that dominates the world economy at the current stage (see Figure 7.2(3)). In such a system, China is no exception.

China's increasing integration into the global system and its entry into the WTO in 2001 seemed consistent with the world-economy theory. Along with its improved understanding of the global system, China has gone through a transition from passively being pulled into the system to actively participating in the system. In recent years the Chinese government played the globalization card actively for its political gains and paid less attention to ideological labels. As a result, the question about the fate of China's socialist practice and its market economy becomes a set of questions about the nature of China's market economy and on the fate of socialism in general and socialism in China in particular. Given the evidence we can gather now, some answers are clear: for example, China is moving away from the old socialist model and toward a capitalist model under the impact of the global system. Some answers are still not evident: For example, will the so-called market socialism transform into full-scale socialism or into full-scale capitalism? The study of China's political economy (as a third-world, peripheral, socialist nation) provides meaningful resources for those questions.

Legalization Process and Its Necessity

Once the economic base was changed, the next question is about possible alternatives in the superstructure. More specifically in this study, one may ask what are possible changes in the Chinese legal system? What is the function of legal reform in China's transition?

Allow me to start with the second question first. Although the economic base (under orthodox Marxism) and the global system (under the world-economy paradigm) have a determinative impact on the development of individual states, scholars have paid increasing attention to the role that a state can play in maneuvering its own system in the process of capital accumulation and operation within the global system (see, e.g., Chase-Dunn, 1982; Girling, 1987). In this analysis, China turns out to be an interesting case. We have seen its political power both at the domestic and the global levels. Globally, China has been controlling its integration pace for its economic and political needs. Domestically, China has been adjusting its structures to maintain its political stability and embrace more changes. In recent years, this adjustment has been completed mainly through the process of legalization.

First, the legalization process becomes a new means for the CCP to relegitimize its authority and power control. As Chinese society changes from a dominantly self-sufficient and agricultural economy under planned administrative policies to an industrialized, open, and commercialized market economy, the old political and ideological control based on the *Zu* and local culture under the rule of man begins to lose its effectiveness and legitimacy. A new means of social control based on a legitimate legal system becomes more appealing (Gong et al., 1999; Zuo & Zhuo, 2000). Theoretically, this power transition corresponds to Weber's analyses of the authority legitimacy transition from one based on a traditional power or a charismatic personal authority to one based on rational legal rules. Although different from the Western model of the rule of law, the CCP is using the "rule by law" as the new means and ideology to justify its political control and governance.

Second, consistent with Weberian theory, the establishment of governance by law and the legal system is inherently connected with capitalist economic operations and functions. When the economic structure in China shifted toward a capitalist model after the reform, an effective legal system was necessary to adjust new relationships among people, business entities, and the government. The legalization process ensures the successful function of the new market economy when substantive economic and political rights are granted to the Chinese people as individual citizens. Each citizen now becomes a legal subject or object, counters local illegitimate controls (from both powerful cadres and organizations), and responds to the central state as the supreme, legitimate authority.

Third, the legalization process recentralizes the power for the Chinese government. In the reform years, decentralization has become a very popular term in China and has been expanded from the economic domain to administrative and legal domains. I call for caution, however, in such expansions. The Chinese government has adopted the legal reform as a new means of governing national affairs, and an effective legal system will counter illegitimate local control (e.g., local protectionism) and give the central government more power and authority. The key is how the center employs the power throughout the legal system.

Fourth, political and legal reform is necessary for China's further integration into the global system. The nation's entry into the WTO in 2001 provided another impetus for China's domestic reform. The Chinese government aims to use both economic and legal changes to strengthen its political and social control and save its one-party political system at home. The integration into the global capitalist system, however, is a double-edged sword and provides both opportunities and challenges to the CCP. On the one hand, it may provide new ways for the CCP to relegitimize its political and legal control through successful transitions; on the other hand, further integration into the global system may erode the CCP's ideology and eventually threaten its one-party control.

In sum, I argue that one reason for the failure of socialist practices in the second half of the 20th century is that socialist nations failed to propose and establish an effective political and legal entity as the superstructure. Many political structures in socialist nations were criticized as authoritarian, tyrannical, or something even worse. In no way were these polities close to the predicted socialist democracy that ensures common wealth and individuals' self-realization. There is a great need for further study of both the economic and the political and legal structures of socialism if socialism will ever survive.

Legalization Process and Its Characteristics

Now go back to the first question posed earlier: What are the changes to China's legal system? What are the characteristics of those changes?

First, China's legalization is being carried out through a process of systemization and professionalization. In recent years, emphases have been put on the openness, fairness, and efficiency of the system along with political reforms. In the judicial system, for example, trials and case documents[1] have been opened to the public. In February 2001, the annual work report by the Shenyang Intermediate People's Court failed to get enough votes (50%) to pass in the fourth meeting of the local people's congress in Shenyang, Liaoning province. The report was eventually approved in August after revisions.[2] This incident signaled a significant change in Chinese legal history. For a long time, local people's congresses were viewed as a rubber stamp, and there were few challenges to the local government, the court, and the procuratorate. This incident showed increasing participation by people's representatives, their determination to execute their political rights and power, and their expectations for the court system in the new era.

Second, as summarized by Mr. Li, a lawyer in Chengdu, China's legalization will have to keep enhancing citizens' human rights. His assertion is critical in four aspects. First, this call is consistent with the requirements of the market economy. When societal structure is becoming more complex with an increased division of labor, new laws are necessary to regulate and protect individual rights. In the last few years, one heated issue was legal protection of private property, and the suggestion gained a wide range of support. In 2004, the amended Constitution for the first time added a new article that guarantees legal protection of private property.[3] On March 16, 2007, the NPC passed a new property law (*wuquan fa* in Chinese) on the final day of its annual 2-week session, which provides sweeping protection for private businesses and property. This new law, finally adopted after 14 years of discussions and revisions, aims to broaden Constitutional protection for private business and property.[4] Second, legal protection also can be a direct and effective means to guarantee citizens' rights against infringements from other individuals, entities, and the government. The enactments of both the Administrative Litigation Law and the State Compensation Law are efforts to serve such purposes. Legal scholars called for more constitutional amendments on human rights protections.[5] Third, the protection of human rights is closely related to other legal practices, especially in criminal proceedings. As reported, from 1998 to 2002, 29,521 charged criminal defendants were found innocent by the courts, a 50% increase from the previous 5-year period.[6] Given China's legal tradition, this is a significant change. Finally, the protection of human rights is consistent with international standards at a time when China is speeding up its integration into the global system. Many scholars indeed called for further improvement on protections of citizens' rights in the wake of China's entry into the WTO.[7] To answer such a call, the amended 2004 Constitution for the first time adopted the exact wording of "human rights" in Article 33, which provides that "the State respects and preserves human rights."

Third, the process of legalization is inherently embedded with characteristics of Chinese legal traditions. There is no definitive answer as to the impact of these characteristics on the legal system. Some of them seem to have a negative effect. For example, based on my court observation, people's lack of respect for the authority of the court system, the traditional preference of substantive justice over procedural justice, and the hierarchal administrative connection between the court system and other governmental branches (e.g., lack of sufficient independence) all seemed to cast shadows on the building and operation of the judicial system. On the other hand, some characteristics seem to have positive effects. Take the practice of people's mediation and judicial mediation as an example. The practice of (people's) mediation was long favored in Chinese legal history, and it was indeed strengthened by the CCP when the function of the formal legal system was weakened in the prereform era (Lubman, 1999). After the reform, while the legal system was being rebuilt, the power of mediation seemed to be reduced. In about 25 years, as shown by Figure 7.3, the number of cases accepted by the courts increased, but the number of cases solved through mediation decreased from more than 8 million in 1982 to less than 4.5 million by 2003. In the new millennium, the total number of cases handled by courts has already surpassed the number of mediations. Given the high percentage of judicial mediation,[8] a significant number of cases could have been transferred to the courts for judicial mediation. My field observation (see Chapter 6) suggests that people go through judicial mediation on purpose, for example, to seek more powerful protection and enforcement. Even though the decreasing trend of people's mediation is obvious, its function is still significant and there were signs that people's mediation has also been transformed and become more and more formal (Fu, 1991). In September 2002, both the MOJ and the SPC published regulations to grant legal status to mediation and ensure legal enforcement of mediation.[9] By the end of 2006, the government initiated another round of media encouragement for mediation practice nationwide, and it favored many local experiments such as financial incentives for successful mediations and integration of mediation with judicial and administrative mediations.[10] In addition, a national people's mediation law was reportedly under construction by the MOJ.[11] At the same time, a new round of encouragement of judicial mediation came out after President Hu Jintao called for "building a socialist harmonious society" at the sixth plenary session of the 16th Central Committee in 2006.[12] Methods such as "(mandatory) clarification after ruling" were praised, and mediation in minor criminal cases and administrative cases was granted.[13] In short, the influence of Chinese legal traditions is a major factor affecting the legalization process (see Cohen et al., 1980; MacCormack, 1996; Ren, 1997). The Chinese legal system will be Chinese because of its unique cultural background and practice.

Fourth, as part of the ongoing political reform, China's legal reform is conducted within a boundary set up by the CCP's political agendas. China's legal system, without independent status, always has had an inherent

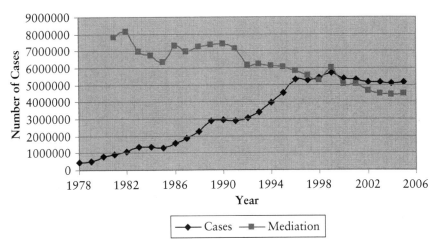

Figure 7.3 Mediation vs. adjudication.

Source: (1) *Law Yearbook of China* (1987–2005); (2) *China Statistical Yearbook* (2001, 2006); (3) Wang (1988, p. 294).

instrumental nature as an administrative tool (Lubman, 1994, 1996). In practice, this instrumental nature (serving political purposes) sometimes goes beyond the legal boundary and contradicts the consistency and the expectation of the legal system (e.g., the severe strike campaign practice as argued in Chapter 4). How far the legal reform can go is determined by the central government's reform decisions. In recent years, for example, we witnessed increasing prestige and power of the court system, and there have been calls, directly or indirectly, to grant more independent status to the court system.[14] Further substantive adjustments to the court system, however, will likely involve changes to the political structure and the Party's principles (e.g., the four cardinal principals).[15] The CCP realizes that the legal reform can be a double-edged sword and has been finding ways to keep control over the legal system. Just before the new year of 2003, all new presiding judges at the Shenyang Intermediate People's Court participated in an oath-taking ceremony,[16] and a similar oath-taking was held 1 year earlier at the Shangdong High People's Court.[17] These ceremonies were not unique and indeed were repeated in many other fields such as prosecutors, lawyers, people's assessors, and non-law-related governmental employees.[18] Many of these ceremonies indeed emphasized "firm support for the leadership of the CCP." Ideological controls such as this one had worked effectively in the prereform era but have been confronted by new ideologies and social values after the reform. The "moral education" proposed by Jiang Zemin in 2001 was another effort to balance the rule of law with the rule of (socialist) morality (see discussions in Chapter 3). How the CCP maintains its control over the growing legal system under both domestic and international pressures will be another key issue in the legalization process.

The study of China's legal reform has important implications for studies of other nations' legal systems and related research on the global system. The economic, political and legal, and social changes in China during the second half of the 20th century and the first years of the 21st century have been dramatic, along with changes in the global system. These changes raised both theoretical and practical challenges to studies in this field. At the same time, the Chinese government faces challenges and opportunities as well in the new millennium. How the government utilizes legal reform to solve problems in the future is the key, especially when China's political reform struggles.

Appendix A
Datelines of China's Negotiation with the WTO

Year/Date	Event
1947	China signed the final documents at the Trade and Employment Meeting of the United Nations (the Final Act of Geneva), in which the GATT was created.
April 21, 1948	China signed a temporary agreement with the GATT.
October 1971	China (the PRC) regained its legal representation in the United Nations.
September 1982	China applied for observer status in the GATT.
November 1982	China gained its observer status in the GATT and was able to attend annual meetings.
July 11, 1986	China formally notified the General Secretary of the GATT and asked for official membership.
March 1987	The GATT established a Working Committee on China and held its first meeting in October.
February 1988	China held its first organization meeting as preparation.
April 15, 1994	At the closing meeting of the Uruguay Round in Monaco, China signed the final agreements for multilateral trade negotiation along with other 122 members. As to the planned establishment of the WTO, China expressed its interest to be a founding member.
December 17–21	The Working Committee on China held its 19th meeting. China failed to reach a mutual agreement with other members on China's founding membership of the WTO.
January 1, 1995	The WTO was officially founded with 134 members. It replaced the GATT with a responsibility to implement the agreements reached in the Uruguay Round and to govern world economic order and trade.
July 1, 1995	The WTO accepted China as an observer.

Year/Date	Event
December 5, 1997	The WTO members of developing nations made their declaration in Geneva, supporting China's application of WTO membership.
May 23, 1997	In its fourth meeting, the WTO Chinese Committee reached agreements on two important issues (the nondiscriminatory and judicial review principles) with regard to China's application.
August 1997	New Zealand, as the first nation, reached mutual agreements with China with regard to China's application. In the same year, China also reached mutual agreements with South Korea, Hungary, and Czechoslovakia.
August 1, 1997	The WTO Chinese Committee closed its fifth meeting in Geneva, in which Long Yongtu announced that China would take important steps to further lower its tariffs, and eradicate nontariff barriers and export subsidies for agricultural products.
April 8, 1998	The WTO Chinese Committee closed its seventh meeting in Geneva. The Committee Chair announced that China's proposal to reduce tariffs in a whole package was welcomed by the Committee, and it was a breakthrough.
April 10, 1999	Shi Guangsheng, Minister of the Ministry of Foreign Trade and Economic Cooperation of the PRC, and U.S. trade representative Barshefsky signed the Sino-U.S. Agricultural Cooperation Agreement in Washington, DC. This is viewed as the prelude for China's participation in the WTO.
April 12, 2000	China reached a bilateral agreement with Malaysia.
May 16, 2000	China reached a bilateral agreement with Latvia.
May 19, 2000	China reached a bilateral agreement with the European Union.
May 29, 2000	After friendly negotiations, China ended its meeting with Switzerland, and signed a mutual agreement.
November 2000	China reached a bilateral agreement with the European Union. At the same time, the representative from Mexico announced that the negotiation between China and Mexico was entering the last phase and would have a positive outcome.
January 10, 2001	China reopened its negotiation with the WTO in Switzerland.
June 6, 2001	The U.S. trade representative Robert Zoellick announced in a press conference in Shanghai that China's participation in the WTO would be beneficial to both China and the world trade system.

Year/Date	Event
June 14, 2001	China and the United States reached full agreements on all remaining issues regarding China's application for a WTO membership.
June 20, 2001	China reached full agreements with the European Union.
July 3, 2001	China's chief representative in the WTO application and Vice Minister of Chinese Ministry of Foreign Trade and Economic Cooperation, Long Yongtu announced that China solved all major problems for its entry into the WTO.
July 3, 2001	The WTO reached general agreements with regard to China's entry into the WTO. After 15 years, China's application was approved.
September 13, 2001	China reached a bilateral agreement with Mexico and therefore finished bilateral negotiations with all WTO members.

Note. From the *China Daily*, July 5, 2001; Online report posted at Xinhuanet, September 18, 2001 (translated by the author).

Appendix B
Case Summary Tables

CHENGDU, SICHUAN PROVINCE

Case	Time	Place	Judge(s) Composition	Secretary	Case Nature	Procedure	Plaintiff/ Prosecutor	Defendant	Representation
*1	2/25/02, early morning	4th courtroom, Qing Yang court	One judge (male)	One (male)	Civil (divorce)	Simplified	Husband	Wife	Self-representation
2	2/27/02, 8:40–9:45 a.m.	3rd courtroom, Qing Yang court	Three judges (2 male, 1 female)	One (female)	Administrative litigation (resettlement dispute)	Normal	Residents (a couple)	Three administrative branches	Self-representation
3	2/28/02, 8:53–10:15 a.m., 10:30–10:45 a.m.	10th courtroom, Chengdu court	Three judges (1 male, 2 female)	One (female)	Administrative litigation, appeal (personal injury caused by police)	Normal	A resident (male)	Police officer	Self-representation
4	2/28/02, 10:22–10:26 a.m.	10th courtroom, Chengdu court	Three judges (1 male, 2 female)	One (female)	Administrative litigation, appeal judgment (legal violation by police)	Normal	A resident (male)	Police officer	Self-representation
5	2/28/02, 2:50–3:05 p.m.	16th courtroom, Chengdu court	Three judges (all female)	One (female)	Civil (loan dispute)	Normal	A company	A company	Self-representation

						Simplified	Wife	Husband	Self-representation
6	3/1/02, 8:30–8:55 a.m.	4th courtroom, Qing Yang court	One judge (male)	One (male)	Civil (divorce)			House builder	
7	3/4/02, 8:45–10:00 a.m.	7th courtroom, Qing Yang court	Three judges (2 male, 1 female)	One (female)	Civil (contract, dispute regarding house-buying)	Normal	House buyer	House builder	Attorneys on both sides (three men, 1 vs. 2)
*8	3/4/02, 2:00–2:40 p.m.	1st courtroom, Qing Yang court	Three judges (2 male, 1 female)	One (female)	Criminal (robbery)	Normal	Procurator (male)	3 codefendants (all male)	Two attorneys (male)
9	3/4/02, 2:45–3:40 p.m.	1st courtroom, Qing Yang court	Three judges (2 male, 1 female)	One (male)	Criminal (robbery)	Normal	Procurator (male)	Male	One attorney (male)
10	3/4/02, 3:45–4:50 p.m.	1st courtroom, Qing Yang court	Three judges (2 male, 1 female)	One (female)	Criminal (blackmail)	Normal	Procurator (male)	Female	One attorney (male)
11	3/5/02, 9:20–10:08 a.m.	6th courtroom, Qing Yang court	Three judges (2 male, 1 female)	One (female)	Civil (loan dispute)	Normal	Bank	D1: Absent D2: A company	D2: One male attorney and legal representative
*12	3/5/02, 10:10–10:24 a.m.	1st courtroom, Qing Yang court	Three judges (2 male, 1 female)	One (male)	Criminal (embezzlement)	Normal	Procurator (male)	Male	One attorney (male)
13	3/5/02, 10:40–11:19 a.m.	1st courtroom, Qing Yang court	Three judges (2 male, 1 female)	One (male)	Criminal (robbery)	Normal	Procurators (1 female, 1 male)	Male	Two attorneys (males)

CHENGDU, SICHUAN PROVINCE

Case	Time	Place	Judge(s) Composition	Secretary	Case Nature	Procedure	Plaintiff/ Prosecutor	Defendant	Representation
14	3/5/02, 11:23–11:35 a.m.	1st courtroom, Qing Yang court	Three judges (2 male, 1 female)	One (female)	Criminal (assault)	Normal	Procurator (female)	Male	Self-representation
*15	3/5/02, 3:35–3:55 p.m.	6th courtroom Qing Yang court	Three judges (2 female, 1 male)	One (female)	Civil (loan dispute)	Normal	Bank	D1: House buyer D2: A company	D1: Self-representation D2: A male attorney and a legal representative
16	3/6/02, 8:44–9:00 a.m.	7th courtroom, Qing Yang court	Three judges (2 male, 1 female)	One (female)	Civil (loan dispute)	Normal	Bank (legal representative and one attorney)	D1: Absent D2: A company	D2: One male attorney
*17	3/6/02, 9:00–9:55 a.m.	6th courtroom, Qing Yang court	Three judges (2 female, 1 male)	One (female)	Civil (contract)	Normal	House buyers (and attorney), all male	House builder	One attorney and a legal representative
18	3/6/02, 10:00–11:30 a.m.	6th courtroom, Qing Yang court	Three judges (2 male, 1 female)	One (female)	Civil (contract, house-buying dispute)	Normal	House buyer (and one attorney), all male	House builder	Two male attorneys
19	3/6/02, 2:39–3:45 p.m.	6th courtroom, Qing Yang court	Three judges (2 female, 1 male)	One (female)	Civil (legal compensation for plaintiff's lost vehicle)	Normal	House renter (and one female attorney)	House builder	Two male attorneys

20	3/7/02, 8:45–10:31 a.m., 11:25–11:45 a.m.	13th courtroom, Chengdu court	Three judges (2 male, 1 female)	One (female)	Civil (contract), appeal and judgment	Normal	Client (female)	Client's former attorney (male)	Self-representation
*21	3/7/02, 10:35–11:10 a.m.	8th courtroom, Chengdu court	Three judges (2 male, 1 female)	One (male)	Criminal (drug trafficking)	Normal	Prosecutor (male)	D1: Male D2: Absent	D1: A male attorney D2: Two attorneys (male and female)
22	3/7/02, 2:40–4:30 p.m., 5:13–5:30 p.m.	13th courtroom, Chengdu court	Two judges (male & female) and 1 female people's assessor	One (male)	Civil (copyright)	Normal	A (male) painter, two attorneys (male & female)	A company	Two male attorneys
23	3/8/02, 8:55–10:35 a.m.	16th courtroom, Chengdu court	Three judges (all male)	One (female)	Civil (compensation for injury at work)	Normal	Worker (male) and one male representative	A shoe factory	A female attorney
24	3/8/02, 4:01–5:59 p.m.; 6:12–6:14 p.m.	13th courtroom, Chengdu court	Three judges (2 male, 1 female)	One (female)	Criminal (theft), planned judgment canceled	Normal	Prosecutor (male)	Three defendants (all male)	Self-representation
25	3/11/02, 8:50–8:51 a.m.	10th courtroom, Chengdu court	Three judges (2 female, 1 male)	One (female)	Appeal judgment announcement	Normal	Unknown	Unknown	Unknown

CHENGDU, SICHUAN PROVINCE

Case	Time	Place	Judge(s) Composition	Secretary	Case Nature	Procedure	Plaintiff/ Prosecutor	Defendant	Representation
26	3/11/02, 8:53–8:57 a.m.	10th courtroom, Chengdu court	Three judges (2 female, 1 male)	One (female)	Administrative appeal judgment, resettlement case, reversed	Normal	Unknown	Unknown	One attorney (female)
27	3/11/02, 9:05–10:42 a.m.	9th courtroom, Chengdu court	Three judges (2 female, 1 male)	One (female)	Civil (contract)	Normal	Construction company	D1: Housing development company D2: Housing development company	D1: One attorney (male) D2: Legal representative (male)
28	3/11/02, 10:50–11:36 a.m.	5th courtroom, Chengdu court	Three judges (2 female, 1 male)	One (female)	Criminal (assault causing death)	Normal	Prosecutors (1 male and 1 female)	Male	Two attorneys (male)
*29	3/11/02, 2:34–2:40 p.m.	2nd courtroom, Qing Yang court	Three judges (2 male, 1 female)	One (female)	Criminal (drug trafficking)	Normal	Prosecutor (male)	Male	Self-representation
30	3/11/02, 2:50–3:45 p.m.	5th courtroom, Qing Yang court	One judge (female)	One (male)	Civil (contract)	Simplified	Company (2 male representatives)	Company	One attorney (male)

*31	3/12/02, 10:31–11:49 a.m.	3rd courtroom, Qing Yang court	Three judges (2 female, 1 male)	One (female)	Administrative litigation (resettlement case)	Normal	Resident (male)	D1: Management office D2: Resettlement office	D1: Legal representative D2: Attorney (male)
*32	3/12/02, 2:55–3:11 p.m.	6th courtroom, Qing Yang court	Three judges (2 female, 1 male)	One (female)	Civil (traffic injury/death)	Normal	The deceased's parents and one male representative	Unknown (driver or the company-hired driver)	Attorney (male)
33	3/14/02, 8:40–9:00 a.m.	7th courtroom, Qing Yang court	Three judges (2 female, 1 male)	One (female)	Civil (investment contract)	Normal	Two investors (male)	Third investor	Legal agent (male)
*34	3/14/02, 9:01–9:09 a.m.	6th courtroom, Qing Yang court	Three judges (2 male, 1 female)	One (female)	Civil (traffic injury/death)	Normal	Victim's agent	Absent, serving criminal sentence	Representative

Note. Qing Yang court = the People's Court at Qing Yang District, Chengdu City, Sichuan province; Chengdu court = Chengdu Intermediate People's Court.
*Incomplete cases, mainly because of my late entry to the trial.

BEIJING

Case	Time	Place	Judge(s) Composition	Secretary	Case Nature	Procedure	Plaintiff/ Prosecutor	Defendant	Representation
35	3/18/02, 1:35–2:07 p.m.	2nd courtroom, Beijing court	Three judges (2 male, 1 female)	Female	Civil (contract)	Normal	One contractor (male)	D: Second contractor (partner) Third party: Company	D: One attorney (male) Third party: One attorney (male)
36	3/19/02, 8:35–9:42 a.m.	23rd courtroom, Beijing High Court	One female (other two absent)	Female	Criminal (theft), appeal judgment	Normal	Prosecutor (absent)	18 defendants (all male)	Unknown
37	3/19/02, 10:00–11:05 a.m.	23rd courtroom, Beijing court	Three judges (2 male, 1 female)	Male	Criminal (robbery and murder)	Normal	Prosecutors (2 female)	Male	One female attorney
38	3/19/02, 1:12–1:30 p.m.	16th courtroom, Beijing court	Male (other two absent)	Male	Criminal (robbery and kidnapping), judgment	Normal	Prosecutor (absent)	Six defendants (4 male, 2 female)	Three out of six have attorneys, only one female attorney appeared
39	3/19/02, 1:31–1:42 p.m.	17th courtroom, Beijing court	Female (other two absent)	Male	Criminal (murder), appeal judgment	Normal	Prosecutor (absent)	Male	One attorney and his mother in representation
40	3/20/02, 9:10–10:51 a.m.	21st courtroom, Beijing court	Three judges (all female)	Male	Civil (contract)	Normal	Two companies	One company	Two attorneys

41	3/21/02, 9:15–10:30 a.m.	Western Central courtroom, Beijing court	Three female judges	Male	Bankruptcy (first creditors' meeting)	N/A	All creditors (banks, enterprises, individuals, etc.)	The 1st General-use machinery factory	Unknown
*42	3/21/02, 10:30–11:12 a.m.	20th courtroom, Beijing court	Three male judges	Male	Civil (patent violation)	Normal	One company	Another company	Unknown
43	3/21/02, 1:35–3:25 p.m.	21st courtroom, Beijing court	Three judges (2 female, 1 male)	Male	Civil (patent violation)	Normal	One company (legal representative and 2 attorneys, male and female)	Three companies	Two attorneys for all three defendants
44	3/22/02, 9:35–10:20 a.m.	23rd courtroom, Beijing court	Three judges (2 female, 1 male)	Male	Criminal (drug trafficking)	Normal	Prosecutors (1 male, 1 female)	Male	One appointed attorney (male)
*45	3/22/02, 10:20–11:20 a.m.	The big courtroom, Beijing court	Three judges (2 female, 1 male)	Several (both male and female)	Appeal, civil contract regarding land transaction	Normal	85 legal peasants (and their families), self-representation	Land contractor	Unknown
46	3/26/02, 9:18–10:35 a.m.	11th courtroom, Hai Dian court	Male	Male	Civil (labor dispute)	Simplified	Three male, one female	Company	Two female legal representatives
47	3/26/02, 1:50–2:09 p.m.	4th (room 209), Hai Dian court	One female, two female People's Assessors	Female	Criminal (unlawful imprisonment)	Normal	Prosecutors (2 male)	Two male	Self-defense

BEIJING

Case	Time	Place	Judge(s) Composition	Secretary	Case Nature	Procedure	Plaintiff/ Prosecutor	Defendant	Representation
48	3/26/02, 2:10–2:26 p.m.	4th (room 209), Hai Dian court	One female, two female People's Assessors	Female	Criminal (fraud)	Normal	Prosecutors (1 female, 1 male)	Male	Self-defense
49	3/27/02, 9:00–10:15 a.m.	4th (room 207), Hai Dian court	One male, two male People's Assessors	Female	Criminal and civil (assault)	Normal	Victim (male, private prosecution)	Male	One male attorney
50	3/27/02, 10:20–10:51 a.m.	4th (room 207), Hai Dian court	One male, two male People's Assessors	Female	Criminal (assault)	Normal	Victim (female, private prosecution)	Female	One male attorney
51	3/27/02, 2:05–2:45 p.m.	4th (room 209), Hai Dian court	One female, two female People's Assessors	Female	Criminal (theft)	Normal	Prosecutors (1 female, 1 male)	Male	One male attorney
52	3/27/02, 3:00–3:14 p.m.	4th (room 209), Hai Dian court	One female, two female People's Assessors	Female	Criminal (selling obscene VCD/DVDs)	Normal	Prosecutors (2 male)	Male	Self-defense

53	3/27/02, 3:15–3:24 p.m.	4th (room 209), Hai Dian court	One female, two female People's Assessors	Female	Criminal (theft)	Normal	Prosecutors (2 male)	Male	Self-defense
54	3/28/02, 9:09–9:25 a.m.	24th (room 419), Hai Dian court	Male	Female	Civil (traffic accident)	Simplified	Taxi drivers (absent), legal representative (female)	D1: Another car driver (absent) D2: Car owner (male)	Self-defense

Note. Beijing court = the Beijing First Intermediate Peoples' Court; Beijing High Court = Beijing High People's Court; Hai Dian court = People's Court at Hai Dian District, Beijing.
*Incomplete cases, mainly because of my late entry to the trial.

Notes

CHAPTER 1

1. My review of previous studies of China's legal system here is mainly confined to studies by Western scholars and scholars with Chinese background but working abroad. There are a number of reasons for such a limitation. First, I have to candidly admit that due to limited access in China, I was unable to do a complete review of all relevant studies. Works done by scholars in China, however, are not completely absent here. Some of them, arguably the best, have been published abroad. Second, based on what I have read and learned, legal studies by Chinese scholars at home are limited both in quantity and quality, although there has been progress in recent years. Historically, legal education and studies were brutally disrupted by class struggle, especially in the Cultural Revolution period (see Chapter 3). Even though efforts have been made to restore legal education and studies after the reform, research and studies on law and society in general and on the legal system in particular are still lagging behind (Ji, 1989). In the spring of 2002 when I talked with Professor Zhu Suli, the dean of the law school at Beijing University, he admitted that there were very few good studies of the Chinese legal system and the legal reform. Nevertheless, I did manage to collect most recent works done by Chinese scholars relevant to my study and include those works in this research (see the section "Books and Articles in Chinese" in the References).

2. Examples of empirical research in this field include Chang (2004), A. Chen (2005), Diamant (2000), Ding (2001), H. Lu (1998), Peerenboom (2001), Potter (1994c), Wall and Blum (1991), L. Zhang and Messner (1995, 1999), and L. Zhang et al. (2000). In addition, see Liang and Lu (2006) for a discussion on methodological issues related to conducting fieldwork in this field in China.

3. Such overestimation was reported in Lardy (1994, 2002), Rawski (2001), and World Bank (1997a). There are a number of other relevant articles by Rawski available online at http://www.pitt.edu/~tgrawski/.

4. See reports in the *People's Daily*, April 18, 2002 & July 18, 2002; in the *Southern Weekend*, June 27, 2002; online news posted at Xinhuanet, May 7, 2002. For local underreporting of their economic growth, see also Roberts (1997).

5. Online news posted at Xinhuanet, August 8, 2002; at Chinanews.com, May 7, 2003; the *People's Daily*, January 21, 2004; the *China Business Post*, January 29, 2005.

6. The *Legal Daily*, August 18, 2006.

7. A friend of mine, who was working in the State Development Planning Commission, reminded me in 2002 that I have to be careful with the interpretation

of the unemployment rate, which is underestimated given the fact that only the registered unemployed number is reported officially. See also relevant discussions in Chapter 4.

8. Official data reported that by the end of 2003, the total number of Internet users reached 7.9 million in China, behind only the United States in the world (*People's Daily*, January 16, 2004).

9. Beijing is the capital of China, sitting in the northeast of China.

10. Chengdu is the capital of Sichuan province, sitting in the southwest of China.

11. A pseudonym is used here for the purpose of protection.

12. In Chinese culture, the term *teacher* is unique. When people call you a teacher, it shows their high respect.

13. Because of its size and importance, Beijing has two intermediate level courts (the First and the Second), and each controls half of the total lower level district courts. The Beijing First Court is the appellate court of the Hai Dian Court. In addition, the Beijing High People's Court is located in the same building as the Beijing First Court, and one of my cases (36) was indeed a case tried by the Beijing High Court.

14. I failed to find court cleaners at the Hai Dian Court and I indeed missed them. This is one in which you want to deal with people, not machines.

15. A people's tribunal is a minibranch (often a small office) of the district court, usually located in faraway areas to help people who have difficulty traveling to the district court (Lee, 1997). The total number of people's tribunals changes quickly, depending on the district courts' decision to add or withdraw tribunals. Numerical information presented here is from the *Law Yearbook of China*. There were 10,345 people's tribunals by 2005 (the *People's Daily*, April 11, 2005).

16. Online news reported that a total of 5.18 million people observed trials in 2004 (posted at www.chinacourt.org, February 12, 2005). In the same year, more than 5.07 million cases were tried by the courts of the first instance (and the number would be even higher if cases heard by courts at other levels were added). On average, there was about one observer in each case!

17. Interestingly enough, the next day, I read an article in a local newspaper, the *Sichuan Workers' Daily*, in which news reporters complained about the fact that note-taking is not allowed in courtrooms even though trials are open to the public. As a matter of fact, several news reporters were beaten, and their equipment (e.g., cameras and tape recorders) was confiscated and destroyed once their "improper behavior" was spotted by the guards (*Sichuan Workers' Daily*, March 5, 2002).

18. There were occasionally reports in the media in which judges refused to honor citizens' rights to observe trials for no legal reasons. For an example, see the *Legal Daily*, December 10, 2004.

19. See discussions on such sampling techniques by Jorgensen (1989), Marshall and Rossman (1989), and Maxwell (1996).

CHAPTER 2

1. It is inaccurate, both theoretically and empirically, to lump almost 30 years (1949–1978) into one historical period, when substantive changes indeed happened in those years. For example, during the Cultural Revolution period (1966–1976), the legal system was almost totally paralyzed. In her study, Xin (1999) further divided the prereform period into four different phases to better represent social and legal changes before 1978. In this research, however, my focus is on economic and political changes before and after 1978, and I

put more emphasis on legal reform after 1978. For the sake of comparison and simplicity, therefore, I adopt the dichotomy between the prereform era and the reform era.

2. Those nonpublic economic means controlled a higher percentage of state capital by then. For example, as Chin (1983) pointed out, the confiscated industrial enterprise of bureaucratic capitalism accounted for 80% of the entire nation's fixed industrial assets, and the private economy accounted the other 20%.

3. See studies on the *Hukou* system by Solinger (1999), Whyte and Parish (1984), and Y. Yan (1994).

4. See H. Lu (1998). For a detailed discussion of the mass-line policy, see Tao (1997).

5. See a more detailed discussion on the damaging impact of the Cultural Revolution on the legal system in Xin (1999).

6. See discussions by P. M. Chen (1973) and Ren (1997). For studies on Chinese legal traditions by domestic scholars, see Huang (2000) and Wu et al. (1994).

7. Data from the *People's Daily*, January 10, 2006; and statistics reported by Qiu, Xiaohua, Commissioner of the National Bureau of Statistics of China (NBSC), posted at www.legalinfo.gov.cn, October 2, 2006.

8. Data from the *People's Daily*, January 26, 2007. For comparison reasons, China's GDP in 2006 was about $2.7 trillion U.S., and the per capita GDP in 2005 was about $1,812 (based on the exchange rate of $1 U.S. = 7.75 Chinese yuan, as of March 2007). In comparison, the U.S. GDP in 2005 was $12.49 trillion, and the per capita GDP was $42,090 (U.S. Census Bureau, 2007, pp. 429, 434).

9. For example, in November 2003, Li Rongrong, Chairman of the State-Owned Assets Supervision and Administration Commission of the State Council, reported to the media that in 7 years from 1995 to 2002, the number of state-owned industrial enterprises (including corporate state-owned enterprises) was streamlined from 77,600 to 41,900, but the profit was raised from 83.8 billion yuan to 220.9 billion yuan. Online news reported at Chinanews.com, November 19, 2003.

10. See report titled, "The Major Breakthrough of Ownership Theory," by Xiao Zhuoji (1997) in the *People's Daily*. This "hand-in-hand development" principle was later added into the 1999 Constitution (The *People's Daily*, January 31, 1999; March 17, 1999).

11. The *People's Daily*, February 28, 2005; November 13, 2006; December 1, 2006.

12. See reports in the *Beijing Evening News*, April 1, 2002; *Beijing Daily*, November 26, 2002.

13. See Keith and Lin (2001) for a discussion of how the government struggled with conceptual differences among various terms such as ownership right, property right, right of possession, right to use, and right to benefit.

14. See J. Chen (1995). See also reports in the *People's Daily*, April 26, 2001; November 14, 2006.

15. The *People's Daily*, November 10, 2002. See also a report in the *Laodong (Labor) News*, November 24, 2002, for specific measures proposed by the Shanghai government to encourage foreign investment in SOEs.

16. Online news reported at Chinanews.com, November 19, 2003.

17. Online news posted at Chinanews.com, October 6, 2001.

18. As reported in the *Beijing Morning Post*, July 22, 2002.

19. Online news posted at Xinhuanet, August 19, 2002; *People's Daily*, August 19, 2002.

20. For more detailed information on the first experience of China's stock market, see Hertz (1998), World Bank (1988).

21. By comparison, China's stock market capitalization in 2004 was about $639.8 billion U.S. and the value of shares traded was about $734.3 billion U.S. In the same year, U.S. stock market capitalization was $16.3 trillion and the value of shares traded was $19.35 trillion (U.S. Census Bureau, 2007, p. 866).

22. Data from the Statistical Communiqué on the 2006 National Economic and Social Development, in the *People's Daily*, March 1, 2007.

23. The *People's Daily*, June 1, 2001; online news posted at Xinhuanet, February 19, 2001.

24. The *People's Daily*, January 4, 2002.

25. Online news posted at Chinanews.com, October 22, 2002.

26. The *People's Daily*, November 12, 2002.

27. The *People's Daily*, November 16, 2001; November 20, 2001; the *Shanghai Security News* (Internet edition), October 21, 2001.

28. The *People's Daily*, November 20, 2001.

29. The *People's Daily*, February 24, 2002.

30. The *People's Daily*, January 22, 2007.

31. It is further added and underscored in the revised 1999 Constitution that "China is going to be at the 'preliminary stage' for a long time" (The *People's Daily*, March 17, 1999).

32. See reports in the *People's Daily*, May 9, 1998; May 11, 1998; May 12, 1998.

33. The *People's Daily*, October 9, 1997; October 10, 1997; May 9, 1998; May 11, 1998. For a detailed study of Chinese politics after Mao and its transition to Dengism, see Baum (1994).

34. The *People's Daily*, June 12, 2001.

35. The *People's Daily*, June 8, 2000.

36. The *People's Daily*, January 31, 1999; March 17, 1999.

37. See reports in the *People's Daily*, June 1, 2000; December 26, 2000; June 12, 2001; November 8, 2001.

38. For the full speech, see the *People's Daily*, July 2, 2001.

39. The *People's Daily*, July 29, 2001; November 8, 2001; February 29, 2002; November 3, 2002; December 10, 2002.

40. See an article by Ye Duchu in the *Outlook Weekly*, July 22, 2002.

41. Online news posted at Xinhuanet, November 14, 2002; the *People's Daily*, November 15, 2002. See the revised new Party's Charter in the *People's Daily*, November 19, 2002.

42. The *People's Daily*, July 18, 2000; July 25, 2000; August 10, 2000; August 29, 2000.

43. The *People's Daily*, June 8, 2000; November 27, 2001.

44. The *Southern Metropolis Daily*, May 2, 2002.

CHAPTER 3

1. The *People's Daily*, December 7, 1999.

2. Article 5 of the 1999 Constitution.

3. See reports in the *People's Daily*, August 9, 2000.

4. The *People's Daily*, September 26, 2002. It was further clarified that the goal of the ninth NPC and its Standing Committee was to set up a preliminary legal system (*chubu xingcheng*) as accomplished by 2002. The preliminary system covered seven major legal areas (including Constitution law, civil and commercial law, administrative law, economic law, social law, criminal law, major procedural law) and three tiers of laws, rules, and regulations (including laws, administrative regulations, and local regulations). The goal of the (current) 10th NPC and its Standing Committee is to further strengthen the basic legal

system (*jiben xingcheng*), and the final goal by the Chinese legislature is to set up a mature system by 2010 (*Outlook Weekly*, March 12, 2007).

5. Official reports based on accumulative data concluded that about one third of all cases were ruled in favor of compensation. The *People's Daily*, June 9, 2004; online news posted at Xinhuanet.com, November 25, 2005. Another report showed that the administrative organization in Baokang County, Hubei province lost all 124 administrative litigations in 1996 and 1997. After years of improvement, the Baokang County administration won 82% of all cases (42) in 2003. The *People's Daily*, August 11, 2004.

6. Official cumulative data showed that from 1995 to November 2004, the procuratorates handled 7,823 cases, and ruled in favor of compensation in 3,167 cases (40%), with a total compensation amount of 58.2 million yuan. Online news posted at www.chinacourt.org, January 3, 2005. Such a high compensation rate, however, did not appear to match official data reported in Table 3.4.

7. See relevant commentaries in the *People's Daily*, October 24, 2001. Another report in the *People's Daily* on March 27, 2002 questioned the limited scope of state compensation (covering tangible losses only), and called for a broader scope to include other intangible losses such as emotional harm.

8. Online news posted at Chinanews.com, January 28, 2003. Based on the most recent statistics in 2006 reported by the NBSC, the average daily wage is raised to 83.66 yuan. Both the Supreme People's Court and the Supreme People's Procuratorate adopted this new standard. See reports in the *People's Court Daily*, the *Procuratorial Daily*, March 27, 2007, and the *People's Daily*, March 29, 2007.

9. Although the goal is to cover "all who need it," legal assistance is primarily provided only to a small group of people presently due to limited resources. To qualify as a recipient, a citizen has to show that one needs legal assistance for infringements of one's rights, and one meets the minimal living standard or social security standard outlined by local governments to prove one's economic needs. The *China Youth Daily*, September 30, 2001. For another example of specific local rules by the Beijing First Intermediate People's Court, see the *Beijing Daily*, December 14, 2001.

10. See the full version of the Regulations in the *People's Daily*, August 1, 2003.

11. The *People's Daily*, January 26, 2007.

12. The *People's Daily*, September 18, 2002; August 13, 2003; February 28, 2007. See also articles by Bai Shuqing and Song Zhijun posted at www.acla.org.cn, October 24, 2003.

13. By comparison, China's 153,846 lawyers in 2005 accounted for a mere 0.0001% of the population, whereas lawyers accounted for 0.32% of the population in the United States and 0.09% in West Germany (based on 1998 data; cited in Peerenboom, 2002b).

14. The *People's Daily*, February 16, 2005.

15. The *Legal Daily*, April 13, 2004.

16. Data from online news posted at Xinhuanet, December 8, 2000; and the *Procuratorial Daily*, March 7, 2001.

17. The *People's Daily*, January 9, 2001.

18. For studies on how Chinese lawyers conduct their practice, meet reform needs, and handle challenges in the new era, see Alford (1995b), B. Li (2001), S. Liu (2006), and Michelson (2006).

19. The *Legal Daily*, January 19, 2006; June 29, 2006.

20. The *People's Daily*, June 17, 2004; January 23, 2007.

21. See Keith and Lin (2001) for a detailed discussion of contributions by Chinese legal scholars and jurists in the reform era.

22. Some of these lectures were reported in the *People's Daily*, October 21, 1998; November 27, 1998; March 1, 1999; April 24, 1999; September 1, 1999; August 26, 2000; November 1, 2000; August 30, 2002; April 29, 2001; December 30, 2001; February 27, 2002; March 1, 2002. See a full list of lectures from 1998 to 2002 on February 19, 2003; and a list of lectures in 2003 on February 25, 2004.

23. The *People's Daily*, October 16, 2002.

24. Some of the major Web sites include www.jcrb.com, www.chinacourt.org, www.legalinfo.gov.cn, www.legaldaily.com.cn, www.cpd.com.cn, www.china peace.org.cn, and www.acla.org.cn.

25. One way to organize activities on the December 4 legal education day is to label each year with a theme. For instance, the identified theme was "(to) enhance the public's awareness of the national Constitution, and continue running the country according to law" in 2001, "running the country according to law and running the office for the people" in 2003, "(to) praise the spirit of Constitution and build a harmonious society" in 2005, and "(to) follow the guidelines of 'five/five' plan, and advance the building of a harmonious society" in 2006. The *People's Daily*, November 20, 2001; December 3, 2001; and special topics on the December 4 legal education day at www.legalinfo.gov.cn.

26. The *People's Daily*, November 22, 2006.

27. See a series of discussions on legal professionalism in the *People's Daily*, July 24, 2002.

28. The *People's Daily*, June 29, 2001; online news posted at Chinanews.com, June 29, 2001.

29. The *Beijing Evening News*, October 12, 2002; the *News Express*, January 1, 2003.

30. See commentaries in the *Beijing Evening News*, May 17, 2002; the *Liaoshen Evening News*, June 15, 2002; online news posted at Xinhuanet, May 30, 2002.

31. According to the reports, the witness had to press his or her left hand on a copy of the PRC's Constitution, and read that "guaranteed by my consciousness, I will faithfully testify according to law, and I thereby guarantee to testify the truth without hiding. (I understand) if I break the oath, I will receive legal punishment and moral admonishment" (translation by the author). Online news posted at Chinanews.com, December 4, 2001; see also the commentary in the *People's Daily*, April 24, 2002.

32. The *China Youth Daily*, July 2, 2001.

33. There are many reports on the first national law exam, and see the following for key information: online news posted at www.chinacourt.org, August 12, 2002; the *People's Daily*, November 1, 2001; and the *Beijing Youth Daily*, March 30, 2002.

34. Online news posted at Xinhuanet, October 19, 2002.

35. The *People's Daily*, April 11, 2002; July 31, 2002.

36. The *People's Daily*, March 2, 1999.

37. The *People's Daily*, February 28, 2007; the *Legal Daily*, March 1, 2007.

38. See reports in the *Beijing Morning Post*, August 9, 2000; the *People's Daily*, October 16, 2002; online news posted at Chinanews.com, November 18, 2000.

39. The *People's Daily*, July 24, 2002. The most recent statistics reported in the *People's Daily* on July 17, 2005 raised the percentage of judges who hold a college degree to 51%. The situation is uneven throughout the nation and it is considerably worse in poor western provinces. For instance, whereas the percentage reached 77% in Guangdong province in 2001, some local people's courts in Shanxi province did not have one single judge who held a college

degree by the end of 2003 (The *Legal Daily*, April 26, 2005; the *Nanfang Daily*, October 6, 2001). According to another source, 25.7% of police working in prisons reportedly held university degrees and another 55.9% held associate's degrees by early 2007 (online news posted at www.legalinfo.gov.cn, March 22, 2007).

40. The *People's Daily*, November 23, 2000; November 25, 2000; online news posted at Xinhuanet, November 22, 2000.

41. Online news posted at Xinhuanet, April 24, 2001; the *People's Daily*, March 23, 2001. It was reported that a total of 13,391 judges voluntarily withdrew from trials based on this new regulation in 2001 (the *People's Daily*, October 16, 2002).

42. The *People's Daily*, October 16, 2002.

43. The *People's Daily*, November 7, 2001. For local practices of such new policies in Hunan province, see a report in the *New Daily of East*, June 19, 2004.

44. The *People's Daily*, October 9, 2002; the *Nanfang Daily*, October 6, 2001.

45. The *People's Daily*, October 26, 2005.

46. The *People's Daily*, September 13, 2006.

47. See, for example, reports in the *Yangcheng Evening News*, September 9, 2002; the *Chongqing Evening News*, October 24, 2002.

48. Data from a survey reported in the *Market Journal*, October 24, 2002.

49. The *People's Daily*, August 6, 2002.

50. The *People's Daily*, March 22, 2002.

51. See also discussions in the *People's Daily*, March 24, 1999; May 5, 1999.

52. The *People's Daily*, June 20, 2001; November 1, 2002.

53. Some scholars coined this term as "rule of virtue." See Keith and Lin (2006). Zou (2006) further questioned this rule of virtue as an equivalent to the rule of man.

54. There were numerous reports on Jiang's proposition of the moral education. See, for example, commentaries in the *People's Daily*, February 1, 2001; February 22, 2001; April 7, 2001; April 29, 2001.

55. The *People's Daily*, November 1, 2002; March 2, 2003.

56. The *People's Daily*, November 4, 2002; March 2, 2003; May 25, 2004.

57. Oi's (1999) study showed that much of the rapid rural industrialization in the 1980s occurred indeed in local government-owned enterprises at the ownership and village levels. Only in the 1990s were private enterprises able to catch up.

58. For detailed discussions on Weber's concept of rationality and bureaucracy (and their relations), see Weber (1954), Giddens (1971), and Turkel (1996).

59. Even though each leader tried to establish his name and fame in books (e.g., the Party Charter and the Constitution), there is little doubt that Jiang Zemin's personal charismatic power is significantly less influential compared to both Mao Zedong's and Deng Xiaoping's power. It is foreseeable that the fourth generation of the Chinese leaders led by Hu Jintao, who never experienced the revolutionary wars, will have even less charisma.

60. In his study of dispute resolution in rural China, Fu (2002) noticed that local rules in many respects were inconsistent with state laws, although they met the substantive requirements of the local governments. The requirement of legality in the new era began to take effect, but the outcome is still difficult to predict.

61. See a series of special reports in *Chinese Law and Government*, 34(4 & 6), 2001, Village Elections in China (I) & (II). See also Li and O'Brien (1999) and Shih (1999).

62. Online news posted at www.people.com.cn, December 9, 2001; the *People's Daily*, May 18, 2005.

63. The *People's Daily*, May 30, 2001.
64. The *People's Daily*, December 10, 2001. For a study of the severe strike campaign in the new era, see Chapter 4.

CHAPTER 4

1. The *People's Daily*, June 28, 2000; January 17, 2001.
2. Online news posted at Chinanews.com, October 29, 2003.
3. The *People's Daily*, January 17, 2001 (translated by the author).
4. The *People's Daily*, June 28, 2000.
5. The *People's Daily*, June 9, 2001; November 5, 2001.
6. The *People's Daily*, December 10, 2000. See also Gao and Song (2001).
7. Data from online news posted at Xinhuanet, March 10, 2002. For actions by the people's procuratorates and the local police departments, see reports in the *People's Daily*, November 16, 2002. Also see He (2003) and Nan (2003) for detailed statistical information.
8. Sometimes, the term was translated as "strike hard," "severe blows," or simply "severe punishment," but in any case it corresponds to the Chinese term *yanda*.
9. Online news report posted at Xinhuanet, November 29, 2002; the *People's Daily*, August 28, 2002.
10. The *Information Times* (Internet edition), August 22, 2002.
11. The *People's Daily*, April 18, 2001.
12. See H. M. Tanner (1999) and Woo (1997) for such quota practices. M. S. Tanner (2005) also revealed how local police often artificially inflated arrest rates by rearresting and recharging past offenders for "newly discovered offenses" (p. 178). Such police practices were confirmed to me by laypeople during my field research in 2002.
13. The *Beijing Evening News*, November 2, 2002.
14. See stories reported in the *Life Week*, July 17, 2002; the *Legal Daily*, July 28, 2002.
15. Note that the Chinese government did not officially claim a severe strike campaign in 1989 (probably because of the political turmoil), but some Western scholars (e.g., Dutton & Lee, 1993; Trevaskes, 2003) definitely saw a continuation of the crackdown in 1989 adopted by the Chinese government from time to time since 1983.
16. The *People's Daily*, May 26, 2006; November 26, 2006.
17. Online news in the *People's Court Daily* (Internet edition), September 30, 2001.
18. Online news in the *People's Court Daily* (Internet edition), April 11, 2002.
19. Some of these violations were even acknowledged as "problems" in these campaigns by governmental officials (see Q. Zhang, 2002).
20. The *People's Daily*, May 15, 2002. In Chinese both the character "severe" and the character "speaking out" share the same pronunciation, *yan*. In this commentary, the author pointed out that both *yan*(s) should be emphasized in the campaign.
21. See, for example, the *People's Daily*, March 4, 2002; December 19, 2002. See also Dutton and Lee (1993) and Bakken (2000). Partially as a result, the NBSC has been conducting national surveys on public safety and publishing relevant results each year since 2001. See the "Public Safety Survey" section at the NBSC Web site.
22. Online news posted at Chinanews.com, July 19, 2002. Later, similar speeches were made on several occasions (e.g., in January, September, and November),

asking for further implementation of the severe strike campaign and the "comprehensive management" under the guidance of the spirit of the 16th Congress. See, for example, online news posted at www.chinacourt.org, January 14, 2003.

23. Online news posted at www.cpd.com.cn, February 5, 2007; the *People's Daily*, September 29, 2006. See also discussion by Dutton (2005).
24. The *People's Daily*, September 29, 2006; November 7, 2006.
25. Online news posted at www.cpd.com.cn, February 5, 2007; the *Legal Daily*, August 16, 2006.
26. The *People's Daily*, February 7, 2001; December 5, 2001; February 4, 2002; April 24, 2002; December 31, 2003.
27. The *People's Daily*, October 9, 2006; October 25, 2006; the *Legal Daily*, February 5, 2007.
28. See a special report in the *Nan Feng Chuang Magazine* (www.nfcmag.com), August 21, 2002.
29. Online news posted at Xinhuanet, December 19, 2002;
30. The *People's Daily*, November 25, 2001; the *Beijing Youth Daily*, November 24, 2001.
31. The *People's Daily*, August 30, 2006.
32. Online news posted at Xinhuanet, October 6, 2002.
33. The *People's Daily*, January 17, 2007.
34. Data from online news posted at Xinhuanet, October 25, 2002.
35. See X. He (2005) for a study of how migrant entrepreneurs in Beijing managed to struggle through life and run their business.
36. Online news posted at Chinanews.com, August 7, 2001. See also Q. Zhu (1995).
37. The *People's Daily*, August 14, 2002.
38. Online news posted at Chinanews.com, September 7, 2001; December 4, 2001.
39. *Yangcheng Evening News*, April 18, 2002.
40. The *Huadong News*, posted at www.people.com.cn, May 20, 2002; the *Qilu Evening News*, July 30, 2002.
41. Online news posted at Xinhuanet, December 1, 2002; the People's Daily, February 24, 2003.
42. "House" in Chinese (*fangzi*) is a bit confusing. In the majority of cases, it refers to an apartment in an apartment building complex.
43. The *Beijing Morning Post*, October 26, 2001; the *Beijing Youth Daily*, October 15, 2001.
44. Online news posted at Xinhuanet, July 22, 2002. It was reported by the Shenzhen government that all peasants were granted resident status by the end of October 2004, and Shenzhen became the first "city without peasants" in China (The *People's Daily*, June 30, 2004).
45. Online news posted at Xinhuanet, December 22, 2001. However, in merely 2 years, the city government halted its "open" policy due to problems created by increased population (over 250,000 in 2 years; *China Youth Daily*, September 15, 2004).
46. It was indeed reported that a reform plan is under discussion by the MPS. Online news posted at www.Chinapeace.org.cn, March 30, 2007; the *People's Daily*, May 9, 2007.
47. Online news posted at Chinanews.com, October 26, 2002; online news posted at Xinhuanet, October 25, 2002; *Global Times* (Chinese), August 31, 2001.
48. It was reported that a total of 400 million new national ID cards had been issued by the end of 2006 (online news posted at www.cpd.com.cn, January 15, 2007).

49. *21st Century Jobs*, November 14, 2002.
50. Gini coefficient is a standard measurement for income inequality. With a range from 0 to 1, the higher the number is, the more inequality the measured location has. See more detailed explanation in Khan, Griffin, Riskin, and Zhao (1992).
51. For a study about the change of occupational structure and the stratification of Chinese peasantry, see X. Lu (1995).
52. The *People's Daily*, February 26, 2002; the *Beijing Youth Daily*, November 23, 2002.
53. *21st Century Jobs*, July 12, 2002.
54. The *People's Daily*, July 9, 2002.
55. *Market Journal*, October 24, 2002; *21st Century Jobs*, July 12, 2002.
56. The *People's Daily*, February 26, 2002.
57. The *People's Daily*, February 26, 2002.
58. The *People's Daily*, July 9, 2002.
59. Online news posted at Chinanews.com, October 16, 2002.
60. Online news posted at Chinanews.com, October 16, 2002; the *People's Daily*, March 26, 2001. See a study on *xiagang* by Qiu and Zheng (1998).
61. The *People's Daily*, September 10, 2002; September 29, 2002.
62. Online news posted at Xinhuanet, October 3, 2001; June 18, 2002; the *Beijing Evening News*, November 2, 2001; the *Market Journal*, September 12, 2001.
63. The *People's Daily*, January 10, 2003; online news posted at Xinhuanet, November 29, 2002; online news posted at Chinanews.com, August 7, 2002.
64. Online news posted at www.people.com.cn, May 16, 2002. Based on a survey in 2002, the average per capita annual salary in Nanjing was about 32,283 yuan, which makes the pool of potential clients rather small (the *Market Journal*, October 24, 2002).
65. After major revisions, the 2006 *China Statistical Yearbook* reported much lower divorce rates compared to numbers in previous versions, as recorded in Table 4.12. However, the increasing trend over time did not change.
66. Online news posted at Xinhuanet, April 22, 2001; the *People's Daily*, October 11, 2001. For a summary of the marriage evolution in contemporary China, see a special report by Ouyang Haiyan in the *New Times Weekly*, September 19, 2006.
67. *Beijing Business Today*, November 5, 2002; *Shanghai Morning Post*, January 1, 2003.
68. The *Legal Daily*, July 3, 2006; online news posted at Xinhuanet, May 23, 2007. See also similar reports on increased divorces in Beijing in the *Beijing Evening News*, December 6, 2004.
69. The *Yangtse Evening Post*, August 17, 2000.
70. For example, see case reports on civil compensation in the *Beijing Evening News*, May 19, 2001; online news reports posted at Chinanews.com, October 25, 2001. See reports on illegal cohabitation in the *Beijing Evening News*, September 11, 2002.
71. See, for example, such calls by the CCCPLC leader (online news posted at Xinhuanet, September 24, 2003; November 16, 2003) and by the SPC president (online news posted at www.chinacourt.org, March 10, 2003; posted at Xinhuanet, November 18, 2006).

CHAPTER 5

1. See reports in the *People's Daily*, January 19, 2001; March 24, 2001; March 26, 2001; May 30, 2000.
2. The *People's Daily*, March 26, 2001 (translation by the author).

3. See a series of reports and commentaries in the *People's Daily*, August 17, 2001.
4. See such reports in the *People's Daily*, March 20, 2001; January 10, 2005.
5. In 1988, Hainan Island was separated from Guangdong province and became a new province in China.
6. Those cities are Dalian, Qinghuangdao, Tianjin, Yantai, Qingtao, Lianyuangang, Nantong, Shanghai, Ningbo, Wenzhou, Fuzhou, Guangzhou, Zhanjiang, and Beihai.
7. Data are taken from the *Collection of Statistics of Foreign Economic Relations and Trade of China* (2001); the *China Statistical Abstract* (2002); and the *WTO International Trade Statistics* (2005).
8. The *People's Daily*, November 15, 2004; September 3, 2005.
9. The *Beijing Youth Daily*, October 21, 2002.
10. The *Shanghai Securities News* (Internet edition), December 8, 2002.
11. Data reported by Qiu Xiaohua, Commissioner of the NBSC, posted at www.legalinfo.gov.cn (October 2, 2006).
12. Data reported by Qiu Xiaohua, Commissioner of the NBSC, posted at www.legalinfo.gov.cn (October 2, 2006).
13. The *People's Daily*, September 12, 2002; the *Beijing Daily Messenger*, September 11, 2002. See also Meredith (2002).
14. Data from Motorola (China) Web site at www.motorola.com.cn (last retrieved on February 13, 2007).
15. See reports from the *People's Daily*, August 10, 2002; November 10, 2002. For specific measures proposed by the Shanghai government to encourage foreign investment in SOEs, see report from the *Laodong (Labor) News*, online news posted at www.eastday.com (November 24, 2002).
16. The *China Economic Times*, August 22, 2002.
17. The *China Economic Times*, August 22, 2002; the *People's Daily*, July 21, 2005; October 9, 2005.
18. Online news posted at Xinhuanet, September 23, 2002.
19. The *Beijing Youth Daily*, October 5, 2004; the *People's Daily*, September 19, 2004.
20. Data from Lardy (2002, p. 56); the *People's Daily*, October 9, 2001.
21. Data from "Invest in China" (www.fdi.gov.cn), Ministry of Commerce of the PRC.
22. For more detailed information about China's entry into the WTO, see reports posted on Xinhuanet, September 18, 2001; the *China Daily*, July 5, 2001; and the *Beijing Youth Daily*, November 11, 2001. See also Appendix A for a dateline of China's entry into the WTO.
23. The *Beijing Youth Daily*, December 11, 2002; online news posted at Xinhuanet, December 9, 2001.
24. Online news posted at Chinanews.com, November 11, 2001.
25. The *People's Daily*, December 12, 2001.
26. The *People's Daily*, November 12, 2002.
27. Online news posted at Xinhuanet, September 10, 2002 on domestic trade issues; online news posted at Xinhuanet, November 8, 2001 on railway operation issues; the *People's Daily*, January 4, 2003; December 2, 2004; the *Legal Evening News*, November 16, 2004, on public facility constructions.
28. The *Beijing Times*, May 2, 2002. Also compare with antidumping statistics from the WTO official Web site.
29. For more detailed information, see the *China Business Times* (online news), September 4, 2002.
30. The *People's Daily*, November 25, 2000.
31. Online news posted at Chinanews.com, October 22, 2002.
32. The *People's Daily*, November 10, 2004.

33. For more detailed information, see the *China Business Times* (online news), September 4, 2002.
34. The *People's Daily*, January 6, 2003.
35. The *People's Daily*, January 9, 2007; the *Legal Daily*, October 11, 2006; December 11, 2006.
36. The 1997 regulation was replaced by the Anti-dumping Regulations of the People's Republic of China and the Anti-subsidy Regulations of the People's Republic of China promulgated by the State Council in 2001.
37. The *People's Daily*, January 6, 2003; February 24, 2003; August 10, 2005.
38. The *People's Daily*, January 15, 2007.
39. The *People's Daily*, October 13, 2006.
40. See reports in the *Beijing Youth Daily*, November 2, 2002; the *People's Daily* (online, English), November 5, 2002; the *People's Daily*, September 16, 205; October 9, 2005; October 19, 2005.
41. Online news posted at www.chinacourt.org, December 8, 2002.
42. See reports in the *People's Daily*, March 21, 2001; the *Beijing Youth Daily*, October 24, 2000. See also Y. Zhao (1997) on the economic contract law.
43. The *People's Daily*, April 22, 2005.
44. The *People's Daily*, December 3, 2001; April 22, 2005.
45. The *People's Daily*, April 22, 2005.
46. See the *2006 Patent Report* of the WIPO at the WIPO official Web site.
47. The *People's Daily*, March 1, 2007; March 13, 2007.
48. In his study of China's anticounterfeiting efforts, Mertha (2005) pointed out a shift for foreign actors in their process of seeking remedies, from civil litigation to administrative enforcement (in the mid- to late 1990s), and then to criminal prosecution (since the late 1990s). This shift reflects not only increasing participation by foreign actors in this process, but also their effort to seek more effective legal protection.
49. See reports in the *People's Daily*, January 31, 2007; March 18, 2007. See also WIPO's report titled *Record year for international patent filings with significant growth from Northeast Asia*, released on February 7, 2007 (available at the WIPO official Web site).
50. Online news posted at Xinhuanet, March 29, 2002; the *Yangcheng Evening News*, September 15, 2001.
51. The *People's Daily*, March 11, 2002; May 30, 2002.
52. The *People's Daily*, December 11, 2002.
53. Online news posted at Xinhuanet, December 3, 2002.
54. The *People's Daily*, April 22, 2005.
55. Online news posted at www.cpd.com.cn, January 18, 2007. Available data on local courts' decisions showed a decent winning rate for foreign litigants in those cases. For example, foreign litigants won 60% of administrative litigations and 80% of civil intellectual property cases at the Beijing First Intermediate Court (the *People's Daily*, January 10, 2007).
56. The *People's Daily*, August 30, 2002.
57. The *Chinese Business View*, September 14, 2001; online news posted at Xinhuanet, September 13, 2001; online news posted at Chinanews.com, December 5, 2001.
58. See reports in the *People's Daily*, February 25, 2006; online news posted at www.legalino.gov.cn, September 25, 2006.
59. See reports in the *People's Daily*, December 16, 2006; December 27, 2006; March 1, 2007; March 12, 2007.
60. Data from Amnesty International reported at least 1,010 executions in 2006, higher than the number in 2003 but lower than most of recent years. See Table 4.7.

61. Online news posted at www.chinacourt.org, March 16, 2007.
62. Data from annual work reports by the SPP to the NPC (2002–2007). See also reports in the *People's Daily*, July 31, 2002; October 11, 2003; December 1, 2003; December 2, 2003; November 19, 2004; October 26, 2005.
63. Data from annual work reports by the Supreme People's Court to the NPC (2004–2006).
64. The *People's Daily*, October 11, 2000. Note that in the 1996 amended Criminal Procedure Law, a new article, Article 12, was added, and it stipulates that "No one shall be found guilty without a judgment rendered by a people's court according to law." There are different opinions among scholars on whether this new stipulation symbolizes an adoption of the principle of "presumption of innocence" (see Luo, 2000, pp. 11–12). In any event, there is a consensus that the legal practice in China is not as satisfactory as the law says.
65. Online news at Xinhuanet, December 7, 2000.
66. The *Procuratorial Daily*, August 29, 2001. See also Cui Rongtao's article posted at www.chinacourt.org, February 4, 2005; Ma and Chen's article posted at www.acla.org.cn, September 16, 2003.
67. The *Yangcheng Evening News*, November 17, 2001.
68. Online news posted at Xinhuanet, March 3, 2003. In this report, several other functions of hooding were also mentioned, such as heightened security and prevention of "illegal" communications among suspects.
69. For some examples, see reports in the *People's Daily*, April 15, 2005; September 21, 2005; the *Legal Daily*, May 9, 2003; online report posted at www.legalinfo.gov.cn, July 3, 2006. The SPP's 2007 annual work report to the NPC recorded that a total of 2,171 people's procuratorates (59% of all procuratorates) have adopted video- and audiotaping (the *People's Daily*, March 22, 2007).
70. Online news posted at Xinhuanet, December 8, 2002; December 22, 2002.
71. The *People's Daily*, May 14, 2002; May 15, 2002; September 19, 2002.
72. The *People's Daily*, August 3, 2001.
73. The *People's Daily*, January 3, 2003.
74. For example, in November 2002, the MPS rescinded 36 ARAs. Most of those ARAs dealt with reviews and approvals of new businesses such as public entertainment, massage parlors, and flea markets. It was reported that the public security organizations would now supervise those businesses "according to laws and regulations" (*Beijing Times*, November 14, 2002).
75. The *People's Daily*, November 4, 2002; March 2, 2003; May 25, 2004.
76. The *China Youth Daily*, July 30, 2001.
77. The *People's Daily*, November 16, 2000.
78. The *People's Daily*, December 6, 2002.
79. The *People's Daily*, August 30, 2000; August 3, 2001.
80. The *People's Daily*, May 16, 2005.

CHAPTER 6

1. According to Chinese laws (e.g., Article 147 of the Civil Procedure Law), a judge panel can be composed of three to seven judges or a combination of judges and people's assessors (see Luo, 2000). However, all judge panels I observed consisted of three judges or a combination of judges and people's assessors. The three-person judge panel is the norm in the current court system in China.
2. Internal official rules are rules promulgated within the court system. Although they are not published laws and regulations, they are binding rules internally.

As a way to effectively organize the court system, those internal rules are arguably necessary.

3. See an introduction of the people's assessor system in Brown (1997). Current laws with regard to the practice of the people's assessor system are included in the Organic Law of the People's Courts, the Civil Procedure Law, the Criminal Procedure Law, and the Administrative Litigation Law.

4. See reports in the *People's Daily* on local courts' practices of simplified procedures, February 6, 2004; October 23, 2006; the *Workers' Daily*, July 20, 2002. In the SPC's 2007 annual work report to the NPC, it was reported that about 38.9% of criminal trials and 71.3% of civil trials by the courts of the first instance were handled through the simplified procedure in 2006, and further expansion is called (the *People's Daily*, March 22, 2007).

5. One main reason for the secretary's different position in Beijing is because of the facility (e.g., the use of a computer). It is easier to plug in a computer on one side near the wall than from a seat in the center. Computers were used by secretaries at all courts in Beijing, but not yet in Chengdu in 2002.

6. One interviewee in Beijing explained to me that the reason why the plaintiff or the prosecutor sits to the right of the judges might have something to do with a tradition in Chinese culture, which states that the right side usually represents a higher official ranking!

7. This was officially confirmed by the SPC, and all new secretaries after 2003 would be hired based on contracts (the *People's Daily*, February 20, 2003).

8. Official data reported that by the end of 2004, there were more than 43,300 female judges in the whole nation, about 22% of all judges. The *People's Daily*, August 25, 2005; online news posted at Xinhuanet, March 8, 2005.

9. See reports posted at *www.chinacourt.org*, November 18, 2002; December 13, 2002; and the *People's Daily*, October 24, 2002. In the SPC's 2007 annual work report to the NPC, it was reported that a total of 48,211 people's assessors participated in 339,965 cases (only about 6.5% of all civil, criminal, and administrative litigation cases by the courts of the first instance) in 2006 (the *People's Daily*, March 22, 2007).

10. The prosecutor has a responsibility of supervising the court according to law (see Corne, 1997).

11. For a discussion of the total domination of the prosecution in a trial and how it can keep a 100% prosecution record because of these "privileges," see an online article posted at www.acla.org.cn, February 28, 2003.

12. Based on law, a Chinese adult citizen could act as a legal representative in litigations.

13. I watched only the sentencing of this case, and the trial was held earlier.

14. When I related this information to one judge in the research group, he was a little surprised and said, "They should have taken it (the handcuffs) off." It is common, however, in news reports to see defendants handcuffed and even shackled in trials.

15. By January 2002, there were about 30,000 female attorneys nationwide, 20% of all attorneys in China (the *People's Daily*, January 9, 2002).

16. All lawyers are required to wear official robes in trials now based on a 2002 regulation from the All China Lawyers Association (see Chapter 3).

17. In addition, there were reports in which criminal defense lawyers were officially arrested or charged because of their alleged "improper" defense. See H. Tanner (1994b), and more stories reported in *China News Week*, September 9, 2002, and *Business Watch Magazine*, July 16, 2002.

18. See Article 24 of the Criminal Law (1997).

19. For a study on how Chinese citizens responded to the development of the rule of law in labor dispute cases, see Gallagher (2006).

20. See discussions of current regulations on witnesses and their testimony in criminal cases and suggestions on further improvements posted at www.acla.org.cn, February 27, 2003.

21. The *China Youth Daily*, May 5, 2002; online news posted at Chinanews.com, May 7, 2002.

22. Online news at Chinanews.com, October 30, 2002; online news at Xinhua.net, August 27, 2002.

23. The *People's Daily*, April 24, 2002.

24. The *People's Daily*, June 1, 2006.

25. See similar discussions by Lubman (1999). In recent years, a new means of conducting moral education (for judges) was to attach a personal letter after the legal verdict, called *faguan houyu*. On the one hand, it shows that judges realized the difference between a verdict based on laws and moral education based on other social values. On the other hand, this new practice is, in essence, an extension of a combination of both. This new practice received some positive feedback. See, for example online news posted at Chinanews.com, September 23, 2002; news posted at www.chinacourt.org, November 23, 2002; the *People's Daily*, January 15, 2003.

26. See Articles 85 to 91 of the Civil Procedure Law, cited in Brown (1997).

27. Note the administrative procedure was significantly simplified in the new regulation on marriage registration in 2003 (see discussion in Chapter 4).

28. I discussed this issue with one judge in the research group. He asked about my opinion first. I told him that I believed the defendants' stories. He nodded and agreed with me. However, he also pointed out that it is not easy to define physical torture in some instances, "Does a slap count so? How about a push?" There are many reports online about coerced confessions based on police abuse of power. See, for example, news posted at Xinhuanet, August 3, 2001; Chinanews.com, December 4, 2001.

29. For examples, see L. Wang (2001), Zuo and Zhuo (2000), and the *People's Daily*, November 27, 2002.

30. See discussions of current criminal defense in legal practice and proposed changes in future reforms posted at www.acla.org.cn, March 22, 2003.

31. Some district courts and intermediate courts recently tried various means to "return" the ruling power and authority to the judge panel, and those moves have been appraised in general. See, for example, reports in the *People's Daily*, June 19, 2002; February 12, 2003. Further impact of these trials, however, remains to be seen.

32. The *Yangcheng Evening News*, January 18, 2003; the *News Express*, January 20, 2003.

33. See online article posted at www.chinacourt.org, November 13, 2003.

34. See online article by Professor Jiang Ping, posted at www.acla.org.cn, February 27, 2003.

CHAPTER 7

1. In December 2002, the SPC published regulations that allow public review of case files and documents in civil litigation. Online news posted at http://www.chinacourt.org, December 17, 2002.

2. The *China Youth Daily*, August 14, 2001. This incident is also cited in Zhao (2006b) and Zou (2006).

3. Article 13, Chapter 1 of the Constitution of the People's Republic of China.

4. The *People's Daily*, March 17, 2007.

5. Online news posted at Chinanews.com, December 8, 2002.

6. The *People's Daily*, March 13, 2003; online news posted at Xinhuanet, December 22, 2002. See also Table 4.6 in Chapter 4.
7. Online news posted at http://www.chinacourt.org, December 8, 2002.
8. According to Lubman's (2000) report, the percentage of cases resolved through judicial mediations could be as high as 60%. Official data show that the average judicial mediation rate was about 40.27% at the level of people's tribunals (online reports posted at www.chinacourt.org, April 8, 2005) and about 50% at other court levels (*People's Daily*, October 10, 2006), despite occasional reports of higher numbers at some local levels (e.g., report posted at www. legalinfo.gov.cn, April 26, 2007). The SPC's 2007 annual report to the NPC showed that the judicial mediation rate in 2006 was 30.4% in all civil cases, and the rate reached 55% in civil cases tried by the courts of the first instance (the *People's Daily*, March 22, 2007).
9. The *People's Daily*, September 29, 2002.
10. The *People's Daily*, October 11, 2006; December 22, 2006. What is missing in this report, with regard to financial incentive, is the potential abuse of power at the local level (e.g., overcharge). Such abuse of power was noticed by Fu (2002).
11. Online news posted at www.legalinfo.gov.cn, November 20, 2006.
12. There are numerous reports and articles on President Hu's "harmonious society" speech. See, for example, a full report by Wu Bangguo, Chairman of the Standing Committee of the NPC, in the *People's Daily*, October 20, 2006.
13. The *People's Daily*, August 15, 2006; January 11, 2007; January 17, 2007; March 11, 2007.
14. See, for example, online discussions posted at http://www.acla.org.cn, March 5, 2003; March 17, 2003; the *People's Daily*, March 19, 2003.
15. Realizing this impossible mission, some Chinese scholars in their reform proposals put more emphasis on individual judges' (or judge panels') independence (from interference from superiors within the court system) and the independence of the court system from administrative interferences. See Tan (2000) and L. Wang (2001). It is not clear at this moment, however, what impact this approach will have and to what extent this approach will solve all problems faced by the judicial system.
16. The *Liaoshen Evening News*, January 1, 2003.
17. The *People's Daily*, October 16, 2002.
18. For prosecutors' oath-taking, see the *People's Daily*, July 24, 2002; for attorneys' oath-taking, see online news posted at www.acla.org, April 1, 2003; the *Yunnan Daily*, December 4, 2003; for people's assessors' oath-taking, see online news posted at www.chinacourt.org, April 21, 2005; for other nonlegal governmental employees' oath-taking, see reports in the *People's Daily*, August 7, 2002; the *Beijing Evening News*, August 6, 2002.

Select Glossary

TERMS IN TEXT

Chinese in Pin-yin	Chinese (Simplified)
bentu ziyuan	本土资源
chaoqi jiya	超期羁押
chengfen	成分
chenmo quan	沉默权
chubu xingcheng	初步形成
cong kuai	从快
cong zhong	从重
dafaguan	大法官
daiye	待业
dang'an	档案
dangbao	党报
danwei	单位
er'shen	二审
faguan	法官
faguan houyu	法官后语
fajing	法警
falü yuanzhu	法律援助
fangzi	房子
fu yuanzhang	副院长

Chinese in Pin-yin	*Chinese (Simplified)*
gaoji faguan	高级法官
Gong, Jian, Fa	公检法
goudui	勾兑
guanxi	关系
hei shehui	黑社会
heyi ting	合议庭
huibi	回避
hukou	户口
jianyi chengxu	简易程序
jiben xingcheng	基本形成
jiuzheng	纠正
kongbian jiaoyi	控辩交易
lesuo	勒索
li	礼
lifa fa	立法法
ling kougong	零口供
maodun	矛盾
pao duan tui	跑断腿
putong chengxu	普通程序
qisu shu	起诉书
renmin fayuan wunian gaige gangyao	人民法院五年改革纲要
renmin peishenyuan	人民陪审员
renmin ribao	人民日报
shenpan duli	审判独立
shenpan weiyuanhui	审判委员会
shenpan yuan	审判员
shenpan zhang	审判长
shenzhe bupan, panzhe bushen	审者不判 判者不审

Chinese in Pin-yin	*Chinese (Simplified)*
shiye	失业
shouxi dafaguan	首席大法官
shuji yuan	书记员
shui zhuzhang, shui juzheng	谁主张 谁举证
ting	庭
tingzhang	庭长
wen zhun hen	稳 准 狠
wuquan fa	物权法
xiagang	下岗
xian pan hou shen	先判后审
xinlang wang	新浪网
xingzheng shenpi	行政审批
yanda	严打
yide zhiguo	以德治国
yifa zhiguo	依法治国
yuanzhang	院长
zhuguan yuanzhang	主管院长
zonghe zhili	综合治理
Zu	族
zuigao renmin fayuan guanyu minshi	中国人民法院关于民事诉讼证据的若干规定
susong zhengju de ruogan guiding	

TERMS IN MEDIA SOURCES

English translation	*Chinese (Simplified)*
Beijing Business Today	北京商报
Beijing Daily	北京日报
Beijing Daily Messenger	北京娱乐信报

English translation	*Chinese (Simplified)*
Beijing Evening News	北京晚报
Beijing Morning Post	北京晨报
Beijing Times	京华时报
Beijing Youth Daily	北京青年报
Business Watch Magazine	商务周刊
China Business Post	财经时报
China Business Times	中华工商时报
Chinese Business View	华商报
China Daily	中国日报
China Economic Times	中国经济时报
Chinanews.com	中国新闻网
China News Week	中国新闻周刊
China Youth Daily	中国青年报
Chongqing Economic Times	重庆经济报
Chongqing Evening News	重庆晚报
Cpd.com.cn	警察网
Global Times	环球时报
Huadong News	华东新闻
Information Times	信息时报
Laodong (Labor) News	劳动报
Legal Daily	法制日报
Legal Evening News	法制晚报
Liaoshen Evening News	辽沈晚报
Life Week	三联生活周刊
Market Journal	市场报
Nanfang Daily	南方日报
Nan Feng Chuang Magazine	南风窗杂志
New Daily of East	东新日报

English translation	Chinese (Simplified)
News Express	新快报
New Times Weekly	新世纪周刊
Outlook Weekly	瞭望新闻周刊
People.com.cn	人民网
People's Court Daily	人民法院报
People's Daily	人民日报
Procuratorial Daily	检察日报
Qilu Evening News	齐鲁晚报
Shanghai Morning Post	上海晨报
Shanghai Security News	上海证券报
Sichuan Workers' Daily	四川工人日报
Southern Metropolis Daily	南方都市报
Southern Weekend	南方周末
21st Century Jobs	21世纪人才报
Workers' Daily	工人日报
Xinhuanet	新华网
Yangcheng Evening News	羊城晚报
Yangtse Evening Post	扬子晚报
Yunnan Daily	云南日报

References

BOOKS AND ARTICLES IN ENGLISH

Alford, W. P. (1995a). *To steal a book is an elegant offense: Intellectual property law in Chinese civilization*. Stanford, CA: Stanford University Press.

Alford, W. P. (1995b). Tasselled loafers for barefoot lawyers: Transformation and tension in the world of Chinese legal workers. *The China Quarterly, 141*, 22–38.

Amnesty International. (1996). *China: No one is safe*. London: Author.

Amnesty International. (1996–2007). *Annual reports on China*. Retrieved from http://www.amnesty.org

Amnesty International. (2004). *People's Republic of China, executed "according to law"?: The death penalty in China* (Rep. No. ASA 17/003/2004). London: Author.

Anderson, A. F., & Gil, V. E. (1998). China's modernization and the decline of communitarianism: The control of sex crimes and implications for the fate of informal social control. *Journal of Contemporary Criminal Justice, 14*, 248–261.

Arrighi, G., Hopkins, T. K., & Wallerstein, I. (1989). *Antisystemic movements*. London: Verso.

Bakken, B. (1991). Modernizing morality? Paradoxes of socialization in China during the 1980's. *East Asian History, 2*, 125–142.

Bakken, B. (1993). Crime, juvenile delinquency and deterrence policy in China. *The Australian Journal of Chinese Affairs, 30*, 29–58.

Bakken, B. (1995). Editor's introduction: Juvenile crime during the reforms. *Chinese Sociology and Anthropology, 27*(3), 3–18.

Bakken, B. (2000). *The exemplary society: Human improvement, social control, and the dangers of modernity in China*. New York: Oxford University Press.

Bakken, B. (Ed.). (2005). *Crime, punishment, and policing in China*. Lanham, MD: Rowman & Littlefield.

Bao, W., Hass, A., & Pi, Y. (2007). Life strain, coping, and delinquency in the People's Republic of China: An empirical test of general strain theory from a matching perspective in social support. *International Journal of Offender Therapy and Comparative Criminology, 51*, 9–24.

Bardhan, P. K., & Roemer, J. E. (Eds.). (1993). *Market socialism: The current debate*. New York: Oxford University Press.

Baum, R. (1994). *Burying Mao: Chinese politics in the age of Deng Xiaoping*. Princeton, NJ: Princeton University Press.

Baum, R., & Shevchenko, A. (1999). The "state of the state". In M. Goldman & R. MacFarquhar (Eds.), *The paradox of China's post-Mao reform* (pp. 333–362). Cambridge, MA: Harvard University Press.

Biddulph, S. (1993). Review of police powers of administrative detention in the People's Republic of China. *Crime and Delinquency, 39*, 337–354.

Bornschier, V., & Chase-Dunn, C. (1985). *Transnational corporations and underdevelopment*. New York: Praeger.

Boswell, T., & Chase-Dunn, C. (2000). *The spiral of capitalism and socialism: Toward global democracy*. Boulder, CO: Lynne Rienner.

Boxer, J. T. (1999). China's death penalty: Undermining legal reform and threatening national economic interest. *Suffolk Transnational Law Review, 22*, 593–618.

Bracey, D. H. (1985). The system of justice and the concept of human nature in the People's Republic of China. *Justice Quarterly, 2*, 139–144.

Bracey, D. H. (1988). Like a doctor to a patient, like a parent to a child—Corrections in the People's Republic of China. *The Prison Journal, 68*, 24–33.

Bracey, D. H. (1989). The regulation of the People's Republic of China concerning punishment for disturbing order: The police and administrative punishment. *Criminal Justice Review, 14*, 154–165.

Brown, F., & Rogers, C. (1997). The role of arbitration in resolving transnational disputes: A survey of trends in the People's Republic of China. *Berkeley Journal of International Law, 15*, 329–351.

Brown, R. C. (1997). *Understanding Chinese courts and legal process: Law with Chinese characteristics*. The Hague, Netherlands: Kluwer Law.

Butler, S. B. (1985). Price scissors and commune administration in post-Mao China. In W. L. Parish (Ed.), *Chinese rural development: The great transformation* (pp. 95–114). Armonk, NY: Sharpe.

Cao, L. (2007). Returning to normality: Anomie and crime in China. *International Journal of Offender Therapy and Comparative Criminology, 51*, 40–51.

Cao, L., & Hou, C. (2001). A comparison of confidence in the police in China and in the United States. *Journal of Criminal Justice, 29*, 87–99.

Cao, S. (1998a). The storm over bankruptcy (I). *Chinese Law and Government, 31*(1), 12–93.

Cao, S. (1998b). The storm over bankruptcy (II). *Chinese Law and Government, 31*(2), 11–96.

Chang, Y. (2004). Courtroom questioning as a culturally situated persuasive genre of talk. *Discourse & Society, 15*, 705–722.

Chao, P. (1982). *Chinese kinship*. London: Kegan Paul.

Chase-Dunn, C. K. (1982). *Socialist states in the world economy*. Beverly Hills, CA: Sage.

Chase-Dunn, C. K. (1989). *Global formation: Structures of the world-economy*. New York: Blackwell.

Chen, A. (2005). Secret societies and organized crime in contemporary China. *Modern Asian Studies, 39*, 77–107.

Chen, J. (1995). *From administrative authorisation to private law: A comparative perspective of the developing civil law in the People's Republic of China*. Boston: Martinus Nijhoff.

Chen, J. (1999). *Chinese law: Towards an understanding of Chinese law, its nature and development*. The Hague, Netherlands: Kluwer Law.

Chen, P. M. (1973). *Law and justice: The legal system in China 2400 B.C. to 1960 A.D.* New YorkDunellen.

Chen, W. (1998). Has the time come for a new ideology in China? The creation of a new authoritative discourse. In J. Cheng (Ed.), *China Review*, 259–280. Hong Kong: Chinese University Press.

Chen, X. (2002). Social control in China: Applications of the labeling theory and the reintegrative shaming theory. *International Journal of Offender Therapy and Comparative Criminology, 46*, 45–63.

Chin, S. (1983). The constitution of China and the economic base. *Chinese Law and Government, 16*(2–3), 45–66.

Christiansen, F., & Rai, S. M. (1996). *Chinese politics and society: An introduction.* New York: Prentice-Hall.

Clark, D., & Feinerman, J. (1996). Antagonistic contradictions: Criminal law and human rights in China. In S. Lubman (Ed.), *China's legal reforms* (pp. 135–154). New York: Oxford University Press.

Cohen, J. A. (1968). *The criminal process in the People's Republic of China, 1949–1964: An introduction.* Cambridge, MA: Harvard University Press.

Cohen, J. A. (Ed.). (1970). *Contemporary Chinese law: Research problems and perspectives.* Cambridge, MA: Harvard University Press.

Cohen, J. A. (1997). Due process? In T. V. Lee (Ed.), *Law, the state, and society in China* (pp. 351–371). New York: Garland.

Cohen, J. A., Edwards, R. R., & Chen, F. C. (Eds.). (1980). *Essays on China's legal traditions.* Princeton, NJ: Princeton University Press.

Corne, P. H. (1997). *Foreign investment in China: The administrative legal system.* Hong Kong: Hong Kong University Press.

Curran, D. J. (1998). Economic reform, the floating population, and crime: The transformation of social control in China. *Journal of Contemporary Criminal Justice, 14,* 262–280.

Davis, D. S. (Ed.). (2000). *The consumer revolution in urban China.* Berkeley: University of California Press.

Davis, D. S., Kraus, R., Naughton, B., & Perry, E. J. (Eds.). (1995). *Urban spaces in contemporary China: The potential for autonomy and community in post-Mao China.* New York: Woodrow Wilson Center Press.

Dellapenna, J. W., & Morton, P. M. (Eds.). (2000). *China and Hong Kong in legal transition: Commercial and humanitarian issues.* Chicago: Section of International Law and Practice, American Bar Association.

Deng, X., & Cordilia, A. (1999). To get rich is glorious: Rising expectations, declining control, and escalating crime in contemporary China. *International Journal of Offender Therapy and Comparative Criminology, 43,* 211–229.

Deng, X., Zhang, L., & Cordilia, A. (1998). Social control and recidivism in China. *Journal of Contemporary Criminal Justice, 14,* 281–295.

Diamant, N. J. (2000). Conflict and conflict resolution in China: Beyond mediation-centered approaches. *Journal of Conflict Resolution, 44,* 523–546.

Diamant, N. J., Lubman, S. B., & O'Brien, K. J. (Eds.). (2005). *Engaging the law in China: State, society, and possibilities for justice.* Stanford, CA: Stanford University Press.

Dicks, A. R. (1995). Compartmentalized law and judicial restraint: An inductive view of some jurisdictional barriers to reform. *The China Quarterly, 141,* 82–109.

Dikotter, F. (2002). *Crime, punishment and the prison in modern China.* New York: Columbia University Press.

Ding, X. L. (2001). The quasi-criminalization of a business sector in China: Deconstructing the construction-sector syndrome. *Crime, Law & Social Change, 35,* 177–201.

Durkheim, E. (1983). *Durkheim and the law* (S. Lukes & A. Scull, Eds.). New York: St. Martin's Press.

Durkheim, E. (1984). *The division of labour in society.* Basingstoke, UK: Macmillan Houndmills.

Dutton, M. (1992). *Policing and punishment in China–From patriarchy to the "people."* Cambridge, UK: Cambridge University Press.

Dutton, M. (2005). Toward a government of contract: Policing in the era of reform. In B. Bakken (Ed.), *Crime, punishment, and policing in China* (pp. 189–233). Lanham, MD: Rowman & Littlefield.

Dutton, M., & Lee, T. (1993). Missing the target? Policing strategies in the period of economic reform. *Crime and Delinquency, 39,* 316–336.

Epstein, E. J. (1991). China's legal reforms. In H. Kuan & M. Brosseau (Eds.), *China Review, 9*.1–9.38. Hong Kong: Chinese University Press.

Epstein, E. J. (1992). A matter of justice. In H. Kuan & M. Brosseau (Eds.), *China Review, 5*.1–5.37. Hong Kong: Chinese University Press.

Feinerman, J. V. (1994). Legal institution, administrative device, or foreign import: The roles of contract in the People's Republic of China. In P. B. Potter (Ed.), *Domestic law reforms in post-Mao China* (pp. 225–244). Armonk, NY: Sharpe.

Feinerman, J. V. (1995). Chinese participation in the international legal order: Rogue elephant or team player? *The China Quarterly, 141*, 186–210.

Feng, S. (2001). Crime and crime control in a changing China. In J. Liu, L. Zhang, & S. F. Messner (Eds.), *Crime and social control in a changing China* (pp. 123–130). Westport, CT: Greenwood.

Feng, Y. (1992). *The law of security in the People's Republic of China: An emerging capitalist device*. Unpublished master's thesis, University of Toronto, Canada.

Frank, A. G. (1980). *Crisis in: The world economy*. New York: Holmes & Meier.

Frank, A. G. (1998). *Reorient: Global economy in the Asian age*. Berkeley: University of California Press.

Frank, A. G., & Gills, B. K. (Eds.). (1993). *The world economy: Five hundred years or five thousand?* New York: Routledge.

Friday, P. C. (1998). Crime and crime prevention in China: A challenge to the development-crime nexus. *Journal of Contemporary Criminal Justice, 14*, 296–314.

Friedmann, J. (2005). *China's urban transition*. Minneapolis: University of Minnesota Press.

Fu, H. (1990). Police reform and its implication for Chinese social control. *International Journal of Comparative and Applied Criminal Justice, 14*, 41–63.

Fu, H. (1991). Mediators and the law: China and America compared. *International Journal of Comparative and Applied Criminal Justice, 15*, 81–88.

Fu, H. (1992). Juvenile delinquency in post-Mao China. *International Journal of Comparative and Applied Criminal Justice, 16*, 263–273.

Fu, H. (1993). *Formalizing popular justice: Police and community in post-Mao China*. Unpublished doctoral thesis, York University, Toronto, Canada.

Fu, H. (2002). Shifting landscape of dispute resolution in rural China. In J. Chen, Y. Li, & J. M. Otto (Eds.), *Implementation of law in the People's Republic of China* (pp. 179–195). The Hague, Netherlands: Kluwer Law.

Gallagher, M. E. (2006). Mobilizing the law in China: "Informed disenchantment" and the development of legal consciousness. *Law and Society Review, 40*, 783–816.

Gao, H., & Song, J. H. (2001). Economic reform, organized crime, and legal administrative response in China. *International Journal of Comparative Criminology, 1*, 91–108.

Garland, D. (1990). *Punishment and modern society*. New York: Oxford University Press.

Garland, D. (2001). *The culture of control: Crime and social order in contemporary society*. Chicago: The University of Chicago Press.

Gaylord, M. S., & Levine, P. (1997). The criminalization of official profiteering: Lawmaking in the People's Republic of China. *International Journal of the Sociology of Law, 25*, 117–134.

Giddens, A. (1971). *Capitalism and modern social theory: An analysis of the writings of Marx, Durkheim, and Max Weber*. Cambridge, UK: Cambridge University Press.

Gil, V. E., & Anderson, A. F. (1998). State-sanctioned aggression and the control of prostitution in the People's Republic of China: A review. *Aggression and Violent Behavior, 3*, 129–142.

Gil, V. E., & Anderson, A. F. (1999). Case study of rape in contemporary China: A cultural-historical analysis of gender and power differentials. *Journal of Interpersonal Violence, 14*, 1151–1171.

Girling, J. (1987). *Capital and power: Political economy and social transformation.* London: Croom Helm.

Gold, T. B. (1991). Youth and the state. *China Quarterly, 127*, 594–612.

Greenberg, J., & Lakeland, J. R. (1998). *A methodology for developing and deploying Internet and intranet solutions.* Upper Saddle River, NJ: Prentice-Hall.

Gross, H. J. (1988). China's special economic zone. *China Law Reporter, 4*(4), 23–40.

Gu, E. X. (2001). Labor market reform [guest editor's introduction]. *Chinese Law and Government, 34*(1), 5–15.

Gu, M. (1999). Criminal procedure law. In G. Wang & J. Mo (Eds.), *Chinese law* (pp. 643–676). The Hague, Netherlands: Kluwer Law.

Harris, R., & Lauderdale, P. (2002). Globalization and South Africa. *Journal of Asian and African Studies, 38*, 243–263.

Harvey, D. (1990). *The condition of postmodernity.* London: Blackwell.

He, X. (2005). Why do they not comply with the law? Illegality and semi-legality among rural-urban migrant entrepreneurs in Beijing. *Law & Society Review, 39*, 527–562.

Herb, P. L. (1988). Economic crime in the People's Republic of China. *ILSA Journal of International Law, 12*, 55–83.

Hertz, E. (1998). *The trading crowd: An ethnography of the Shanghai stock market.* Cambridge, UK: Cambridge University Press.

Hobler, B. H. (1989). Correctional education in the People's Republic of China. *Journal of Correctional Education, 40*, 64–69.

Hopkins, T. K., & Wallerstein, I. (Eds.). (1980). *Processes of world-system.* Beverly Hills, CA: Sage.

Hopkins, T. K., & Wallerstein, I. (1982). *World-systems analysis: Theory and methodology.* Beverly Hills, CA: Sage.

Hopkins, T. K., & Wallerstein, I. (1996). *The age of transition: Trajectory of the world-system, 1945–2025.* Atlantic Highlands, NJ: Pluto Press.

Hu, H. C. (1948). *The common descent group in China and its functions.* New York: Viking Fund.

Hu, Z. (1989). More on the five modes of production. *Chinese Law and Government, 21*(2), 71–97.

Hughes, J. A. (1995). *Understanding classical sociology: Marx, Weber, Durkheim.* Thousand Oaks, CA: Sage.

Inverarity, J. M., Lauderdale, P., & Feld, B. C. (1983). *Law and society: Sociological perspectives on criminal law.* Boston: Little, Brown.

Ji, W. (1989). The sociology of law in China: Overview and trends. *Law and Society Review, 23*, 903–914.

Johnson, E. H. (1986). Politics, power and prevention: The People's Republic of China case. *Journal of Criminal Justice, 14*, 449–457.

Jones, S. (Ed.). (1999). *Doing Internet research: Critical issues and methods for examining the net.* Thousand Oaks, CA: Sage.

Jorgensen, D. L. (1989). *Participant observation.* Newbury Park, CA: Sage.

Keith, R. C. (1991). Chinese politics and the new theory of "rule of law". *The China Quarterly, 125*, 109–118.

Keith, R. C. (1994). *China's struggle for the rule of law.* Houndmills, UK: St. Martin's.

Keith, R. C. (1997). Legislating women's and children's "rights and interests" in the PRC. *The China Quarterly, 149*, 29–55.

Keith, R. C., & Lin, Z. (2001). *Law and justice in China's new marketplace.* London: Palgrave.

Keith, R. C., & Lin, Z. (2006). *New crime in China: Public order and human rights.* London: Routledge.

Khan, A. R., Griffin, K., Riskin, C., & Zhao, R. (1992). Household income and its distribution in China. *China Quarterly, 132,* 1029–1061.

Kim, H. I. (1981). *Fundamental legal concepts of China and the West: A comparative study.* Port Washington, NY: National University Publications, Kennikat Press.

Lardy, N. R. (1994). *China in the world economy.* Washington, DC: Institute for International Economics.

Lardy, N. R. (2002). *Integrating China into the global economy.* Washington, DC: Brookings Institution Press.

Lauderdale, P., & Cruit, M. (1993). *The struggle for control: A study of law, disputes, and deviance.* Albany: State University of New York Press.

Lauderdale, P., & Toggia, P. (1999). An indigenous view of the new world order. *Journal of Asian and African Studies, 34,* 157–177.

Lee, T. V. (Ed.). (1997). *Law, the state, and society in China.* New York: Garland.

Leng, S. (1982). Crime and punishment in post-Mao China. *China Law Reporter, 2,* 5–33.

Leng, S. (1985). *Criminal justice in post-Mao China: Analysis and documents.* Albany: State University of New York Press.

Levy, R. (1995). Corruption, economic crime and social transformation since the reforms: The debate in China. *The Australian Journal of Chinese Affairs, 33,* 1–25.

Li, J. (1996). The structural strains of China's socio-legal system: A transition to formal legalism? *International Journal of the Sociology of Law, 24,* 41–59.

Li, L. C. (2000). The "rule of law" policy in Guangdong: Continuity or departure? Meaning, significance and processes. *The China Quarterly, 161,* 199–220.

Li, L., & O'Brien, K. J. (1999). The struggle over village elections. In M. Goldman & R. MacFarquhar (Eds.), *The paradox of China's post-Mao reform* (pp. 129–144). Cambridge, MA: Harvard University Press.

Li, V. H. (1978). *Law without lawyers: A comparative view of law in China and the United States.* Boulder, CO: Westview.

Li, Y. (2002). Court reform in China: Problems, progress and prospects. In J. Chen, Y. Li, & J. M. Otto (Eds.), *Implementation of law in the People's Republic of China* (pp. 55–84). The Hague, Netherlands: Kluwer Law.

Liang, B., & Lauderdale, P. (2006). China and globalization: Developments in economic and legal change. *Journal of Developing Societies, 22,* 197–220.

Liang, B., & Lu, H. (2006). Conducting fieldwork in China—Observations on collecting primary data regarding crime, law, and the criminal justice system. *Journal of Contemporary Criminal Justice, 22*(2), 1–16.

Liang, B., Lu, H., Miethe, T. D., & Zhang, L. (2006). Sources of variation in pro-death penalty attitudes in China: An exploratory study of Chinese students at home and abroad. *British Journal of Criminology, 46,* 119–130.

Lin, G. (1989). The Asiatic mode of production and ancient Chinese society: A criticism of Umberto Melotti's distortion of Chinese history in his book "Marx and the third world." *Chinese Law and Government, 21*(2), 47–70.

Liu, F. (1987). Some aspects of the protection of industry property in China. *China Law Reporter, 4,* 155–160.

Liu, J. (2005). Predicting recidivism in a communitarian society: China. *International Journal of Offender Therapy and Comparative Criminology, 49,* 392–409.

Liu, J. H., Zhang, L. N., & Messner, S. F. (Eds.). (2001). *Crime and social control in a changing China.* Westport, CT: Greenwood.

Liu, J., Zhou, D., Liska, A. E., Messner, S. F., Krohn, M. D., Zhang, L., et al. (1998). Status, power and sentencing in China. *Justice Quarterly, 15*, 289–300.

Liu, S. (2006). Client influence and the contingency of professionalism: The work of elite corporate lawyers in China. *Law & Society Review, 40*, 751–781.

Lo, C. W. (1995). *China's legal awakening: Legal theory and criminal justice in Deng's era.* Hong Kong: Hong Kong University Press.

Lowe, D. M. (1996). *The function of "China" in Marx, Lenin, and Mao.* Berkeley: University of California Press.

Lu, H. (1998). *Community policing—Rhetoric or reality? The contemporary Chinese community-based policing system in Shanghai.* Unpublished doctoral dissertation, Arizona State University, Tempe, AZ.

Lu, H. (1999). Bang Jiao and reintegrative shaming in China's urban neighborhoods. *International Journal of Comparative and Applied Criminal Justice, 23*, 115–125.

Lu, H., & Drass, K. A. (2002). Transience and the disposition of theft cases in China. *Justice Quarterly, 19*, 69–96.

Lu, H., & Miethe, T. D. (2002). Legal representation and criminal processing in China. *British Journal of Criminology, 42*, 267–280.

Lu, H., & Miethe, T. D. (2003). Confessions and criminal case disposition in China. *Law and Society Review, 37*, 549–578.

Lu, H., & Miethe, T. D. (2007). Provincial laws on the protection of women in China: A partial test of Black's theory. *International Journal of Offender Therapy and Comparative Criminology, 51*, 25–39.

Lu, H., & Zhang, L. (2005). Death penalty in China: The law and the practice. *Journal of Criminal Justice, 33*, 367–376.

Lu, X. (1995). Rethinking the Chinese peasantry: Ten years of transformation. *Chinese Law and Government, 28*(1), 39–80.

Lubman, S. B. (1994). Introduction. In P. B. Potter (Ed.), *Domestic law reforms in post-Mao China* (pp. 3–16). Armonk, NY: Sharpe.

Lubman, S. B. (Ed.). (1996). *China's legal reforms.* New York: Oxford University Press.

Lubman, S. B. (1999). *Bird in a cage: Legal reform in China after Mao.* Stanford, CA: Stanford University Press.

Lubman, S. B. (2000). Sino-American relations and China's struggle for the rule of law. In J. W. Dellapenna & P. M. Norton (Eds.), *China and Hong Kong in legal transition: Commercial and humanitarian issues* (pp. 9–60). Chicago: Section of International Law and Practice, American Bar Association,

Lukes, S. (1985). *Marxism and morality.* New York: Oxford University Press.

Luo, W. (2000). *The amended criminal procedure law and the criminal court rules of the People's Republic of China: With English translation, introduction, and annotation.* Buffalo, NY: Hein.

Ma, G. (2001). Population migration and crime in Beijing, China. In J. Liu, L. Zhang, & S. F. Messner (Eds.), *Crime and social control in a changing China* (pp. 65–71). Westport, CT: Greenwood.

MacCormack, G. (1996). *The spirit of traditional Chinese law.* Athens: The University of Georgia Press.

Marshall, C., & Rossman, G. B. (1989). *Designing qualitative research.* Newbury Park, CA: Sage.

Mathaus, M. (1989). Residence control in present-day China. *Asian Affairs, 20*, 184–194.

Maurer-Fazio, M., Rawski, T. G., & Zhang, W. (1999). Inequality in the rewards for holding up half the sky: Gender wage gaps in China's urban labour market, 1988–1994. *The China Journal, 41*, 55–88.

Maxwell, J. A. (1996). *Qualitative research design: An interactive approach*. Thousand Oaks, CA: Sage.

Mayer, A. (1989). The rocky way to democracy: A few comments on legal developments in China since the Cultural Revolution. *China Law Report, 6*, 1–10.

Meredith, R. (2002, September 2). Brown and brains: Engineers and scientists, not just factory workers, now come cheap in China. *Forbes, 170*(4), 94.

Merry, S. E. (1990). *Getting justice and getting even: Legal consciousness among working-class Americans*. Chicago: University of Chicago Press.

Mertha, A. C. (2005). Shifting legal and administrative goalposts: Chinese bureaucracies, foreign actors, and the evolution of China's anti-counterfeiting enforcement regime. In N. J. Diamant, S. B. Lubman, & K. J. O'Brien (Eds.), *Engaging the law in China: State, society, and possibilities for justice* (pp. 162–192). Stanford, CA: Stanford University Press.

Michelson, E. (1998a). Tradition in the shadow of modern legal practice: Continuing and change in the delivery of justice in China. *Chinese Law and Government, 31*(5), 5–108.

Michelson, E. (1998b). Tradition in the shadow of modern legal practice: Continuing and change in the delivery of justice in China. *Chinese Law and Government, 31*(6), 3–104.

Michelson, E. (2006). The practice of law as an obstacle to justice: Chinese lawyers at work. *Law and Society Review, 40*, 1–38.

Mo, J. S. (1997). Alternative dispute resolution. In C. Wang & X. Zhang (Eds.), *Introduction to Chinese law* (pp. 367–407). Hong Kong: Sweet & Maxwell Asia.

Mo, J. S. (1999a). Law of intellectual property. In G. Wang & J. Mo (Eds.), *Chinese law* (pp. 497–556). The Hague, Netherlands: Kluwer Law.

Mo, J. S. (1999b). Non-judicial means of dispute settlement. In G. Wang & J. Mo (Eds.), *Chinese law* (pp. 757–805). The Hague, Netherlands: Kluwer Law.

Monthy, J. T. (1998). Internal perspectives on Chinese human rights reform: The death penalty in the PRC. *Texas International Law Journal, 33*, 189–226.

Nai-kwai Lo, L. (1993). The changing educational system dilemma of disparity. In H. Kuan & M. Brosseau (Eds.), *China Review*, 22.1–22.42. Hong Kong: Chinese University Press.

Ngai, N. (1994). Youth deviance in China. In H. Kuan & M. Brosseau (Eds.), *China Review*, 18.1–18.21. Hong Kong: Chinese University Press.

Oechsli, C. G. (1988). The developing law of mortgages and secured transaction in the People's Republic of China. *China Law Report, 5*, 1–26.

Oi, J. C. (1989). *State and peasant in contemporary China: The political economy of village government*. Berkeley: University of California Press.

Oi, J. C. (1999). *Rural China takes off: Institutional foundations of economic reform*. Berkeley: University of California Press.

Oliverio, A., & Lauderdale, P. (2005). *Terrorism: A new testament*. Whitby, ON, Canada: de Sitter.

Ollman, B., & Schweichart, D. (1998). *Market socialism: The debate among socialists*. New York: Routledge.

Palmer, M. (1996). The re-emergence of family law in post-Mao China. In S. Lubman (Ed.), *China's legal reforms* (pp. 110–134). New York: Oxford University Press.

Parish, W. L. (Ed.). (1985). *Chinese rural development: The great transformation*. Armonk, NY: Sharpe.

Peerenboom, R. P. (1993). *Law and morality in ancient China: The silk manuscripts of Huang-Lao*. Albany: State University of New York Press.

Peerenboom, R. (2001). Seek truth from facts: An empirical study of the enforcement of arbitral awards in the People's Republic of China. *American Journal of Comparative Law, 49*, 249–327.

Peerenboom, R. (2002a). *China's long march toward rule of law*. Cambridge, UK: Cambridge University Press.

Peerenboom, R. (2002b). Law enforcement and the legal profession in China. In J. Chen, Y. Li, & J. M. Otto (Eds.), *Implementation of law in the People's Republic of China* (pp. 125–147). The Hague, Netherlands: Kluwer Law.

Peerenboom, R. (Ed.). (2004). *Asian discourses of rule of law: Theories and implementation of rule of law in twelve Asian countries, France, and the U.S.* New York: Routledge.

Ping, H. (2006). Is money laundering a true problem in China? *International Journal of Offender Therapy and Comparative Criminology, 50*, 101–116.

Polumbaum, J. (1994). To protect or restrict? Points of contention in China's draft press law. In P. B. Potter (Ed.), *Domestic law reforms in post-Mao China* (pp. 247–269). Armonk, NY: Sharpe.

Potter, P. B. (1992). *The economic contract law of China: Legitimation and contract autonomy in the PRC*. Seattle: University of Washington Press.

Potter, P. B. (1994a). The administrative litigation law of the PRC: Judicial review and bureaucratic reform. In P. B. Potter (Ed.), *Domestic law reforms in post-Mao China* (pp. 270–304). Armonk, NY: Sharpe.

Potter, P. B. (Ed.). (1994b). *Domestic law reforms in post-Mao China*. Armonk, NY: Sharpe.

Potter, P. B. (1994c). Socialist legality and legal culture in Shanghai: A survey of the getihu. *Canadian Journal of Law & Society, 9*(2), 41–72.

Potter, P. B. (1995). *Foreign business law in China: Past progress and future challenges*. San Francisco: The 1990 Institute.

Potter, P. B. (1998). The Chinese legal system (?): Continuing tensions over norms and enforcement. In J. Cheng (Ed.), *China Review*, 25–60. Hong Kong: Chinese University Press.

Potter, P. B. (1999). The Chinese legal system: Continuing commitment to the primacy of state power. *The China Quarterly, 159*, 673–683.

Potter, P. B. (2001a). *The Chinese legal system: Globalization and local legal culture*. New York: Routledge.

Potter, P. B. (2001b). The legal implications of China's accession to the WTO. *The China Quarterly, 167*, 592–609.

Potter, P. B. (2004). Legal reform in China: Institutions, culture, and selective adaptation. *Law & Social Inquiry, 29*, 465–495.

Qiu, Z., & Zheng, Y. (1998). Xia-Gang and its sociological implications of reducing labour redundancy in China's SOEs. In G. Wang & J. Wong (Eds.), *China's political economy* (pp. 227–248). Singapore: Singapore University Press.

Rawski, T. G. (2001). What's happening to China's GDP statistics? *China Economic Review, 12*, 347–354.

Reichel, P. L. (2005). *Comparative criminal justice systems: A topic approach* (4th ed.). Upper Saddle River, NJ: Prentice-Hall.

Ren, X. (1997). *Tradition of the law and law of the tradition: Law, state, and social control in China*. Westport, CT: Greenwood.

Roberts, A. L. (1997). *The political impact of China's new private entrepreneurs*. Unpublished doctoral dissertation, University of California, Berkeley, CA.

Roemer, J. E. (1993). Can there be socialism after communism? In P. K. Bardhan & J. E. Roemer (Eds.), *Market socialism: The current debate* (pp. 89–107). New York: Oxford University Press.

Roemer, J. E. (1994). *A future for socialism*. Cambridge, MA: Harvard University Press.

Roemer, J. E. (1996). *Equal shares: Making market socialism work*. London: Verso.

Rojek, D. G. (1985). The criminal process in the People's Republic of China. *Justice Quarterly, 2*, 117–125.

Rojek, D. G. (1989). Social control in the People's Republic of China. *Criminal Justice Review, 14*, 141–153.

Rojek, D. G. (2001). Chinese social control: From shaming and reintegration to "getting rich is glorious." In J. H. Liu, L. Zhang, & S. F. Messner (Eds.), *Crime and social control in a changing China* (pp. 89–103). Westport, CT: Greenwood.

Schweichart, D., Lawler, J., Ticktin, H., & Ollman, B. (1998). *Market socialism: The debate among socialists.* New York: Routledge.

Scobell, A. (1988). Strung up or shot down?: The death penalty in Hong Kong and China and implications for post-1997. *Case Western Reserve Journal of International Law, 20*, 147–167.

Scobell, A. (1990). The death penalty in post-Mao China. *China Quarterly, 123*, 503–520.

Selden, M. (1985). Income inequality. In W. L. Parish (Ed.), *Chinese rural development: The great transformation* (pp. 193–218). Armonk, NY: Sharpe.

Seymour, J. D. (1988). Editor's introduction. *Chinese Law and Government, 21*(3), 3–13.

Seymour, J. D., & Anderson, R. (1998). *New ghosts, old ghosts: Prisons and labor reform camps in China.* Armonk, NY: Sharpe.

Shen, J. (1997). A critical analysis of China's first regulation on foreign dumping and subsidies and its consistency with WTO agreement. *Berkeley Journal of International Law, 15*, 295–328.

Shih, C. (1999). *Collective democracy: Political and legal reform in China.* Hong Kong: The Chinese University Press.

Shirk, S. L. (1994). *How China opened its door.* Washington, DC: The Brookings Institution.

Shue, V. (1988). *The reach of the state: Sketches of the Chinese body politics.* Stanford, CA: Stanford University Press.

Situ, Y., & Liu, W. (1996). Comprehensive treatment to social order: A Chinese approach against crime. *International Journal of Comparative and Applied Criminal Justice, 20*, 95–115.

Solinger, D. J. (1984a). *Chinese business under socialism: The politics of domestic commerce, 1949–1980.* Berkeley: University of California Press.

Solinger, D. J. (Ed.). (1984b). *Three visions of Chinese socialism.* Boulder, CO: Westview.

Solinger, D. J. (1993). *China's transition from socialism: Statist legacies and market reforms, 1980–1990.* Armonk, NY: Sharpe.

Solinger, D. J. (1995). The floating population in the cities: Chances for assimilation? In D. S. Davis, R. Kraus, B. Naughton, & E. J. Perry (Eds.), *Urban spaces in contemporary China: The potential for autonomy and community in post-Mao China* (pp. 113–139). New York: Woodrow Wilson Center Press.

Solinger, D. J. (1999). *Contesting citizenship in urban China: Peasant migrants, the state, and the logic of the market.* Berkeley: University of California Press.

Special Topic Team, Chinese People's University. (1989–1990). China's plan for economic structural reform, 1988–1995. *Chinese Law and Government, 22*(4), 71–95.

Stern, R. H. (1997). China: A most favored nation or a most feared nation—The PRC's latest anti-crime campaign and a possible U.S. response. *George Washington Journal of International Law & Economics, 31*, 119–140.

Stiglitz, J. E. (2002). *Globalization and its discontents.* New York: Norton.

Sun, Y. (2001). The politics of conceptualizing corruption in reform China. *Crime, Law & Social Change, 35*, 245–270.

Tanner, H. M. (1994a). Chinese rape law in comparative perspective. *The Australian Journal of Chinese Affairs, 31*, 1–23.

Tanner, H. M. (1994b). *Crime and punishment in China, 1979–1989*. Unpublished doctoral dissertation, Columbia University, New York.

Tanner, H. M. (1999). *Strike hard! Anti-crime campaigns and Chinese criminal justice, 1979–1989*. Ithaca, NY: East Asia Program, Cornell University.

Tanner, M. S. (1994). Organizations and politics in China's post-Mao law-making system. In P. B. Potter (Ed.), *Domestic law reforms in post-Mao China* (pp. 56–93). Armonk, NY: Sharpe.

Tanner, M. S. (1999). *The politics of lawmaking in post-Mao China: Institutions, processes and democratic prospects*. Oxford, UK: Clarendon.

Tanner, M. S. (2000). State coercion and the balance of awe: The 1983–1986 "Stern Blows" anti-crime campaign. *The China Journal, 44*, 93–125.

Tanner, M. S. (2005). Campaign-style policing in China and its critics. In B. Bakken (Ed.), *Crime, punishment, and policing in China* (pp. 171–188). Lanham, MD: Rowman & Littlefield.

Tao, L. (1997). Politics and law enforcement in China. In T. V. Lee (Ed.), *Law, the state, and society in China* (pp. 99–142). New York: Garland.

Tifft, L. L. (1985). Reflections on capital punishment and the "campaign against crime" in the People's Republic of China. *Justice Quarterly, 2*, 127–137.

Townsend, D. E. (1987). The concept of law in post-Mao China: A case study of economic crime. *Stanford Journal of International Law, 24*, 227–258.

Trevaskes, S. (2003). Public sentencing rallies in China: The symbolizing of punishment and justice in a socialist state. *Crime, Law & Social Change, 39*, 359–382.

Troyer, R. J., Clark, J. P., & Rojek, D. G. (Eds.). (1989). *Social control in the People's Republic of China*. New York: Praeger.

Turkel, G. (1996). *Law and society: Critical approaches*. Needham Heights, MA: Allyn & Bacon.

Turner, K. G., Feinerman, J. V., & Guy, R. K. (Eds.). (2000). *The limits of the rule of law in China*. Seattle: University of Washington Press.

Van Ness, P. (1984). Three lines in Chinese foreign relations, 1950–1983: The development imperative. In D. J. Solinger (Ed.), *Three visions of Chinese socialism* (pp. 113–142). Boulder, CO: Westview.

Vermeer, E. B., & d'Hoohe, I. (Eds.). (2002). *China's legal reforms and their political limits*. Richmond, UK: Curzon.

Wai, T. (1994). Ideology & the ethos of reform. In M. Brosseau & C. Lo (Eds.), *China Review*, 3.1–3.21. Hong Kong: Chinese University Press.

Walder, A. G. (1986). *Communist neo-traditionalism: Work and authority in Chinese industry*. Berkeley: University of California Press.

Walder, A. G. (Ed.). (1995). *The waning of the communist state: Economic origins of political decline in China and Hungary*. Berkeley: University of California Press.

Wall, J. H., Jr., & Blum, M. (1991). Community mediation in the People's Republic of China. *Journal of Conflict Resolution, 35*(1), 3–20.

Wallerstein, I. (1984). *The politics of world economy: The states, the movements, and the civilizations*. Cambridge, UK: Cambridge University Press.

Wang, C., & Zhang, X. (Eds.). (1997). *Introduction to Chinese law*. Hong Kong: Sweet & Maxwell Asia.

Wang, G., & Mo, J. (Eds.). (1999). *Chinese law*. The Hague, Netherlands: Kluwer Law.

Wang, G., & Wong, J. (Eds.). (1998). *China's political economy*. Singapore: Singapore University Press.

Wang, H., Cheng, W., Yang, X., & Yang, W. (1995). Industrialization and social differentiation: Changes in rural social structure in China since reform. *Chinese Law and Government, 28*(1), 9–38.

Wang, H. (1996). *Transnational networks and international capital flows: Foreign direct investment in China.* Unpublished doctoral dissertation, Princeton University, Princeton, NJ.

Wang, J. (1988). *The role of law in contemporary China: Theory and practice.* Unpublished doctoral thesis, Cornell University, Ithaca, NY.

Wang, J. (1997). *Reform on legal profession in China: Comparative analyses with the experience of the United States.* Unpublished thesis, University of Wisconsin-Madison, Madison, WI.

Wang, S. (1995). The rise of the regions: Fiscal reform and the decline of central state capacity in China. In A. G. Walder (Ed.), *The waning of the communist state: Economic origins of political decline in China and Hungary* (pp. 87–113). Berkeley: University of California Press.

Wang, X. (1998). Whither troubled Chinese state-owned enterprises. In J. Cheng (Ed.), *China Review*, 363–394. Hong Kong: Chinese University Press.

Wang Y. (1989). An inquiry into Marx's concept of the AMP. *Chinese Law and Government, 21*(2), 98–108.

Wank, D. L. (1999). *Commodifying communism: Business, trust, and politics in a Chinese city.* Cambridge, UK: Cambridge University Press.

Ward, R. H. (1985). The police in China. *Justice Quarterly, 2,* 111–115.

Weber, M. (1954). *Max Weber on law in economy and society* (M. Rheinstein, Ed.). New York: Simon & Schuster.

Weber, M. (1978). *Economy and society: An outline of interpretive* sociology (G. Roth & C. Wittich, Eds.). Berkeley: University of California Press.

Weber, M. (1984). *Confucianism & Taoism.* London: London School of Economics.

Weber, M. (1988). *The protestant ethic and the spirit of capitalism.* Gloucester, MA: P. Smith.

Whyte, M. K., & Parish, W. L. (1984). *Urban life in contemporary China.* Chicago: University of Chicago Press.

Wong, K. C. (1994). Public security reform in China in the 1990s. In M. Brosseau & C. Lo (Eds.), *China Review,* 5.1–5.39. Hong Kong: Chinese University Press.

Wong, K. C. (2000). Black's theory on the behavior of law revisited IV: The behavior of Qing law. *International Journal of the Sociology of Law, 28,* 327–374.

Wong, K. C. (2001a). Community policing in China: Philosophy, law and practice. *International Journal of the Sociology of Law, 29,* 127–147.

Wong, K. C. (2001b). The philosophy of community policing in China. *Police Quarterly, 4,* 186–214.

Wong, K. C. (2002). Policing in the People's Republic of China: The road to reform in the 1990s. *British Journal of Criminology, 42,* 281–316.

Woo, M. Y. (1997). The right to a criminal appeal in the People's Republic of China. In T. V. Lee (Ed.), *Law, the state and society in China* (pp. 176–212). New York: Garland.

Woo, M. Y. (1999). Law and discretion in the contemporary Chinese courts. *Pacific Rim Law & Policy Journal, 8,* 581–614.

Woo, M. Y. (2000). Law and discretion in contemporary Chinese courts. In K. G. Turner, J. V. Feinerman, & R. K. Guy (Eds.), *The limits of the rule of law in China* (pp. 163–195). Seattle: University of Washington Press.

World Bank. (1988). *China: Finance and investment.* Washington, DC: Author.

World Bank. (1990). *China: Macroeconomic stability and industrial growth under decentralized socialism.* Washington, DC: Author.

World Bank. (1992). *China: Strategies for reducing poverty in the 1990s.* Washington, DC: Author.

World Bank. (1994). *China: Foreign trade reform.* Washington, DC: Author.

World Bank. (1995). *China: Macroeconomic stability in decentralized economy.* Washington, DC: Author.

World Bank. (1996). *The China economy: Fighting inflation, deepening reforms.* Washington, DC: Author.

World Bank. (1997a). *China 2020: Development challenges in the new century.* Washington, DC: Author.

World Bank. (1997b). *China's management of enterprise assets: The state as shareholder.* Washington, DC: Author.

World Bank. (1999). *China: Weathering the storm and learning the lessons.* Washington, DC: Author.

World Intellectual Property Organization. (2006). *WIPO patent report: Statistics on worldwide patent activities.* Geneva, Switzerland: Author.

World Intellectual Property Organization. (2007). *Record year for international patent filings with significant growth from Northeast Asia.* Geneva, Switzerland: Author.

Wu, D. (1989). The Asiatic mode of production in history as viewed by political economy in its broad sense. *Chinese Law and Government, 21*(2), 27–46.

Wu, Jinglan Study Group. (1989–1990). The economic structure for China's midterm reform. *Chinese Law and Government, 22*(4), 18–34.

Xiang, G. (1999). Delinquency and its prevention in China. *International Journal of Offender Therapy and Comparative Criminology, 43*, 61–70.

Yan, X. (1992). *Regulation of foreign investment in Chinese law.* Unpublished master's thesis, McGill University, Montreal, Canada.

Yan, Y. (1994). Dislocation, reposition and restratification: Structural changes in Chinese society. In M. Brosseau & C. Lo (Eds.), *China Review*, 15.1–15.24. Hong Kong: Chinese University Press.

Yang, S. (2002). Money laundering in China: A policy analysis. *Journal of Contemporary Criminal Justice, 18*, 370–380.

Yang, V. (1996). *How to specify? Vagueness in definitions of crimes in Chinese law and receptions of Western legal concepts.* Unpublished doctoral thesis, Simon Fraser University, Burnaby, BC, Canada.

Yu, O. (1998). *The underrecording of crime by police: An international spin.* Paper presented at the annual meeting of the American Society of Criminology. November, Washington, D.C.

Yu, O., & Zhang, L. (1999). The under-reporting of crime by police in China: A case study. *Policing: An International Journal of Police Strategies & Management, 22*, 252–263.

Yuan, C. (1995). *Law and social organization in contemporary China.* Unpublished doctoral dissertation, Stanford University, Stanford, CA.

Zhang, L. (2003). Official offense status and self-esteem among Chinese youths. *Journal of Criminal Justice, 31*, 99–105.

Zhang, L., & Messner, S. F. (1995). Family deviance and delinquency in China. *Criminology, 33*, 359–387.

Zhang, L., & Messner, S. F. (1999). Bonds to the work unit and official offense status in urban China. *International Journal of Offender Therapy and Comparative Criminology, 43*, 375–390.

Zhang, L., Messner, S. F., & Lu, Z. (1999). Public education and inmates' perceptions of the legitimacy of official punishment in China. *British Journal of Criminology, 39*, 433–449.

Zhang, L., Messner, S. F., Lu, Z., & Deng, X. (1997). Gang crime and its punishment in China. *Journal of Criminal Justice, 25*, 289–302.

Zhang, L., Messner, S. F., Zhou, D., Liska, A. E., Krohn, M. D., Liu, J., et al. (2000). Organization of ownership and workplace theft in China. *International Journal of Offender Therapy and Comparative Criminology, 44*, 581–592.

Zhang, T. (2001). Guest editor's introduction. *Chinese Law and Government, 34*(3), 3–8.

Zhao, D. (1997). Decline of political control in Chinese universities and the rise of the 1989 Chinese student movement. *Sociological Perspectives, 40,* 159–182.

Zhao, S. (Ed.). (2006a). *Debating political reform in China: Rule of law v. democratization.* Armonk, NY: Sharpe.

Zhao, S. (2006b). Political liberalization without democratization: Pan Wei's proposal for political reform. In S. Zhao (Ed.), *Debating political reform in China: Rule of law v. democratization* (pp. 41–57). Armonk, NY: Sharpe.

Zhao, Y. (1997). Contract law. In C. Wang & X. Zhang (Eds.), *Introduction to Chinese law* (pp. 235–273). Hong Kong: Sweet & Maxwell Asia.

Zheng, Y. (1998). *From rule by law to rule of law? A realistic view of China's legal development.* Singapore: East Asian Institute, National University of Singapore.

Zhong, L. Y., & Broadhurst, R. G. (2007). Building little safe and civilized communities: Community crime prevention with Chinese characteristics? *International Journal of Offender Therapy and Comparative Criminology, 51,* 52–67.

Zhou, J. (1991). The Chinese correctional system and its development. *International Journal of Comparative and Applied Criminal Justice, 15,* 15–32.

Zhu, J. (1991). Political religion: The case of the Cultural Revolution in China. *SA: Sociological Analysis, 52*(1), 99–110.

Zhu, Q. (1995). The urban–rural gap and social problems in the countryside. *Chinese Law and Government, 28*(1), 81–101.

Zhu, S. (1989). *The change of law and its characteristics in the People's Republic of China: 1978 to present.* Unpublished master's thesis, Arizona State University, Tempe, AZ.

Zhu, S. (1992). *A critique of social control in cross-cultural studies.* Unpublished doctoral dissertation, Arizona State University, Tempe, AZ.

Zou, K. (2006). *China's legal reform: Towards the rule of law.* Boston: Martinus Nijhoff.

BOOKS AND ARTICLES IN CHINESE

Gong, P., Xia, J., & Liu, W. (Eds.). (1999). *Dangdai Zhongguo De Falü Geming* [Chinese law revolution at the contemporary era]. Falü Chubanshe [Law Press, China].

He, B. (2001). *Xin Zhongguo Chengli hou Zhongguo Dalu Heishehui (Xingzhi De) Fanzui De Yanbian Guocheng, Guilü Jiqi Fazhan Qushi* [The evolution, law and trend of crime (and/or in the nature) of Underworld]. Soochow University.

He, B. (Ed.). (2003). *Heishehui Fanzui Jiedu* [An analysis of underworld organization crimes]. Zhongguo Jiancha Chubanshe [China Procuratorial Press].

Huang, W. (2000). *Dangdai Zhongguo Falü Fazhan Yanjiu* [Research on contemporary Chinese law development]. Jilin Daxue Chubanshe [Jilin University Press].

Li, B. (2001). *Zhongguo Lüshi Ye Fazhan Wentie Yanjiu* [Research on issues in the development of lawyer profession in China]. Jilin Renmin Chubanshe [Jilin People's Press].

Meng, F., & Li, Q. (2004). Guowai Duihua Fanqingxiao De Xianzhuang Fenxi [An analysis of anti-dumping cases against China]. *Shangye Yanjiu* [Commercial Research], *293,* 157–160.

Nan, Y. (Ed.). (2003). "Dahei Chu'e" Shenpan Cankao [Trial references on crackdowns against underworld organizations]. Renmin Fayuan Chubanshe [Court Press, China].

Su-li. (2000). *Song Fa Xia Xiang* [Bring the law to the rural area]. Zhongguo Zhengfa Daxue Chubanshe [University of Political Sciences and Law Press].

Tan, S. (Ed.). (2000). *Zhongguo Sifa Gaige Yanjiu* [Research on Chinese legal reform]. Falü Chubanshe [Law Press, China].

Wang, L. (2001). *Sifa Gaige Yanjiu* [Research on judicial reform]. Falü Chubanshe [Law Press, China].

Wang, Y., & Zhang, G. (Eds.). (1992). *Zhongguo Falixue Zongshu Yu Pingjia* [The summary and evaluation of Chinese legal theory study]. Zhongguo Zhengfa Daxue Chubanshe [University of Political Sciences and Law Press].

Wu, S., Li, G., Qiao, C., Ma, X., & Li, L. (1994). *Zhongguo Chuantong Falü Wenhua* [The Chinese traditional legal culture]. Beijing Daxue Chubanshe [Beijing University Press].

Xiao, Z. (1997, October 10). The major breakthrough of the ownership theory. *People's Daily*.

Xin, C. (1999). *Zhongguo De Falü Zhidu Jiqi Gaige* [The Chinese legal system and current legal reform]. Falü Chubanshe [Law Press, China].

Zhang, Q. (Ed.). (2002). *"Yanda" Zhengche De Lilun Yu Shiwu* [Theory and practice of the "yanda" policy]. Zhongguo Jiancha Chubanshe [China Procuratorial Press].

Zuo, W., & Zhuo, C. (2000). *Bianqian Yu Gaige: Fayuan Zhidu Xiandaihua Yanjiu* [Changes and reforms: A study of the modernization of the court system]. Falü Chubanshe [Law Press, China].

STATISTICAL COLLECTIONS

Almanac of China's Finance and Banking (2001, 2004, 2005)

Almanac of China's Population (2001)

China Industry Economy Statistical Yearbook (2001)

China Judicial Administration Yearbook (1995–2000, 2003–2004)

China Private Economy Almanac (1978–1993, 1996–1999)

China Population Statistics Yearbook (2001)

China Statistical Abstract (2002, 2005)

China Statistical Yearbook (1980–2006)

Collection of Statistics of Foreign Economic Relations and Trade of China (2001)

Law Yearbook of China (1986–2005)

The Procuratorial Yearbook of China (1988–1995, 1997–2000)

The Yearbook of The People's Courts (1988–1992)

U.S. Census Bureau, *Statistical Abstract of the United States* (2007)

Index